P9-BIQ-490

PROPHETS
of PEACE

PROPHETS
of PEACE

*Pacifism and Cultural Identity
in Japan's New Religions*

ROBERT KISALA

University of Hawai'i Press
Honolulu

©1999 University of Hawai'i Press
All rights reserved
Printed in the United States of America

04 03 02 01 00 99   5 4 3 2 1

Library of Congress Cataloging-in-Publication Data
Kisala, Robert, 1957–
Prophets of peace: pacifism and cultural identity
in Japan's new religions / Robert Kisala.
p. cm.
Includes bibliographical references and index.
ISBN 0–8248–2228–5 (cloth : alk. paper).
—ISBN 0–8248–2267–6 (pbk. : alk. paper)
1. Pacifism—Religious aspects.
2. Japan—Religion—1868–1912.
3. Japan—Religion—20th century.
BL2207.5.K58 1999
291.1'7873'0952—dc21   99–35260
CIP

Camera-ready copy prepared by the author.

University of Hawai'i Press books are printed
on acid-free paper and meet the guidelines
for permanence and durability of
the Council on Library Resources.

Printed by Edwards Brothers Inc.

Contents

Acknowledgments

This book developed out of research done for a doctoral degree in Religious Studies from the University of Tokyo. Professor Shimazono Susumu's assistance was invaluable in planning the research, making contacts with the groups involved, and seeing the project through to completion. I would like to thank him for both his mentoring and his friendship.

Several colleagues in the graduate school at the University of Tokyo offered advice in preparing the questionnaire used in this research and in arranging interviews. In this connection I would especially like to thank Yamada Mamoru, Nagai Mikiko, and Tsushiro Hirofumi.

Numerous members of the six groups treated at length in this book, as well as Shinnyoen, included in the questionnaire survey, kindly cooperated in sharing their time, their stories, and their faith. Although I have been somewhat critical here of their approaches to peace, I hope that my respect and gratitude for their kindness and trust is also apparent in these pages.

Several friends in Tokyo and at Divine Word Seminary in Nagoya helped in transcribing the tapes of the interviews used for my research. At the risk of forgetting some names, let me at least mention Mogi Reiko, Tanaka Eiko, Isaka Mari, Kikuta Akiko, Akao Michio, Ishida Makoto, Narui Daisuke, and Shintate Daisuke.

My colleagues and several visiting professors at the Nanzan Institute for Religion and Culture read over an early draft of the manuscript and offered invaluable advice for clarifying the argument and presentation. Ian Reader also read a very early draft of some of the initial chapters and offered detailed comments. Finally, comments provided by two anonymous reviewers helped considerably in preparing the final draft.

Ed Skrypczak kindly proofread the entire manuscript, twice. Bendan Kelleher also read numerous drafts of the chapters and offered comments regarding style and content.

Pat Cosby at the University of Hawai'i Press has been very encouraging and supportive ever since I first mentioned some vague ideas I had about writing something in English on my doctoral work. I also thank the other editors and production staff at the University of Hawai'i Press for their help in preparing the final copy.

Jim Heisig and Paul Swanson patiently taught me all I know about preparing camera-ready copy, an education that was invaluable in preparing this book. I thank them for spending long hours in going over the process with me, and for putting up with my impatience.

My brothers in the Society of the Divine Word have been continually supportive of my work throughout the long years of study and since I started working at the Nanzan Institute for Religion and Culture. I cannot thank them enough for their encouragement and interest.

Finally, I dedicate this book to my parents. Like all members of their generation they were, each in their own way, "tempered by war, disciplined by a hard and bitter peace," and my thoughts on peace have been largely shaped by the basic values I learned from them.

PROPHETS
of PEACE

Introduction

On 27 February 1991, I stood looking out over the ocean from the Mabuni Cliffs on the southern part of the main island of Okinawa. The news in the preceding days had been filled with reports of the ground attack against Iraqi troops occupying Kuwait, an attack that almost seemed to be timed to coincide with my long-planned spring vacation on the southern Japanese island. I had spent the day visiting the war memorials clustered between Naha and Mabuni, listening to the recorded accounts of survivors of one of the fiercest battles of World War II.[1] In the battle for Okinawa almost two hundred thousand people died between the onset of battle on 1 April 1945, and its conclusion at the end of June: more than 107,000 Japanese troops, 75,000 Okinawan civilians, and 7,000 American troops.[2] Many of the Americans lost their lives on the cliffs at Mabuni, where Japanese defenders hiding in the numerous caves on the face of the cliffs mowed down the Americans coming ashore for the final assault. Almost 28,000 Japanese were cremated with flamethrowers or blown up with grenades in the caves that dot that part of the island, and it was the ferociousness of the battle for Okinawa that arguably contributed to the decision to use atomic weapons on Hiroshima and Nagasaki, events that have become perhaps the defining influence on the Japanese psyche in the postwar years.

It was the confluence of images of these two wars—the recorded memories of survivors and live broadcasts from the Middle East—that led to my decision at Mabuni to research the concept of peace promoted by the Japanese new religious movements. Since my arrival in Japan in 1985 I have been interested in the social ethic of the New Religions. I should perhaps acknowledge right from the start that my interest here is not purely academic. I believe that religion has a positive role to play in society, and it is this belief that has in part motivated many of the key decisions in my life—to become a Catholic priest, to ask for assignment in Japan, and to choose new religious movements as the focus of my research in Japan. In contemporary Japanese society it is not generally recognized that religion can fulfill a positive social function, and it is this skepticism that has, in part, motivated my desire to explore the social activism of Japanese religious groups, especially the New Religions.

The choice of New Religions as a means to explore the positive role of religion in society is not an obvious one. In the wake of the poison gas attack on the Tokyo subways by a new religious group on 20 March 1995, these groups are often looked upon with suspicion, as at least a degenerate form of religion if not, in fact, dangerous, either to their believers or to society at large. This view is prevalent in Japan, similar to the image of "cults" in the West, despite the fact that perhaps fifteen percent of the population are members of one or the other of these groups—a considerable number of people in a society where only thirty percent of the population profess any religious belief at all.[3] I would argue that these figures indicate that it is precisely these new religious groups that mediate the religious traditions of the country most effectively to the contemporary population, and that is the reason for my interest in them.

Despite lingering theoretical questions in the field of religious research,[4] "New Religions" has become established as an independent category in the study of Japanese religion. Its boundaries remain fluid, and occasionally arbitrary, but some general characteristics have been identified to distinguish the groups included in this category from the "established religions." These religions are innovative and syncretistic, transforming and combining religious elements from the preexisting cultural milieu. They are usually founded by a charismatic person, and sometimes possess a unique body of revelation left by the founder. Perhaps the most important characteristic is the date of their foundation; most studies include in this category groups established since the mid-nineteenth century, against the backdrop of the modernization of Japanese society.

For the sake of convenience we can talk about three waves of new religious groups on the basis of the period of emergence or growth and the predominant religious tradition reflected in the faith of the group.[5] The groups that emerged in the nineteenth century were generally based on the Shinto or folk-religious traditions of the rural society out of which they emerged. The second wave, of groups popular shortly after World War II, can be described generally as urban, lay Buddhist movements, offering both a sense of community and a means to perform the rituals for the dead to a population that had left the countryside temples behind. In the 1970s yet a third wave emerged, emphasizing spiritist practices and offering the opportunity for a transformation of consciousness, often linked with the attainment of psychic powers. Rather than the religious traditions of Japan these latter groups mediate a religious experience found broadly in contemporary postindustrial societies, with specific influence from nineteenth century American spiritist movements.

Despite the various religious traditions that they reflect, and the innovations introduced by their founders, these groups share much in common, most fundamentally a common worldview based on the popularization of common Confucian, or more specifically Neo-Confucian, principles in the eighteenth century. The world is seen as an interconnected whole, and activity on one level will affect all other levels. Therefore, a transformation on the most immediate level of the inner self will have repercussions within one's family, the surrounding society, and eventually on the universe as a whole. Consequently, emphasis is placed on individual self-cultivation, centering on the virtues of thankfulness, sincerity, and harmony. When confronted with some hardship or misfortune, the believer is called upon to reflect on his or her daily life and relationships within the family, with neighbors, and with coworkers. Have you been appropriately thankful for favors received, most basically for the gift of life itself? Are your relationships marked by sincerity, or have you rather been the cause of disharmony by the assertion of selfish

3

desire? Such reflection should lead to a change of heart, a process that implies that any situation can be transformed through a change in attitude—from one of forgetfulness to thankfulness, from selfish desire to meekness.

Such a worldview is obviously not conducive to the formation of an attitude of social activism, since such activity is based on the belief that social structures are at least in part accountable for individual suffering. There are other aspects of the doctrine and activity of these groups, however, that can motivate positive action for social change, and these aspects have perhaps not received the attention they deserve. Many of the first-wave new religions were quite critical of the social situation in the nineteenth century, when the rural population suffered disproportionately in the transition from a feudal to capitalist economy, and advocated the establishment of a new social order under the banner of *yonaoshi*, or world reform. The principles of solidarity and fundamental equality were maintained with particular strength by these early new religious groups, and this led to their involvement in various social welfare and volunteer activities. In this way, altruism and self-sacrifice are included in the constellation of virtues to be cultivated as part of the believer's self-transformation, and positive action towards the alleviation of suffering is encouraged. This tradition of charitable involvement has been carried on by many of the postwar new religions as well, and, under the influence of modern social theory, an awareness of the social-structural causes of individual misfortune is often found, to a greater or lesser degree, alongside the individual moral explanation outlined above.[6]

In addition to social welfare and civic volunteerism, peace activities are a major expression of the social concern of the New Religions. Entries contained in the *New Religions Dictionary*,[7] for example, make explicit reference to such activities in over forty cases. Various explanations can be offered to account for this widespread interest in peace. Certainly the experience of World War II itself is a major contributing factor in the concern for peace seen broadly in Japanese society and the self-dedication of many religious groups to the pursuit of this cause. Additionally, Michael Pye has argued that the concern for peace can help these religious groups to achieve a "world identity" that breaks through the confines of particularism and nationalism.[8] The very public expression that dedication to peace takes in the various activities of these groups can also help to enhance their image in Japanese society, a matter of no small concern. Within the doctrine and self-understanding of these groups, however, peace is seen as a natural concern of religion, and work towards its establishment is accepted as a truly religious social concern.

In choosing groups as the objects of the present research I aimed for a cross section of New Religions in terms of size, religious tradition, variety of activity, and social base. Small, somewhat obscure groups such as Nipponzan Myōhōji and Shūyōdan Hōseikai are included as well as the relatively well-known mass movements of Sōka Gakkai and Risshō Kōseikai. Myōhōji and the latter two groups represent the Buddhist tradition, while Hōseikai and Shōroku Shintō Yamatoyama could be described as folk-religious groups, and Byakkō Shinkōkai as a spiritist group. The latter group promotes the Prayer for World Peace—whose opening words, "May peace prevail on earth," can be found on stickers and poles across Japan and in many unexpected places throughout the world—as its primary peace activity. Meanwhile, the monks and nuns of Nipponzan Myōhōji engage in nonviolent direct action, protesting against United States military bases in Japan and staging hunger strikes for peace. Sōka Gakkai, on the other hand, has published numerous volumes of recollections of World War II, as part of their campaign to educate the postwar generations on the reality of war. Finally, in regard to social base, while five of the groups have their headquarters in the Tokyo metropolitan area and attract a mostly urban following, Yamatoyama's headquarters can be found in the mountains of Aomori in the north, and its believers are largely drawn from the rural areas of northern Honshu and Hokkaido.

The methodology I employed in my research of these movements was multifaceted. It was partly descriptive: an exposition of the history of the groups, focusing on the groups' own view of their history, but also using independent sources when appropriate. A particular concern here was to explore their response to Japanese militarism in the years prior to 1945, as well as their peace activities in the postwar period. Moving beyond the descriptive, I hoped to identify the concept of peace that motivates and directs their activity. To this end, I sought to analyze the doctrine of each group from the viewpoint of its teaching on peace, as well as to obtain a sampling of believers' personal opinions, through the use of a questionnaire survey and structured interviews.[9]

In analyzing the concept of peace that emerged through this research I use two theoretical measures: the question of pacifism and what is described in these pages as a "civilizational" idea of peace. Postwar Japan is generally assumed to have adopted pacifism as its national policy, and many religious groups see themselves as the defender of this position against those at home and abroad who would have the country rearm in order to play a more active role in international politics. One needs to question, however, just what is meant by pacifism here. Many people use pacifist rhetoric without a clear understanding of its implications, leading to glaring contradictions in Japanese society and muting public debate on an issue of increasing importance in the post–Gulf War period. My first concern, therefore, was to clarify the positions of the groups under study here, placing them within the broader ethical debate on war and peace currently being pursued internationally.

However, I was also interested in highlighting what might be unique to the Japanese idea of peace. To this aim, I identified two elements reflected to a greater or lesser degree in the doctrine and practice of the groups I was researching. The first is based on the more general worldview of the New Religions, that is, the emphasis on individual moral cultivation. Here such cultivation is seen as the primary means to the establishment of world peace. The second element has its roots in the cultural and intellectual heritage of Japan, but is also part and parcel of the idea of a unique national or ethnic mission that we can see broadly in cultures around the world: the idea that peace will be established through the spread of the benefits of "civilization." I have combined the two elements of personal cultivation and the spread of civilization in the concept of a "civilizational" idea of peace, and would propose that this concept is characteristic of the Japanese idea of peace. Let me turn now to the two issues of pacifism and the civilizational idea of peace, in order to outline the approach I took in writing this book.

THE PACIFIST OPTION AND ITS LIMITS

Pacifism is a position taken on the basis of an absolute moral decision; that is, it allows for no compromise with the principle that human life is not to be taken under any circumstances. It seems clear that this position, based on the injunction "Thou shalt not kill," was the orthodox Christian view for the first three centuries of that religion's existence, and similar proscriptions against the taking of life can be found in other religious traditions as well. Within the Christian tradition, pacifism was replaced as the mainstream position early in the fourth century by the just war theory. This position is based on the premise that the proscription against the taking of life is not absolute; that there are other values in competition with the preservation of life, values that can be summarized by the term "justice," whose preservation can on certain occasions require the sacrifice of life. Here the proscription against the taking of life is seen as an ideal to be worked at, but nonetheless an ideal that must occasionally be sacrificed in the preservation of other values.

It is no accident that just war theories became predominant in the Christian world from the fourth century. It was at that time that Christianity changed from being a minority religion in opposition to the Roman Empire to the officially recognized religion of the empire. As a "mainstream" religion it had to deal more systematically with questions such as self-defense and public order, and the force necessary to uphold those values. Inevitably, power and zealotry breed corruption and excess, and indeed, in the history of the Christian West, much harm has been done in the name of justice, most notably in the Crusades, the Inquisition, and European religious wars. In its essence, however, the just war theory was meant to minimize the use of force, limiting its application to situations where there was a clear need to redress wrong, and doing it in a way that would cause the least harm to the fewest number of people.

Recent scholarship has emphasized the commonality of the pacifist and just war positions by pointing out that both are based on a presumption against harm and that it is only in the breach that the just war theory allows for the use of force.[10] In fact, in its popular usage, "pacifism" is often employed to describe this latter position, that is, the presumption against the use of force, rather than its absolute proscription. For example, in their various studies of Christian groups in England and the United States in the interwar period, David Martin and Martin Marty point out that many of these groups adopted a "pacifist" stance, largely in revulsion to the slaughter of troops on both sides in World War I.[11] Their pacifism was quickly abandoned, however, when their countries geared up for war against the fascists at the end of the 1930s, indicating that it was not of the absolute variety called for in the strict definition of the term.[12]

The situation in Japan today is, in some ways, quite similar to that of interwar England and the United States. *Heiwashugi*, the Japanese term, is translated as pacifism, but in its popular usage it often refers to the presumption against the employment of force, rather than its absolute rejection. Japan's defeat in World War II and the destruction that it entailed, including the only use of atomic weapons yet seen in human history, is undoubtedly the single most important influence on the adoption of this position in the postwar period. The pacifist ideal is enshrined in the 1946 constitution, which "forever renounce[s] war as a sovereign right of the nation and the threat or use of force as [a] means of settling international disputes" (Article 9). However, this is not normally interpreted to be an absolute rejection of force, and military spending on "Self-Defense Forces" is among the highest in the world. Many "pacifists" in Japan seek to limit the scope of the Self-Defense Forces, prohibiting their deployment outside of Japan, for example, rather than rejecting outright any possible use of force.

On the other hand, there are those in Japan who do argue for pacifism in its strict sense. For example, the Japan Communist Party continues to maintain that the Self-Defense Forces are unconstitutional, a position that one source indicates is supported by 80% of constitutional scholars in Japan.[13] In contrast, the Democratic Socialist Party of Japan recently abandoned this position, in fulfillment of a condition to enter into a coalition government with the conservative establishment. This reversal on the part of the socialists illustrates a point I alluded to earlier, that the pacifist option becomes untenable for a group that wants to become part of the establishment, where questions of defense and order need to be addressed. David Martin makes the same point regarding the religious groups he studied in England; in his analysis it is only groups that are somewhat removed from society that can be strictly pacifist.[14] Once groups enter the mainstream they must compromise on the absolute prohibition against the taking of life. Perhaps order can be maintained in the limited society of fellow believers, or, when all else fails, members of such pacifist groups may be prepared to lay down their own lives rather than harm another, but that is not a decision that can be applied to society as a whole.

Strict pacifism, then, would seem to be an ideal that is restricted to monastics, commune-like groups that have removed themselves from society, or outstanding individuals like Dorothy Day. Indeed, as Roland Bainton points out, even the so-called Christian Peace Churches, the Anabaptists, Quakers, and Brethren, have had to compromise on pacifism to the varying degrees that they have become a part of mainstream society.[15] Since it is such an extreme position, the question must be raised as to whether it is a useful tool to use in evaluating the Japanese New Religions being studied here. It is certainly not my goal to set an impossibly high standard with which to criticize these groups and their peace activities. Rather, I have two reasons for dwelling on the question of pacifism. The first has been raised above: the need to introduce some clarity into the public debate in Japan on issues of security and world order. The confusion of ideals with realistic strategies has only served to muddle thinking on these crucial moral issues, and stymied popular participation in the political process. My second reason is that ideals are important; society does need the witness of strict and absolute pacifism in order to avoid the temptation to employ force too easily. To be a credible witness, however, pacifists need to be clear about the implications of the absolute stance that they have taken.

I do not believe that all religious or moral leaders must be pacifist. On the contrary, I believe that the vast majority of people would, in good conscience, acknowledge some need for force in the protection of values that are seen to be as compelling as life itself. The question then raised is how one is to judge when such force is necessary. The just war theory has been the Christian approach to supplying that answer, and there seems to have been a resurgence of popular interest in that theory in recent years—at least to judge from some of the rhetoric employed in public discourse in the United States around the time of the Gulf War.[16] However, there are problems with the theory. The destructive force of modern warfare seems to mock its attempts to limit war, fundamentally calling into question its utility in the contemporary situation. Furthermore, in Japan (and much of Asia) the concepts of justice and rights are themselves criticized as fundamentally opposed to tolerance and harmony, key elements of what is proposed as "Asian values." Given these problems with the just war theory we might ask what alternatives are possible to provide guidelines for the moral use of force.

These questions are the focus of chapters two through four of the present volume. These chapters present material on five of the six groups chosen for this study. In Chapter Two we will take a look at the two groups that are more or less faithful to a strict rendering of the pacifist ideal, Nipponzan Myōhōji and Byakkō Shinkōkai. As mentioned above, Nipponzan Myōhōji is a Buddhist monastic sect in the Nichiren tradition, active in organizing marches, sit-ins, and hunger strikes to promote disarmament and the peaceful resolution of conflict. Their nonviolent activism is consciously modeled after that of Mahatma Gandhi, and the members of this group are well known to peace activists throughout the world. In contrast, Byakkō Shinkōkai rejects any kind of political activism in favor of its own spiritual solution to the problem of how to establish world peace. To this end, its peace activities have a single focus, the promotion of the Prayer for World Peace, formulated by the founder of the group. Typical of other religious groups that have become popular in Japan and elsewhere since the 1970s, Byakkō Shinkōkai presents its believers with a dualistic worldview, denying the ultimate reality of the material world and encouraging an awakening to a higher, spiritual, existence. The believers are called upon to channel these spiritual energies in order to bring about world peace. Consequently, Byakkō Shinkōkai's separation from the world is of a vastly different character from the monasticism of Nipponzan Myōhōji, but it nevertheless offers its members the opportunity to fulfill the absolutist demands of the pacifist position.

Chapter Three focuses on the case of Sōka Gakkai. As the largest new religious group in Japan, with perhaps more than eight million members and branches in over 120 countries and territories worldwide, the activities of this group in the promotion of world peace are of particular importance. Sōka Gakkai actively employs pacifist rhetoric, and the persecution of its founder and postwar leader during World War II is often offered as an explanation for its abhorrence of all war. In the postwar period, however, it has become a major player in Japanese politics, establishing its own political party in the 1960s, a party that was formally part of a coalition government during the post–Gulf War debate on Japan's role in the world. The active role it has taken on in Japanese society has made the absolute pacifist position untenable. What this group advocates instead is an internationalist approach: the building of world peace through the establishment of international structures to ensure stability.

The last chapter in this section deals with the just war theory and its critics. Two of the groups examined in this study, Risshō Kōseikai and Shōroku Shintō Yamatoyama, identify pacifism as an ideal that is not readily realized in the present world, and try to offer a specifically religious path towards the transformation of the world. As many of the New Religions do, Risshō Kōseikai has inherited much of its character from the personality of its founder, by all accounts a magnanimous and tolerant man who has led the group from an early stage down the path of dialogue and interreligious cooperation. This religious group has been a leader in the ecumenical movement in Japan, as well as the driving force behind the creation of the World Conference on Religion and Peace, an international body of religious leaders working to establish world peace. Shōroku Shintō Yamatoyama, although much smaller than Risshō Kōseikai and lacking the natural international connections that Kōseikai's Buddhist background offers, is nonetheless equally involved in interreligious efforts at dialogue and cooperation. It is likewise an active member of the World Conference on Religion and Peace, and its postwar leader was instrumental in launching perhaps the most effective grassroots program to promote international cooperation and peace in Japan. These groups are more explicit than the other groups covered in this survey in recognizing that there is real evil in the world, which must occasionally be met with force. However, they fail to offer clear criteria as to when the use of force is justified, no doubt a difficult task in an atmosphere where uncritical pacifist rhetoric abounds.

The focus on pacifism and pacifist rhetoric in these groups will help to clarify the terms of discourse regarding war and peace in contemporary Japanese society, and indicate areas where religion could take a more active position in guiding public discussion on moral issues in that country. These are issues that I will return to in the concluding chapter. Let me now turn to the "civilizational" idea as the Japanese cultural concept of peace.

A "CIVILIZATIONAL" CONCEPT OF PEACE

Research into the concept of peace often attempts to delineate differences in understanding the concept across cultures. For example, in his study Bainton begins by pointing out differences in various

Mediterranean cultures: the Hebrew idea is equated with prosperity, the Greek idea with order and coherence, and the Roman idea with the absence of war.[17] In contrast, Ishida Takeshi and others propose harmony as the distinguishing characteristic of the Japanese concept of peace.[18] Their argument is not unpersuasive, for we have already seen that harmony is one of the prime virtues promoted by the Confucian ethic that dominates moral discourse in Japan. On the basis of the research that I will be presenting here, however, I would propose that the Japanese concept might more accurately be described as being based on the idea of civilization, and that this can be developed under two aspects.

First of all, civilization refers to a refined moral state of being, and the idea of peace that we will be looking at here is often seen fundamentally as a matter of moral self-cultivation. In line with the worldview of the Japanese New Religions outlined earlier, the establishment of world peace is often described as dependent on the internal change of heart of each individual human being. Although international agreements, confidence building activities, economic development, and social structural changes might all contribute to building a world at peace, unless people themselves change, it is argued, these will all ultimately fail. Such reasoning is not foreign to religious groups working for world peace outside of Japan as well, but the degree to which it is emphasized in Japan, especially by the New Religions, makes it one part of a distinctly Japanese approach to peace.

Secondly, civilization is also often used as a discriminating concept, to distinguish between areas where such a state exists and where it is absent. In this sense it can, at times, issue in an oppositional schema derived from a feeling of ethnic or cultural superiority. Under this aspect, work for peace primarily consists in the spread of the benefits of civilization as they are enjoyed in one's own country or culture. In Western colonial rhetoric this takes on a sense of national mission, expressed as the "white man's burden." While modern Japanese colonialism was in large part motivated by a desire to counter the policies of the Western powers and avoid the fate that had befallen China, there is evidence already in the sixteenth century of the rhetoric of national mission and cultural superiority supporting a colonial policy towards other countries in Asia. The focus of our interest here will be to see how this rhetoric has changed in the postwar period, and how it continues to play a significant, although sometimes unconscious, role in the concept of peace promoted by the new religious groups under study in this volume.

Chapters Five and Six deal specifically with the dual aspects of this civilizational idea of peace as found in the doctrine and practice of the six groups under study. Chapter Five deals with the first aspect of this concept, the emphasis on moral self-cultivation. On the basis of the common worldview espoused by many of the Japanese New Religions, individual moral cultivation is thought to be the foundation of world peace—the concentric circles of peace are centered, it is believed, in the individual heart and from there move out to the family, surrounding society, nation, world, and, eventually, the whole universe. While this idea is expressed, with varying emphases, by all of the groups chosen for this project, it is perhaps most clearly present in Shūyōdan Hōseikai. Shūyōdan is a subcategory of Japanese New Religions, and it literally means Association for the Cultivation of Morals. In the postwar period Hōseikai explicitly made the establishment of world peace its primary goal, a goal that is to be achieved specifically through the individual moral cultivation of the members of the group. Following a look at how this element is presented by the five groups dealt with earlier, this chapter will focus on the dynamic of this process in Shūyōdan Hōseikai, the sixth group that comprises this study.

Chapter Six will deal with the issue of cultural superiority and how it is transformed by some religious groups in the postwar period. Echoing Japanese popular culture, the establishment of world peace has been promoted by many of these religious groups as the unique mission of Japan in the postwar era. Occasionally, prewar terms are used to describe this mission. For example, *hakkō ichiu* (literally, the whole world under one roof) was one of the expressions of Japanese colonialism. It was meant to convey the ideal of world unity under Japanese direction, leading to the establishment of peace. In this way it is a prime example of the prewar idea of establishing peace through the spread of Japanese civilization. In an interview as part of my research, the leader of Yamatoyama made an attempt to retrieve the term as an expression of universal brother- and sisterhood, based on respect for cultural differences. Such expressions of a pluralistic ideal seem to predominate in these groups, and indicate some degree of success in erasing notions of cultural superiority. In some of the New Religions studied here, however, there seems to be merely a shift from ethnic categories to religious categories, and the clash is now described as one between religious or spiritual civilization and material civilization. Especially in the case of Nipponzan Myōhōji, this schema seems to be nothing more than a code for Eastern (or Buddhist) civilization and Western civilization, indicating that the oppositional aspect of this concept of peace might still be operative.

In order to introduce the themes that make up this theoretical framework, Chapter One serves to place pacifism, just war, moral self-cultivation, and national mission within the context of Japanese intellectual history. A defining influence on the development of this intellectual tradition is the fact that prior to the modern period the maintenance of internal social order was of relatively more concern than conflicts with foreign powers. In the early modern period this contributed to the popularization of both an ethic of self-cultivation as well as rhetoric that identified good social order as a distinctively Japanese trait. The establishment of world peace through the spread of this order was promoted as a national mission, culminating eventually in the Japanese colonization of Asia in the first half of the twentieth century. Western concepts of pacifism and the just war were introduced only in the latter half of the nineteenth century, as relations with foreign powers took a more central place in the evolving concept of peace. These concepts were promoted especially in the writing of prominent Japanese Christians, where they were often combined with ideas of national mission and self-cultivation, and occasionally took expression in a tendency towards withdrawal and quietism. A thematic rather than a comprehensive approach to these issues is taken in this chapter, and the presentation will perhaps seem eclectic and incomplete. While a thorough, diachronic study of the development of the concept of peace in Japanese intellectual history would be more satisfying, I must admit that it is beyond my ability at this time. Perhaps this essay will help to encourage others to attempt such a study.

Finally, in a concluding chapter I attempt an evaluation of the concept of peace identified in the doctrine and practice of these groups, and offer some reflections on the role of religion in contemporary Japanese society. It is not only the New Religions that have an "image problem" in Japan; suspicion of religious institutions extends to the established religions as well. Public opinion surveys indicate that in the minds of many Japanese religion has "sold its soul" for wealth and political power.

If it is to establish a place for itself beyond the fringes of Japanese society it needs to find a moral voice. In light of both the importance of the current debate in Japanese society regarding security issues and the long-standing involvement of religious groups with the question of peace, this issue offers religion a unique opportunity to do so.

This work is intended primarily as a study of Japanese New Religions from a perspective that has previously been largely neglected, that is, their social ethic and social activism. In this way I hope that it will make some contribution to the ever-expanding body of research on these movements. However, as I pointed out at the beginning of this introduction, I do not approach the subject dispassionately. My research has led me to critique popular notions of pacifism and national mission, as well as the efficacy of individual moral cultivation as a solution to social problems. It has also made me an advocate for a more positive role of religion in Japanese society. I hope, in the end, that these concerns do not detract from but rather enhance the value of this work as a study in social ethics and new religious movements.

ONE

Elements of a Japanese Cultural Concept of Peace

Peace studies in Japan in the post–World War II period have been almost exclusively concerned with the concept of pacifism. In line with the postwar intellectual environment that rejects all war, a major concern of these studies has been to search for the foundations of antiwar and pacifist sentiments. In doing this, the figures they have turned to as models are mostly from the Meiji period, and many of them are either Christians or socialists.[1] I am not aware of any attempt to develop a comprehensive intellectual history of the development of the concept of peace in Japan. Neither will this chapter be able to fill that void, for my purpose is more limited. What I hope to do is point out some of the major intellectual movements that contribute to the development of the concept of peace that I found in the doctrine and practice of the New Religions chosen for my research, namely, the elements of self-cultivation, national mission, and, later, pacifism and the just war.

In considering what is characteristic of the Japanese idea of peace reflected in these groups we might begin with the overall historical context that nurtured that concept. In contrast to the situation in Europe, where Christian pacifist and just war theories were developed, one defining characteristic of the Japanese historical situation regarding war and peace is that, until the modern period, the country had been involved in very few conflicts with foreign powers. Until the nineteenth century its conflicts with groups outside of Japan had been limited to a disastrous invasion of the Korean peninsula in the seventh century, some attacks by pirates on the southern island of Kyushu in the ninth century, two attempted Mongol invasions of Japan in the thirteenth century, and another invasion of Korea at the end of the fifteenth century. On the other hand, in the centuries leading up to the inauguration of the Tokugawa regime in 1603 Japan was racked by a series of internal conflicts among rival warlords, culminating in a century-long civil war that was only brought to an end with the institution of the new regime. Consequently, perhaps the most important influence on the pre-Meiji Japanese concept of peace is the experience of internal conflict and the consequent emphasis on stability and social order. As a result, pre-Meiji discourse on peace in Japan tends to emphasize internal social order, and there is little development of theories regarding international relations.

Having only recently obtained the submission of rival warlords and faced with the encroachment of Western powers in Asia—the beginning of Western colonialism—the new regime chose to isolate itself from the rest of the world and consolidate the stability it had brought to the nation. Weapons were confiscated from the peasant class, and a rigid social structure was instituted. This situation changed dramatically with the opening of the country in 1868. As part of its policy of becoming a modern nation-state, on a par with the Western powers, and thus avoiding colonization by those powers, in short order a national army was created and universal conscription introduced. Japan went to war with China in 1894 over spheres of influence on the Korean peninsula, and gained Taiwan as a colony as a result of that war. Ten years later Japan fought Russia, and with its victory was granted privileges in Manchuria. Korea was annexed in 1910, and by allying itself with European forces fighting Germany in World War I, Japan was able to expand its control in China. It was in this context that Western pacifist and just war ideas entered intellectual and public discourse in Japan, largely through the activities of several influential Christians.

The emphasis on stability and order, therefore, precedes Meiji-era discourse on pacifism and is an important element in the Japanese concept of peace that is commonly overlooked in contemporary peace studies. In Japanese intellectual history this emphasis becomes entwined with the Confucian idea that inner moral rectitude contributes to good social and cosmic order, issuing in the emphasis placed on individual moral cultivation that remains as a key element of the worldview of the Japanese New Religions. Furthermore, other movements in Japanese intellectual history identify stability and order as the hallmark of Japanese civilization, as well as the guarantor of Japanese ethnic superiority, and this element of spreading the benefits of Japanese civilization becomes part of the constellation of ideas concerning peace in the early modern and modern periods.

While the elements of stability, moral cultivation, and ethnic superiority are thus essentially entwined, in the following pages I will consider them individually, in each case providing illustrations of how they have been expressed in various intellectual developments and movements. In doing this I will concentrate on material beginning with the establishment of the early modern social order inaugurated by the Tokugawa regime, since this material is more directly pertinent to the concept of peace that emerges in the New Religions. In the latter part of this chapter we turn to modern pacifist and just war rhetoric, concentrating on the Meiji Christian intellectuals. While such rhetoric is essentially a new element introduced into the Japanese concept of peace since the mid-nineteenth century, we will see that in the writings of these intellectuals it is often combined with the cultural constructs treated earlier in the chapter, those of moral cultivation and ethnic or national mission.

THE VIRTUE OF STABILITY AND ORDER

In recent years it has become commonplace to argue that rhetoric concerning the maintenance of proper relationships and harmony masks a considerable amount of dissent and conflict in Japanese society. The treatment of bushido in the intellectual history of Japan is one example of this phenomenon. Although modern tracts on bushido, including the famous work by Nitobe Inazō that we will treat at length later in this chapter, emphasize loyalty as the foundation of the social order, the increasing emphasis on loyalty was in fact one of the results of the establishment of the Tokugawa order. The century-long period of civil strife that preceded the Tokugawa regime testifies to the presence of a more rough-and-tumble warrior ethic that marked this period of personal advancement through shifting loyalties. Indeed, some scholars argue that pragmatism and disloyalty were more the norm, contrary to the image portrayed in emerging rhetoric on the warrior ethic.[2] In this section we will take a look at two developments in Japanese intellectual history from the first half of the Tokugawa era that illustrate the emphasis on stability and order, *Tokugawa Ieyasu's Testament* and the work of the Confucian scholar Ogyū Sorai.

While intrigue and self-promotion did not end with the institution of the Tokugawa regime, from the end of the fifteenth century there is an identifiable attempt to construct an ideological system to promote stability and order. Herman Ooms argues that this was accomplished by freely borrowing ideological constructs from the Buddhist, Shinto, and Confucian traditions in order to supply a transcendental foundation to the new regime.[3] This ideology emphasized the virtues of loyalty, benevolence, and trust, and affirmed the use of military power to preserve good order. In this way it glorified bushido, the warrior ethic, but transformed it from the rough-and-tumble practice of the previous centuries that promoted personal advance through the use of arms to one of loyalty and stability.

A summary of this ideology can be found in a document that purports to be *Tokugawa Ieyasu's Testament*, published in the early seventeenth century. Tokugawa Ieyasu was the warlord who finally united the country under his rule in 1603 and thus instituted a regime that survived more than two and a half centuries, until the beginning of the Meiji period in 1868. In the *Testament*, Tokugawa rule is given the transcendental basis of being sanctioned by Heaven's Mandate, a Confucian concept used to express the cosmic will. The presence of this mandate is confirmed by Tokugawa's very success, and this should in turn elicit loyalty on the part of his subjects—loyalty is not addressed to Ieyasu himself, but rather to the higher principle that has sanctioned his rule. Disloyalty is thus a rejection of the cosmic principle that has determined the natural order of things.

Imbued in this way with loyalty to the Tokugawa line as the recipient of Heaven's mandate, the warrior was to be the tool of social control.

The *Testament* proclaims that Heaven's Way is upheld by the Way of the Warrior (*budō*), which is used to stamp out evil and keep chaos at bay.[4] In the *Testament*, however, the application of such force was to be tempered by *jihi*, a Buddhist concept usually rendered as compassion but translated by Ooms as benevolence. *Jihi* arises from the knowledge that all people are equal as Heaven's children, and needlessly harming anyone is therefore a crime against Heaven. In the end, military power is indispensable for the maintenance of a just, peaceful society, but it must be tempered by benevolence.[5]

In a later development of this discourse on social order, benevolence is transformed from a tempering influence on the application of force to the very use of that force in preserving order. *Bendō* and *Taiheisaku* are treatises written by the Confucian scholar Ogyū Sorai (1666–1728) almost one hundred years after the *Tokugawa Testament*, about halfway through the Tokugawa period. In these works the preservation of order is given an even more prominent place, in reaction to a deterioration in the social situation.

By the eighteenth century, weaknesses had begun to appear in the Tokugawa system, especially as a result of its fiscal mismanagement. The financial policies of the regime bankrupted first the warrior class and later the peasant class, leading to a number of uprisings in the countryside. It was against the background of this social unrest that Sorai tried to reinforce the ideological underpinning of the Tokugawa regime. Accordingly, in *Bendō* and *Taiheisaku*, Sorai argues that it is the duty of the sovereign to assure that the realm is at peace, and, indeed, maintenance of order is offered as the true expression of benevolence. For example, in *Bendō* Sorai explains:

> The government prohibits violence but uses military law to execute people. Can this be called benevolence? But it all stems from the need to maintain peace in the land.[6]

In *Taiheisaku*, which means a "Plan for Peace," Sorai is even more explicit in arguing that the true content of benevolence is the preservation of peace, meaning good order.

> Confucians of later ages speak of benevolence and explain the principles of sincerity and commiseration. But even if they possess the spirit of sincerity and commiseration, if they fail to bring peace to the people, they are not benevolent; however much compassion

they have, it will all turn out to be wasted benevolence, the benevolence of a woman.[7]

Later in the Tokugawa period this emphasis on stability and order found expression in the ethnocentric belief that stability was, in fact, the hallmark of Japanese civilization. Before we turn to this development, however, let us first take a look at how a religious worldview that emphasized inner moral cultivation as the means to effect change in the social environment was popularized in Japan, paralleling these other developments.

MORAL CULTIVATION

Stability and order are emphasized when society is threatened by internal conflict. In the early Tokugawa period this emphasis was meant to reverse the strongman ethic that had led to centuries of conflict and provide ideological support for the new regime. As the new order began to unravel, intellectuals like Ogyū Sorai sought to strengthen the emphasis on stability by promoting the role of the warrior class in preserving order. At about the same time several popular movements emerged among the merchant and peasant classes emphasizing personal morality as the solution to social problems.

Yasumaru Yoshio identifies the common dynamic of these movements as a "philosophy of the heart" (*kokoro no tetsugaku*).[8] This philosophy of the heart, as described by Yasumaru, identifies inner spiritual activity as the foundation for all change. It posits an essentially unlimited potentiality to the human heart, and offers a means to the realization of the power of the human spirit through the practice of a "conventional morality" (*tsūzoku dōtoku*). The cultivation of the virtues of filial piety, loyalty, thrift, frugality, diligence, and so on was offered as the answer to the social problems caused by the economic upheavals of the time, in essence reducing these problems to a matter of personal ethics. Emerging in the seventeenth century in the major urban areas of the country, these movements spread throughout the countryside in the nineteenth century, becoming firmly implanted in the popular culture by the end of that century.

Robert Bellah highlighted one of these movements in his study of early modern Japanese religion, *Tokugawa Religion*. The *shingaku* movement of Ishida Baigan (1685–1744) became popular among the urban merchant class as a type of common morality that emphasized Confucian notions of proper relationship and the virtues of honesty, sincerity, frugality, and hard work.[9] This type of popular ethic also took hold in the countryside, popularized by *shingaku* followers as well as other preachers such as Ninomiya Sontoku (1787–1856). Ninomiya was an agricultural philosopher and technologist who enjoyed considerable success in increasing crop yields in the area north of Edo through precise calculation of irrigation and fertilizer requirements. In addition to this technical aid, however, he encouraged farmers to improve their own lot through the ethical ideas of *hōtoku*, or the repaying of benefits received from Heaven, nature, and other human beings. According to Ninomiya *hōtoku* was to be achieved through the practice of common virtues such as sincerity, diligence, thrift, filial piety, and cooperation, and this would lead to the creation of a prosperous and peaceful society.

Yasumaru and others have pointed out the ambiguous nature of the results obtained by the application of the philosophy of the heart to social problems, an issue we will return to in Chapter Five of this study, when we explore the use of moral cultivation as the means to the establishment of world peace. On the one hand, the philosophy of the heart is a tremendously empowering concept, assuring the individual that his or her own efforts not only contribute to, but are, in fact, decisive towards, effecting change in the social environment. Indeed, it would seem that the emphasis on personal morality did contribute towards the establishment of a prosperous trading class, the foundation of modern Japanese capitalism. On the other hand, however, such an ethic clearly has a greater effect within the confines of interpersonal relationships, largely ignoring the structural reality of social life. Although these movements were involved in extending educational opportunities as well as welfare activities that sought to alleviate suffering and improve the lot of the common people, the ethic they promoted tended to mask the need for systemic changes in the political structure.

ETHNOCENTRISM IN THE CONCEPT OF PEACE

Having briefly sketched some developments that contributed to the emphasis on stability and order in the concept of peace and the popularization of a common morality that emphasized internal personal cultivation, in the following rather long section I want to indicate how these two elements become entwined with Japanese ethnocentrism, issuing in developments that define the concept of peace in the prewar period. We begin with Kokugaku, a nativist school of thought that emerged in the eighteenth century.

Eighteenth-Century Nativism

Kokugaku is at once a literary, political, and religious movement whose foundation lies at least partly in a reaction to the increasing influence of Confucian ideas and scholarship in Tokugawa society, as seen, for example, in the person of Ogyū Sorai. Kokugaku evolved from the philological study of Japanese classical literature and ancient writings whose purpose was generally to identify peculiarly Japanese cultural traits or a distinctive Japanese mentality. This study can be traced back to Keichū (1640–1701), a Buddhist monk of the Shingon sect who took up the study of the *Man'yōshū*, an anthology of eighth-century poetry. Keichū insisted that in order to understand the ancient classical literature one had to allow one's mind to become unfettered by intellectual concepts so as to come in touch with the naive emotions of a direct, human response, a primitivism that is reflected in later Kokugaku writings.

Another early influence on Kokugaku was Kada no Azumamaro (1669–1736), a descendant of a family of Shinto priests who focused his study on ancient documents as well as literary works. He opened a school for Japanese studies in Kyoto and had a direct influence on Kamo no Mabuchi (1697–1769), also from a family of Shinto priests. Like Keichū, Mabuchi took up the study of the *Man'yōshū*, finding there an honest and direct expression of emotion without the artificiality he thought had been introduced by foreign, specifically Buddhist and Confucian, influences.

Motoori Norinaga (1730–1801), usually acknowledged as the central figure of this movement, came to Kokugaku through a study of Keichū's work, later becoming a disciple of Mabuchi. Norinaga completed a study of the *Kojiki,* a foundational text of Japanese mythology from the eighth century, that had been started by his mentor. Continuing in the primitivist tradition of his teachers, Norinaga propounded his belief that in order to understand the text one needs a sensitivity to the appearance of objects and events in the human and natural

23

world and the emotions that they arouse, unfettered by Confucian or Buddhist doctrinal interpretations. Norinaga believed that the *Kojiki* text was a factual record of the activity of the gods and people in ancient times, and that it reflected a natural moral sense. He maintained that ancient Japanese texts do not contain the word *michi*, or "way" in the sense of a correct moral path, because the ancients had a natural feel for what was right, and were in this way superior to the Chinese, who were in need of the moral guidance supplied by Confucian principles.

In another work, the *Naobi no mitama*, Norinaga develops at length this idea of Japanese cultural superiority, identifying stability as the basis of that superiority. Relying on Japanese mythology, Norinaga states that Japan is the land of the appearance of Amaterasu Ōmikami, the central native goddess, and that the land is ruled by the emperor, the descendant of the goddess.[10] For that reason, he argues that the rule of the emperor is in fact the rule of the gods, as it was, unchanging from ancient times, and that in turn is why Japan is referred to as the Land of the Gods.[11] In foreign lands, namely China, there is no end to revolution and unrest, with people of lower status trying to seize power from those above. In Japan, however, the emperor's reign continues unbroken, and the people follow naturally that order as it has been established in ancient times, ensuing in profound peace.[12] If there is unrest in Japan it is a result of the fact that people have tried to learn foreign ways and have allowed their spirit to become separated from the spirit of the emperor.[13] This situation can only be corrected if people are loyal and obedient to their superiors and do what they know naturally to be right; they are endowed with this natural ethical sense because all share in the spirit of the gods that is the foundation of Japanese culture.[14]

These ideas of cultural superiority based on the perceived presence of an unparalleled social stability did not originate with Norinaga or Kokugaku, but can be traced back at least several centuries prior to the material that we are dealing with here. Satomi Kishio, for example, outlines the development of the *shinkoku* (Land of the Gods) idea in his intellectual history of the concept of *kokutai*, or national polity.[15] Satomi finds the first recorded use of *shinkoku* in the *Nihon shoki*, purportedly an early history of Japan compiled in the eighth century, where the use of the term is still rather ambiguous. *Shinkoku* apparently becomes connected with the defense of the nation a century later, since it appears in records of prayers offered at Ise in 870 to protect the nation from pirate attacks on the southern island of Kyushu. The belief that Japan enjoys special protection as the Land of the Gods was strengthened by the unsuccessful Mongol invasion attempts in the thirteenth century. Furthermore, Satomi points out that around this time the concept of the Land of the Gods comes to be connected with the idea of justice, resulting in the belief that Japan and its rulers embody justice, by virtue of the fact that Japan is the Land of the Gods. By the time of the Muromachi Shogunate in the fourteenth century this concept becomes connected with beliefs concerning the unbroken reign of the imperial family, an indication of order and stability that is adjudged to be both the result of the special favor of the gods and a proof of cultural superiority.

In Satomi's tracing of the development of this concept we see a movement from a plea for protection to the affirmation of a unique cultural identity that success in war brings. The focus on order and stability, expressed in beliefs regarding the unbroken imperial reign in Japan, is clear already from the fourteenth century, and, in Satomi's reading, this stability is already taken as a concrete indication of cultural superiority at that time. These ideas came even more to the fore and began to be codified into a national ideology in the early part of the nineteenth century, as new developments increased the threat to the Tokugawa order and the policy of national isolation became increasingly untenable.

Jōi and the Mito School

As the Tokugawa policy of national isolation was threatened by the appearance of Western and Russian ships in Japanese coastal waters early in the nineteenth century, the two elements of an emphasis on moral cultivation and a sense of cultural superiority were combined in the thought of the so-called Mito School. Mito was a domain northeast of Edo, and the school of thought that bears its name had strong Confucian and Kokugaku influences. Pertinent to our discussion is the development of discourse on the concept of *jōi* within this school.

Jōi is the Japanese reading of a Chinese Confucian concept that literally means "expel the barbarian(s)." Various interpretations of this concept are offered both in Chinese and Japanese Confucian thought, clustered around two ideational frameworks. The first offers a worldview that differentiates Confucian moral civilization from barbarism, usually territorially, and the *jōi* injunction can be taken as a call to strengthen the borders to keep the barbarians out. The second framework is more fluid in its view of where "civilization" can be found, and the injunction here is to expel what is barbarian, applied to any culture.[16] While the former reading was the more direct meaning applied to the use of this concept by the Mito school, the latter reading also influenced the discourse emerging in Japan at this time, for the "strengthening of the borders" against the barbarians was to be accomplished through a process that relied primarily on moral cultivation.

Aizawa Seishisai (1782–1863), a retainer of the Mito domain, composed in 1825 the *Shinron*, or *New Theses*, as a kind of manifesto, calling on the Tokugawa regime to defend the nation from the threat posed by the increasingly frequent appearance of foreign ships off the Japanese coast. At this point the ships were fishing or trade vessels rather than warships, but these vessels did threaten the enforced isolation of Japan imposed at the beginning of the Tokugawa period. In this work Aizawa draws heavily on the arguments of Kokugaku scholars, as seen in the following introductory paragraph:

> Our Divine Realm is where the sun emerges. It is the source of the primordial vital force sustaining all life and order. Our Emperors, descendants of the Sun Goddess, Amaterasu, have acceded to the Imperial Throne in each and every generation, a unique fact that will never change. Our Divine Realm rightly constitutes the head and shoulders of the world and controls all nations. It is only proper that our Divine Realm illuminates the entire universe and that our dynasty's sphere of moral suasion knows no bounds. But recently the loathsome Western Barbarians, unmindful of their base position as the lower extremities of the world, have been scurrying impudently across the Four Seas, trampling other nations underfoot. Now they are audacious enough to challenge our exalted position in the world.[17]

Although the "barbarians" thus act contrary to the moral laws of nature in ignoring their lowly status, they are given free reign because, "When the power of men is immense, they overcome Heaven." What is needed then is a great warrior to come to Heaven's aid: "Unless a Great Hero bestirs himself to assist Heaven's normative processes, all creation will fall prey to the wily, meat-eating barbarians."[18] The most potent weapon of the barbarians in their effort to overturn the natural order of things, however, is identified as spiritual in nature:

For close to three hundred years now the Western barbarians have rampaged on the high seas. Why are they able to enlarge their territories and fulfill their every desire? Does their wisdom and courage exceed that of ordinary men? Is their government so benevolent that they win popular support? Are their rites, music, laws, and political institutions superb in all respects? Do they possess some superhuman, divine powers? Hardly. Christianity is the sole key to their success.[19]

Aizawa calls Christianity a "truly evil and base religion," arguing that its doctrines are simple to grasp, and thus that it is a potent tool to deceive "stupid commoners." Charitable acts are employed as part of this deception, to win over the people and pave the way for the propagation of Christian doctrines. In this way, the Christian religion functions as the ultimate weapon in the Western arsenal, a key part of the West's strategy for world domination.

Whenever they seek to take over a country, they employ the same method. By trading with that nation, they learn about its geography and defenses. If these be weak, they dispatch troops to invade the nation; if strong, they propagate Christianity to subvert it from within. Once our people's hearts and minds are captivated by Christianity, they will greet the barbarian host with open arms, and we would be powerless to stop them.[20]

To counter such a spiritual threat, Aizawa concludes that it is ultimately an awareness of Japan's unique cultural identity and an adherence to the fundamental virtues of loyalty and filial piety that will provide peace and security for the nation. While acknowledging the importance of military preparedness to repel incursions by the foreign powers, and calling on the government to implement a policy of forcibly expelling foreign ships in Japanese waters, Aizawa calls ultimately for a spiritual and moral defense:

The barbarians are triumphant everywhere and have begun to disseminate their poisonous doctrines in our Divine Realm....Yet we in the Middle Kingdom remain without an unswerving moral basis of action; our people lack unity and spiritual cohesion, our leaders can dream up nothing better than stop-gap, gloss-it-over measures to tide them over each day's crises. Our Land of Illustrious Gods has fallen to such depths that we now sit by idly and allow these foreign beasts to lure the common people away from us. Have we lost all sense of shame?[21]

The solution thus offered is a recognition of a national consciousness, expressed above all in the virtues of loyalty and filial piety, and the establishment of a national religion based on these beliefs and virtues, including the performance of national rituals centered on the Imperial Household in order to enhance the unity of the people. When the Tokugawa regime collapsed because of its inability to keep the country closed to foreigners, these policies were largely adopted by the new Meiji government, in order to preserve order and stability.

Meiji Religious Policy

Although Aizawa's aim was to bolster the resolve and standing of the Tokugawa regime, his *New Theses* in fact became a rallying point for mid-nineteenth-century reformers who sought to overthrow the Tokugawa government because of its abandonment of the *jōi* policy. With the ascendancy of these reformers, the *New Theses* became a kind of blueprint for governing, issuing initially in the policy of establishing State Shinto as the national religion. To this end, an attempt was made to reverse centuries of Buddhist-Shinto syncretism and Buddhism was actively persecuted for a time; local shrines were consolidated to enhance state control; new national shrines were established; and an attempt was made to introduce a set of national holidays based on imperial feasts and seasonal agricultural rites to be performed by the emperor. This religious policy had to be continuously adapted to changing conditions in the early decades of the Meiji period, until finally it took the form of a civic creed summarized in the Imperial Rescript on Education at the end of the nineteenth century.[22]

The Meiji Constitution, instituting a constitutional monarchy, was promulgated in 1889. The introduction of the new political system, with its guarantees of religious freedom (granted under pressure from the Western powers), heightened concern for a spiritual glue to hold the nation together. The Rescript on Education was promulgated the following year in response to this concern. The text of the rescript is as follows:

> Know ye, Our Subjects:
> Our Imperial Ancestors have founded Our Empire on a basis broad and everlasting and have deeply and firmly planted virtue; Our subjects ever united in loyalty and filial piety have from generation to generation illustrated the beauty thereof. This is the glory of the fundamental character of Our Empire, and herein lies the

source of Our education. Ye, Our subjects, be filial to your parents, affectionate to your brothers and sisters; as husbands and wives be harmonious, as friends true; bear yourselves in modesty and moderation; extend your benevolence to all; pursue learning and cultivate arts, and thereby develop intellectual faculties and perfect moral powers; furthermore advance public good and promote common interests; always respect the Constitution and observe the laws; should emergency arise, offer yourselves courageously to the State; and thus guard and maintain the prosperity of Our Imperial Throne coeval with heaven and earth. So shall ye not only be Our good and faithful subjects, but render illustrious the best traditions of your forefathers.

The Way here set forth is indeed the teaching bequeathed by Our Imperial Ancestors, to be observed alike by Their Descendants and the subjects, infallible for all ages and true in all places. It is Our wish to lay it to heart in all reverence, in common with you, Our subjects, that we may all thus attain to the same virtue.[23]

As Carol Gluck points out, the rescript consists of a Mito school beginning and a Confucian center, promoting the virtues that had by then become part of both the popular morality and national ideology.[24] To these is added an imperial ending that made the unbroken line of emperors, "coeval with heaven and earth," the source of these virtues. In this way it succinctly combines the elements we have identified here as part of the Japanese concept of peace: stability, inner moral cultivation, and beliefs in a unique cultural identity. The rescript itself was revered as an icon, and together with the other elements of State Shinto it was proclaimed to be a matter of morals, rather than religion, and while citizens were free to choose the latter, the former remained a duty incumbent on all. In the years leading up to World War II, religious groups were enlisted—some voluntarily, others displaying varying degrees of resistance—in the propagation of this national ideology.

A Buddhist lay religious movement was particularly important in the propagation of this ideology, and became a vehicle for the popularization of Nichiren Buddhism, contributing to the development of many new religious movements in the immediate prewar and postwar period. As a final illustration of the Japanese cultural concept of peace combining stability, moral cultivation, and ethnic superiority let us take a brief look at the development of civilizational discourse in Nichirenism.

Tanaka Chigaku and Nichirenism

Nichirenism, or *Nichiren shugi*, is a term applied to a number of popular religious organizations, largely lay, that began to emerge within the tradition of Nichiren Buddhism from the middle of the nineteenth century. These groups to a certain extent grew out of lay confraternities within that religious tradition, and, like many of the New Religions, they often emphasized practices such as faith healing and the attainment of this-world benefits. Tanaka Chigaku (1861–1939), a lay preacher from Tokyo, is the best-known representative of these movements, and because of his contribution to civilizational discourse on peace he will be the focus of our investigation.

Shortly after his father's death in 1870, Tanaka was enrolled as a novice in a Nichiren temple in northeastern Tokyo, and began a period of doctrinal study that was to last for much of the next decade. After repeated illness and, reportedly, disillusionment with the leaders of the sect regarding accommodation to the state's religious policy in the early Meiji period, Tanaka renounced his priestly vows in 1879 and embarked the following year upon a career as a lay preacher of Nichiren Buddhism. Three recurrent messages can be found in Tanaka's preaching: criticism of the priestly establishment, a concern that Buddhism had become separated from the daily life of most Japanese, and the belief that the true Buddhist faith presented by Nichiren would guarantee the security of the nation. This last point is one of the central tenets of Nichiren Buddhism. The thirteenth-century monk after whom the sect was named denounced other popular forms of Buddhist practice as false and malicious, proclaiming that faith in the *Lotus Sutra* was the only path to salvation in the corrupt age of *mappō*. *Mappō* is the final stage in a degenerate view of history, and, because of a historically incorrect dating of the Buddha's death, it was widely believed to have been inaugurated in the twelfth century. Famine, epidemic, earthquakes, and conflict were all seen as indications of the arrival of *mappō*, and Nichiren called for conversion to the true faith of his own preaching as the means to save the nation from these threats. His exhortations were summarized in the *Risshō ankokuron* [Treatise on pacifying the state by establishing orthodoxy], presented to the Kamakura shogunate in 1260.

Developments at the end of the nineteenth century led to Tanaka Chigaku's fusing of Nichiren doctrine with the notions of stability and cultural superiority we have been discussing, issuing in the clearest expression of the "civilizational" concept of peace in the prewar period. It seems that Tanaka was greatly influenced by the outpouring of patriotism accompanying the Sino-Japanese War in 1894–1895, and from about that time a national mission to unify the world under the reign of the Japanese emperor became a major theme of his teaching. For example, he presented a document entitled *Bukkyō fūfu ron* [Treatise on Buddhist married life] to the Emperor and Empress in November 1894, on the occasion of their twenty-fifth wedding anniversary. While this treatise on one level reflected his earlier concern with presenting Buddhist principles for daily life, in this case by developing a Buddhist doctrine of marriage, it was also an argument for Japan's mission of world unification. Tanaka argued here that Nichiren Buddhism and the Japanese state were inseparably linked, like man and wife, for the accomplishment of this goal.

From about 1903, Tanaka began to develop a syncretic blend of Nichiren and nativist, or Shinto, ideas in order to promote this sense of national mission. Unlike Norinaga's use of the *Kojiki*, however, Tanaka turned to the other ancient text of Japanese mythology, the *Nihon shoki*, where the first Japanese emperor, Jinmu, is exalted as the unifier of the country. Borrowing an expression from the *Nihon shoki*, *hakkō ichiu*, whose meaning is usually rendered as the unity of the whole world under one roof, Tanaka maintained that it was the divine mission of the imperial line of Japan, founded by Jinmu, to lead the whole world into a unity that would bring about peace.

It seems that Tanaka himself was ambiguous concerning the means necessary to accomplish this unification. In his analysis of the tenets of Nichirenism, Edwin Lee states that in a treatise calling for the unification of Japanese Buddhism in 1901, *Shūmon no ishin* [Reform of religion], Tanaka uses military images to call for an aggressive implementation of Japan's "heavenly mandate to unite the world."[25] In his later work on the *Nihon shoki*, however, Tanaka called for a "unification by righteousness," the peaceful recognition of the divinely ordained world order.[26] These two elements are brought together in a collection of Tanaka's articles translated into English and published in 1935 by his son, Satomi Kishio, under the title, *What is Nippon Kokutai? Introduction to Nipponese National Principles.* There a two-stage implementation of world unity is called for: first "spiritual absorption" through the promotion of the Japanese national principles, followed by military pacification, where the unruly and lawless people of the world are brought under Japan's control.[27] It is worth noting that what we see here is an interesting inversion of Aizawa's thoughts on the role of Christianity in the implementation of the Western colonial mission.[28]

Hakkō ichiu, as promoted by Tanaka and other Nichirenists in the early half of the twentieth century, proclaimed that it was Japan's national mission to extend the benefits of civilization, primarily that of stability under the emperor's rule, to the rest of the world, and thus establish profound peace.[29] Foreign conflicts had become a matter of increasing concern from the beginning of the nineteenth century, but in both the *jōi* concept and twentieth-century Nichirenism the need for military might to defend the borders or fulfill the national mission was always combined with recourse to spiritual means, with much emphasis given to moral cultivation as a requisite to the establishment of peace at home and abroad.

Christian peace discourse, centering on pacifism and the just war theory, was introduced into this environment with the reestablishment of the Christian mission to Japan in the latter half of the nineteenth century. We turn now to a consideration of that discourse, and how it was developed in line with the native ideas concerning peace that we have focused on in this chapter.

MEIJI CHRISTIAN INFLUENCES ON PEACE DISCOURSE

Japanese Christian intellectuals in the Meiji period often found themselves caught between two cultures, and occasionally they took it upon themselves to be a bridge between the West and Japan. In this section we will take a look first at perhaps the two most influential examples of this position, Nitobe Inazō and Uchimura Kanzō. Although lifelong friends, these two figures took very different approaches to the task of explaining the two cultures to each other. We begin with Nitobe's presentation of bushido, the warrior ethic, as "the soul of Japan."

Nitobe Inazō's Bushido

Nitobe Inazō (1862–1933) was born just six years prior to the dawn of the modern Japan that he has come to represent to the West. From the north of Japan, Nitobe studied at Sapporo Agricultural College, which had been founded in 1876 with the help of the American Christian missionary William S. Clark. It was while in Sapporo that Nitobe himself was converted to Christianity, and after further studies at Tokyo University he set out in 1884 to study abroad, first in the United States and later in Germany. Following six years of study in the West, Nitobe married an American Quaker, Mary Elkington, and returned to teach at his alma mater in Sapporo. Poor health led him to move to the West Coast of the United States in 1897, but by 1900 he had recovered sufficiently to become a consultant on sugar production in Taiwan, which had by then become a Japanese colony. He later became a professor of colonial policy at Tokyo University, a position he held until he was appointed under secretary general of the League of Nations in Geneva. Nitobe returned home to Japan in 1926 and remained active in foreign relations until his death in 1933, shortly after he had to defend Japan's military action in Manchuria to his academic and diplomatic colleagues at a conference held in Canada.

Although Nitobe's writings total sixteen volumes, perhaps his most famous work is a short book called *Bushido: The Soul of Japan*, written while he was convalescing on the West Coast of the United States. In this book, Nitobe calls upon the warrior ethic of the Tokugawa period to explain the ethical foundations of Japanese society to a Western audience, in answer, he says, to "the frequent queries put by my wife as to the reasons why such and such ideas and customs prevail in Japan."[30] In his explanation of this ethic Nitobe highlights many of the elements we have identified as important to the prewar Japanese concept of peace. Despite the fact that his wife and many of his teachers were Quakers, Nitobe himself does not adopt a pacifist position but, as his positive evaluation of bushido indicates, he recognizes that the use of force is at times unavoidable. Although he does not use the term "just war," in many respects his arguments reflect the main concerns of this theory.

First of all, justice or rectitude is identified as the prime virtue of bushido. *Gi* in Japanese, justice or rectitude is related to duty, or *giri*, specifically the obligations to parents, superiors, inferiors, and society at large, the relationships highlighted in Confucian ethics.[31] Nitobe also translates *giri* literally as Right Reason, in order to point out how such relationships are central to proper order. As a motive, *giri* is described as "infinitely inferior to the Christian doctrine of love," but its central place in the moral code of bushido is a recognition that love is often insufficient as a motivation in human affairs:

> Since if love does not rush to deeds of virtue, recourse must be had to man's intellect and his reason must be quickened to convince him of the necessity of acting aright.[32]

Nitobe decries the fact that *giri*, which as Right Reason should be the "categorical imperative" for moral behavior, has "in time degenerated into a vague sense of propriety called up to explain this and sanction that." The reasons for this decline are what he labels "the conditions of an artificial society":

> a society in which accident of birth and unmerited favour instituted class distinctions, in which the family was the social unit, in which seniority of age was of more account than superiority of talents, in which natural affection had often to succumb before arbitrary man-made customs.[33]

Although in tension with his earlier acceptance of right relationships and the obligations that these relationships entail, these sentiments of Nitobe echo the arguments of Motoori Norinaga and Kokugaku for a natural sensitivity, stripped of foreign artificiality, or an inherent sense of what is right. In his argument bushido is saved from a degraded concept of duty by its second virtue, courage. Nitobe defines courage as acting in rectitude or justice, plainly put as "doing what is right,"[34] once again reflecting the naivete or primitivism of Kokugaku arguments. Courage is self-sacrificing, and its cultivation requires a sternness verging on cruelty. As an example of the popular image of this native ethic that Nitobe's work helped to create, I quote at length from his argument regarding the inculcation of courage in the young:

> Samurai's sons were let down to steep valleys of hardship, and spurred to Sisyphus-like tasks. Occasional deprivation of food or exposure to cold, was considered a highly efficacious test for inuring them to endurance. Children of tender age were sent among utter strangers with some message to deliver, were made to rise before the sun, and before breakfast attend to their reading exercises, walking to their teachers with bare feet in the cold of winter; they frequently—once or twice a month, as on the festival of a god of learning—came together in small groups and passed the night without sleep, in reading aloud by turns. Pilgrimages to all sorts of

uncanny places—to execution grounds, to graveyards, to houses reputed of being haunted, were favourite pastimes of the young. In the days when decapitation was public, not only were small boys sent to witness the ghastly scene, but they were made to visit alone the place in the darkness of night and there to leave a mark of their visit on the trunkless head.[35]

Such training is positively evaluated, for in addition to stoic courage it also contributes to the cultivation of benevolence, an affection for others that is called *bushido no nasake,* the tenderness of the warrior. Such tenderness is supposed to temper righteousness, but the two are always held in balance:

> Rectitude carried to excess hardens into stiffness; benevolence indulged beyond measure sinks into weakness.[36]

While reflecting Tokugawa discourse on benevolence here, Nitobe also makes a comparison with Western, Christian practice, pointing out that courtesies offered the fallen enemy, including medical treatment, is not a practice limited to the West with their conventions regarding conduct in war, but is also a part of the bushido tradition. We might use this as a stepping off point, to introduce some of the parallels found in the bushido code as presented by Nitobe and the Christian just war tradition. Nitobe himself advocated a presumption against the use of force, writing that "fighting in itself, be it offensive or defensive, is, as Quakers rightly testify, brutal and wrong."[37] The same idea is expressed in the bushido apothegms:

> "To be beaten is to conquer," meaning true conquest consists in not opposing a riotous foe; and "The best won victory is that obtained without the shedding of blood."[38]

Nitobe also speaks of limits placed on the redress of wrongs, specifically that of exacting vengeance.

> Injury must be recompensed with justice—and yet revenge was justified only when it was undertaken in behalf of our superiors and benefactors. One's own wrongs, including injuries done to wife and children, were to be borne and forgiven.[39]

Thus, although Nitobe does not specifically refer to the just war theory, in presenting the warrior ethic to the West he indicates a concern with pointing out parallels with the Christian doctrine, in terms of the presumption against force, limiting the conditions when force can be applied, and conduct in war. In the midst of the postwar concern to establish the foundations of Japanese pacifism, Nitobe's contribution to Meiji-era discourse on war and peace is often ignored. In fact, *Bushido* was translated into Japanese and became influential as part of the right-wing bushido revival in Japan in the 1930s, no doubt contrary to Nitobe's own intent in writing the book. Indeed, it could be that the popularization of Nitobe's explanation of bushido by the rightists has contributed to the rejection of just war ideas in the postwar period, a point we will return to in Chapter Four.

Nitobe was in many ways very much a man of his times. Accepting, even embracing, the new reality of a Japan open to the West, he sought to present the dynamics of his own culture in terms that would be discernible to its new partners, and rivals. He also accepted, seemingly unquestioningly, military and colonial exploits as part of the new reality into which Japan had stepped in its drive to become a modern nation state, equal to the Western powers. One of his contemporaries, Uchimura Kanzō, also initially accepted, but later rejected, these developments. Uchimura made an explicit attempt to explain his positions in terms of both Christian just war and pacifist theories, and it is to him that we turn next.

Uchimura Kanzō's Conversion to Pacifism

Born one year earlier than Nitobe Inazō, Uchimura Kanzō (1861–1930) also studied at the Sapporo Agricultural College, where the two met, were converted to Christianity together, and became lifelong friends. Uchimura shared Nitobe's desire to bridge the two cultures that had so influenced his own life, writing extensively on Japan in English and lecturing on Christianity in Japanese. After a short, failed marriage he went to study at Amherst College and Hartford Theological Seminary in the United States before returning to Japan in 1888. His career as a teacher in Japan was short-lived and stormy, marked by frequent clashes with the authorities over his principles. The most famous of these incidents occurred in 1891, when he was accused by journalists and scholars of *lèse majesté* for refusing to bow before the Imperial Rescript on Education. Finding that he could support himself as a writer, he quit teaching and became editor of a succession of magazines and newspapers.

Furthermore, although he had decided against becoming an ordained minister during his theological studies in the States, he began a series of popular lectures on the Christian scriptures and religion. In time Uchimura gathered a number of followers sympathetic to his view that Christianity works best without ecclesiastical structures, and he is recognized as the founder of the Mukyōkai, or Non-Church Movement.[40]

Through his extensive writings Uchimura has become identified with the Christian pacifist movement in Japan. Early on, however, he was a supporter of Japan's intervention in Korea, using just war rhetoric to voice his agreement with that policy. In a rather long essay published in *The Japan Weekly Mail* on 11 August 1894 entitled "Justification for the Korean War," Uchimura lays out the reasons for war with China over spheres of influence on the Korean peninsula.

The essay begins by recognizing problems with the just war thesis, especially as it has been used in the West. Uchimura acknowledges that greed, which he calls "lusts," is the normal cause for war, and rhetoric concerning "righteousness" is often merely a justification of greed. This is particularly so in the "materialistic" nineteenth century, when the nations of the West—of "Christendom"—have embarked on wars for personal gain. Uchimura argues, however, that nobler motives can still be found in the East.

> Heathenism if dark is earnest, and it may yet retain enthusiasm which Christendom has lost with its superstitions. A sort of Chivalric spirit is yet with us, a spirit akin to Spartan courage, and Roman valour to crush the proud. If the West has passed its era of enthusiasm, the East is still in it, and a righteous war is still *possible with us.*[41]

Uchimura goes on to list Japan's grievances against China, as well as to point out that Japan had tried to avoid war with its "haughty and impudent" neighbor for more than a decade already. In answer to the argument that Japan has as little right to interfere in Korean affairs as China, he mounts a spirited defense of an activist policy in order to save Korea from a worse fate:

> [W]e *have* right to interfere, and it is our duty to interfere, when they are dying of hunger, when they are attacked by robbers, when our plain common-sense shows us that they are rapidly going toward the brink of destruction....We interfere with Korea because

her independence is in jeopardy, because the world's most backward nation is grasping it in her benumbing coils, and savagery and inhumanity reign there when light and civilization are at her very doors. Right we have not to disturb her healthy peace, much less to degrade her; but to save her and free her from evils too glaringly apparent, our sacred right of neighbourhood compels us to vigorous interference on her behalf.[42]

Indeed, Uchimura sees Japan as the savior of all Asia, and the present war as an inevitable conflict between a small, modern country and a large, ancient civilization that will determine the future of the continent:

Japan's victory will mean free government, free education, free religion, and free commerce for 600,000,000 souls that live on this side of the globe, while her defeat and China's victory will mean— what, let the reader judge for himself.[43]

Uchimura's essay is notable for the role given the East, especially Japan, as the agent of justice and purveyor of civilization, as well as for the strident tone that it takes in asserting that role. Uchimura soon regretted this stand. Less than a year after the publication of "Justification for the Korean War," Uchimura reveals his embarrassment with his arguments in a letter to a supporter in the United States:

The trouble with China is over; or rather, it is said to be over. The war developed all the goodness and boldness in our national temper, and the kind Providence gave us a check for the latter aspect of our nature. A "righteous war" has changed into a *piratic* war somewhat, and a prophet who wrote its "justification" is now in shame.[44]

His disappointment with the policies of his government, however, had not yet led him to abandon the notion that some battles are better fought than avoided. In a short essay published in *Sekai no Nihon* [Japan in the World] on 1 August 1897 entitled *Heiwa zuki no tami* [A Peace-Loving People], Uchimura takes exception to the argument made by the philosopher Inoue Tetsujirō that, in contrast to the West, Japan has from ancient times been a country of gentle, peace-loving people. Uchimura's objection is not directed at the claim made by Inoue, but rather at the fact that the Japanese are perhaps too eager to accept peace at any price:

There are in the world people who love an ignoble peace. Although war is to be avoided, it should not be avoided merely for the sake of peace. Righteousness is more important than life itself. For the sake of justice and truth we should sacrifice our lives, we should fight even if the future of the nation is at stake. The Japanese are so in love with peace that they are willing to sacrifice what is clearly a just and noble cause.[45]

Given Uchimura's combative, uncompromising character, we can imagine that it must have taken a considerable amount of soul-searching before he adopted the pacifist option. It would appear that it was the approach of another war, the Russo-Japanese War of 1904–1905, that precipitated his conversion to this position. In a short essay published on 30 June 1903 entitled *Sensō haishiron* [The Abolition of War], Uchimura declares, "I am not only against the commencement of hostilities with Russia, I am for the absolute abolition of all wars. War is murder, and murder is a crime."[46]

Although an essay written in English at the outbreak of war early in 1904 tends to justify Japan's actions as a response to insults suffered at the hands of Christendom (represented here by Russia),[47] an essay published later in the year entitled *Yo ga hisenronsha to narishi yurai* [Why I Became an Antiwar Advocate] both confirms Uchimura's conversion to pacifism and offers reasons for his about-face on this issue. Along with his reading of scripture and some personal experiences, Uchimura offers his disappointment at the outcome of the war with China a decade earlier—a war that he notes he defended in the essay we looked at above—as his reasons for adopting the pacifist position. Concerning the Sino-Japanese War he writes:

> The result of the Sino-Japanese War taught me that war is destructive and offers no benefits. Korean independence, the motivation for the war, is in fact less secure than ever; morality in Japan, the victor, has been immensely corrupted, and no one has been able to rein in marauders in China, the vanquished enemy. These are the results of the war, the victory, that I see in Japan, the land of my birth.[48]

The pacifism advocated by Uchimura, however, was not as thoroughgoing as we might assume. Specifically, in an article written just one month after the pacifist manifesto mentioned above, Uchimura encourages like-minded conscripts to "swallow your tears and follow the order" to report for military service. He offers several reasons for his advice: that the refusal to serve will be seen as self-serving cowardice and reflect unfavorably on the pacifist position; that others will end up fighting in their place and so their refusal will result in the sacrifice of these others; and, using the Christian idea of reparation, that the evil of war can only be atoned for by the sacrifice of many innocent pacifists.[49] As high-minded as these reasons are, they indicate that Uchimura was willing to make some compromise with society, or with the realities of war, in trying to apply the pacifist position. The difficulty in maintaining the absolute pacifist position has already been alluded to in the introduction to this present study, and it will be a major theme as we look at the doctrine and practice of the New Religions in the following chapters.

Finally, we turn briefly to one more Japanese Christian figure from the Meiji period who both illustrates the problem of maintaining the absolute pacifist position and provides an example of how the Japanese cultural emphasis on moral cultivation can lead to a radical quietism.

Pacifism's Discontents

Kinoshita Naoe (1869–1937) was a well-known journalist who became active at an early age in political affairs, motivated by his Christian faith. Kinoshita attended Tokyo Senmon Gakkō, later renamed Waseda University, one of the renowned Christian academies in the capital. After graduation he returned to his hometown of Matsumoto and became a reporter for the local newspaper. It was while in Matsumoto that he first became involved in Christian lay activities, including the prohibition movement, eventually accepting baptism at the age of twenty-four. He later also joined the seminal socialist movement there.

His hard-hitting reporting on corruption in Matsumoto landed him in prison in Tokyo, and after acquittal he decided to remain in the capital, finding employment with the *Mainichi Shinbun*, a major national newspaper. While a reporter for the *Mainichi* he was sent to investigate copper pollution at the Ashio Mine north of Tokyo, and the resulting articles, later published as a book, document perhaps the earliest modern environmental scandal in the world.[50]

Kinoshita was an eloquent orator, and from the time of the Sino-Japanese War in 1894–1895 he took a consistently pacifist position, based on his Christian beliefs. In 1906, however, he decided to remove himself from all political activity, and devoted the rest of his life to meditation. Kinoshita explains this decision in an essay published that year entitled *Zange* (Penitence):

> We often use the words "radical revolution," and we have grown used to hearing the expression from others as well. But what do we mean by "radical?"…Now I feel only shame at the shallowness of the idea that the world can be saved through political action. When I decided to become a Christian, I dove right into the movement to "realize the gospel of Christ through political action." Of course, hidden behind the desire for political success was the hunger for my own fame. All of my efforts were in fact directed towards the "king of this world." Although I said that I was sacrificing myself for the world, in fact in my heart I sought to sacrifice the world for myself. For this, as far as I was concerned, the whole world could be destroyed. Ahh, is this the spirit of someone who calls himself a pacifist?[51]

As a consequence of this reflection on his own motives and how he had been led astray by his desires, Kinoshita advocated an inner, spiritual revolution in the latter half of his life. His turn to the inner life, as dramatic in its own way as that of Uchimura from just war theories to pacifism, is not necessarily reflective of the demands that most pacifists feel in living out the implications of the absolute moral position that they have taken. It does reflect, however, a more general movement away from society in an effort to live out that choice, a matter that we will take up directly in the next chapter. As an example of the emphasis placed on internal moral cultivation it is also extreme—pursuit of this aim does not normally issue in such a radical quietism. An explicit decision to eschew political activity, such as that made by Kinoshita, can be seen in the doctrine of only one of the groups under study here, Byakkō Shinkōkai. The degree to which interest in such activity can be maintained in an atmosphere that emphasizes internal solutions to life's problems, however, will also be a major theme of this book.

◆   ◆   ◆

Historical circumstances in combination with the various religious traditions found in Japan contributed to the development of a concept of peace that emphasized stability and order, individual moral cultivation, and a sense of mission to spread the benefits of civilization, namely a stable society under the rule of the Japanese emperor. While a more comprehensive study of the development of the concept of peace in Japanese intellectual history might reveal other important elements, as well as provide context and nuance to the elements highlighted here, the present study has at least succeeded in identifying some of the more obvious material that played an important part in forming the ideas of peace that were prominent in the prewar period, as well as providing a necessary corrective to the exclusive concern with pacifism in postwar peace studies. Additionally, in dealing with the Meiji Christian contribution to peace discourse, I have highlighted just war rhetoric alongside the pacifist position usually identified with the Meiji Christians in most current studies on peace. Although these Christians may not have been instrumental in promoting the Christian just war theory as such, they doubtless contributed to the rhetoric of just war in the prewar period. Indications of the prevalence of such rhetoric can be found in the wartime doctrine and activities of some of the groups used in this study. We will also see how such rhetoric is almost universally rejected in the postwar period, contributing to confusion concerning the pacifist position and legitimate security issues.

We turn now to an examination of the doctrine and practice of peace in the six groups chosen for this study. In the next three chapters, dealing with pacifism and the just war, material on five of the groups will be presented in turn. Given the pervasiveness of pacifist rhetoric in postwar Japan we will want to take a close look at just what these groups mean by *heiwa shugi,* not in order to judge them against some ideal standard, but rather in the hope of introducing some clarity to the current discussion in Japan on war and peace. The sixth group will be highlighted in Chapter Five, when we examine the role that moral cultivation plays in the concept of peace proposed by all six of the groups. In Chapter Six we will once again return to material from all six of the groups in order to explore how ideas of ethnic superiority and national mission are reinterpreted in the postwar period.

TWO

The Pacifist Option

In the Christian tradition, after the fourth century, pacifism, as an absolute moral position, has been largely restricted to religious orders and the so-called peace churches (Anabaptists, Quakers, and Brethren).[1] As David Martin points out, these groups were able to maintain the pacifist position by removing themselves somewhat from society—religious orders through their vows, and the peace churches by segregating themselves, to varying degrees, from society.[2] This separation is necessary because the absolute rejection of force cannot be reconciled with the responsibilities of guaranteeing national defense and preserving good order, considerations that must be faced if one seeks to participate in government.

Of the peace churches, the Quakers have been most active politically, running for elective office and supporting a legislative lobbying effort in the United States. Therefore their case might be most instructive in pointing out how the pacifist option can only be maintained by separation from society. Founding their own colonies in the Americas, Quakers were a major force in the politics of Pennsylvania and New

Jersey. Unable to accept the increasing demands to compromise their conscientious beliefs, however, most of the Quaker legislators in Pennsylvania resigned in the mid-1750s, during the French and English wars. Conflicts over slavery led to a move towards more complete separation among Quakers in the United States in the 1820s, and it was only in 1943 that the Quakers returned to politics institutionally, through the establishment of the Friends Committee on National Legislation, formed to lobby the national government on issues related to social justice and world peace.

Quaker believers, as well as members of the other peace churches, were granted conscientious objector status, exempting them from compulsory military service, by various governments from around the beginning of the nineteenth century, in recognition of the pacifist stance taken by these groups rejecting participation in any war. Since it was more difficult for believers of the mainline churches, with their just war theories, to receive such status, this is a concrete example of the obligations that society imposes on its members, as well as of how the peace churches remove themselves from society in order to pursue the pacifist option.

The apparent necessity to be somewhat removed from society in order to fulfill the demands of the pacifist position becomes problematic when one considers the situation in postwar Japan. The constitution adopted in 1946, the so-called Peace Constitution, explicitly renounces the threat or use of force as a policy tool available to the government.[3] Although the intent of the article is clearly pacifist, this position has been heavily compromised from early in the postwar period. Following the outbreak of hostilities on the Korean Peninsula in 1950, the allied forces occupying Japan urged the government to form a National Police Reserve, renamed the Self-Defense Force in 1954, to assist in the defense of the islands should the need arise. This body, divided into land, sea, and air defense units, constitutes in all but name the military force proscribed by Article 9 of the constitution, and the recognition of the need, and right, to defend the nation by force is clearly contrary to the pacifist position. This compromise with the exigencies of national security was accomplished not through constitutional change, which might have served to clarify peace discourse in postwar Japan, but by administrative interpretation of the constitution, a practice followed by subsequent governments in determining the size of the force, its budget allocation, and, initially, its deployment outside Japanese territorial limits in an auxiliary capacity to allied forces in the wake of the Persian Gulf War. While the "Peace Constitution" remains intact, Japanese pacifism has long ago been abandoned to the realities of life in international society. The process by which this has been done, however, has contributed greatly to the popular confusion regarding the implications of the pacifist position, as well as the limited availability of this option.

Two of the groups examined in this study have, to varying degrees and in very different ways, separated themselves from mainstream society sufficiently to maintain a somewhat strict pacifism. This chapter will outline their beliefs and explore the implications of their pacifism. We begin with a monastic Buddhist sect, Nipponzan Myōhōji.

NICHIREN MONASTICISM IN NIPPONZAN MYŌHŌJI

Nipponzan Myōhōji is a small group of both lay and monastic Nichiren Buddhists, numbering about 1,500 people. Each of the Nipponzan Myōhōji temples is nominally independent, and the group appears to have a very loose organizational structure, with activities coordinated by discussion among the members. The lay members usually participate in the activities of one of the Myōhōji temples, while the monks and nuns are more prominent in the group's activities both nationally and internationally. The origins of the group can be traced back to early in this century, with the establishment of the first Nipponzan Myōhōji temple by Fujii Nichidatsu (1885–1985) in Northern China in 1918.

Fujii was born in Kumamoto Prefecture, in the southern part of Japan. At the age of 19 he decided to become a Nichiren Buddhist monk and studied extensively in Tokyo and Kyoto before leaving on a missionary trip to China in 1917. Following the establishment of his first temple the following year, Nipponzan Myōhōji temples were established in five other places in Manchuria within the next six years. In 1923, as Fujii was preparing to expand his missionary work into Russia, he heard word of the Great Kanto Earthquake, and, in the tradition of Nichiren, fearing for the safety of his homeland he changed his plans and returned to Japan. The following year a Nipponzan Myōhōji temple was established at the foot of Mt. Fuji, that prayers might be made there for the sake of the nation. The same year, Fujii was arrested as he tried to get near to the compound where the Taishō Emperor was convalescing, in order to offer prayers for the emperor's health.

The picture Fujii paints of himself in his autobiography is that of a fearless rebel and ascetic.[4] He tells us that his decision to take monastic vows led to his disinheritance by his father, and that his first mission, a meeting hall for a small group of believers near Lake Biwa outside of Kyoto, was established in circumvention of government policy at that time limiting the opening of new Buddhist facilities. He left that mission in only a year, and, after a brief period of conscription in the infantry, adopted the life of an itinerant monk, beating a drum and chanting the *daimoku*[5] as he walked, a practice called *gyakku shōdai*.[6] His prayers for the Taishō Emperor took this form, and the resulting commotion near the emperor's villa led to his arrest and detention. He attributes his early release on this occasion to the fact that he embarked on a hunger strike, and in the more detailed Japanese version of his autobiography he recounts that after his release he rented a storefront across from the police station where he had been detained, and from there he harangued the police chief to come out and answer why he was persecuting monks who only sought to pray for the emperor in his time of need.[7]

Fasting and cold water austerities are fairly common religious practices in Japan, often adopted by Buddhist and other mountain ascetics as part of their spiritual training. Fujii was no exception, incorporating week-long fasts and periods of prayer under waterfalls as part of his normal practice. In addition, he made use of a particularly painful ascetic method at key points in his life, when faced with major decisions concerning his missionary work. The English account of his autobiography describes this practice in vivid detail:

> One often loses his way in his lifetime. When one has no idea how he should live the rest of his life, how he should make up his mind, or what decisions he should make, he should really wager his whole body and soul and wait for instructions from Heaven. To do so, he must be prepared to give up his life.
>
> In Chapter XXIII of the Lotus Sutra, the story of the Boddhisattva Medicine-King, an exercise of "paying homage by means of burning one's own body and arms" is referred to. That is what induced me to burn my body.... Specifically, I performed it by burning a bundle of incense sticks fixed horizontally to my arm. The skin became inflamed and a blister formed. The blister soon broke,

Nipponzan Myōhōji monks chanting at a ceremony held at the
Tama Dōjō, west of Tokyo.

and a foul smelling liquid drained out of it, which moistened both
the skin and incense sticks. Normally a bundle of incense sticks
burns in half an hour, but the moisture delayed this. This process
was repeated over and over again for hours. Afterward, the skin was
quite inflamed, and an open wound resulted, giving me quite a bit
of pain. The wound of course needed medical treatment, but I
could not rely on either a surgeon or medicine to cure it. So I put

47

the white and green parts of a green onion on it. After a while, the wound ceased to be painful. I remember it took the wound about 100 days to heal, leaving a scar. I have six such scars on my body.[8]

The defiant, unyielding spirit depicted in Fujii's autobiography permeates Nipponzan Myōhōji's activities, and no doubt helped to attract another generation of rebels, the student protesters of the 1960s, to its particular brand of monastic life. Katō Hiromichi, a Myōhōji monk I interviewed as part of this research project, was one of those rebels.[9] Katō dropped out of college in 1970, at the height of the student rebellion in Japan, and set out on a three-year trip through Asia. He describes his decision as follows:

> When I was a student, there was something about the peace movement, the leftist kind of ideology of the peace movement, that just didn't sit right with me. Of course, I agreed with a lot of what they were saying, and I participated in it myself to a certain extent. But there was this feeling that something was missing. So, I didn't know what to do, and like many people in the 60s I figured if I traveled abroad—not that anything would change really, but there might be something there—I just had this vague feeling that if I went someplace else that I would find something there.

After traveling through Australia, Indonesia, Malaysia, Thailand, all the way to Afghanistan, supporting himself through odd jobs and the generosity of the people met along the way, Katō found himself in India, where he received the hospitality of Myōhōji monks.

> I myself didn't care much for beating the drums and all that. But they would let you sleep at the temple, and even feed you at that. I was living on whatever I could get, you know. And you could speak Japanese there as well, so I would go to the temple from time to time, but I really didn't care for the prayers.

Wavering in his rebellion against society after three years on the road, and beginning to feel guilty about abandoning his parents for such a long time, Katō contemplated returning to Japan and settling down. Fujii himself, however, convinced Katō to reconsider his plans, telling him that the best service he could perform for his parents would be to take vows as a Myōhōji monk, thus offering Katō a way to continue his life opposed to society and its demands. Looking back on that decision from the perspective of twenty years as a monk, Katō agrees with its wisdom.

I really couldn't find my way in society. I can't just be quiet and accept society as it is. I just can't see myself following the establishment. We call it unyielding, defiant, a defiant spirit. I guess I still have that defiance, even today.

It is perhaps significant that Katō first met Nipponzan Myōhōji monks in India, for that country held a special meaning for Fujii's work. Following the death of his mother in 1930 Fujii once again left Japan, this time embarking upon what he considered his most important missionary endeavor, the return of Buddhism to India, the land of its birth. After a visit to the Indian border with Nepal, where the Buddha is reputed to have been born, he proselytized in Calcutta and Bombay for the next three years, without much success. In 1933 he interrupted his mission to India to travel to Ceylon, and in that Buddhist country he was able to attract a number of disciples. In October of 1933 he returned to India for an audience with Mahatma Gandhi, the leader of the Indian independence movement and exponent of nonviolent resistance. Fujii apparently spent about a month at Gandhi's ashram at Wardha, and during that time he was allowed two audiences with Gandhi, which lasted only twenty and five minutes respectively. Despite the shortness of these encounters, in later years Fujii placed great importance on them, for he often identified his own postwar philosophy of nonviolent activism with Gandhi's example.

In the postwar years, the monks and nuns of Nipponzan Myōhōji have been in the foreground of the peace movement in Japan. They can often be seen leading peace marches, protesting at military bases, conducting hunger strikes at major urban intersections, all the while beating their drums and chanting the *daimoku* for peace. During the Persian Gulf War, for example, this group staged a hunger strike in the square in front of Shibuya Station, one of the major commuter stations in Tokyo, in protest of the war. Their activities, moreover, are not limited to Japan, for they have been active in Cambodia, Sri Lanka, Nicaragua, and Bosnia, demonstrating for peace in the midst of strife, and have been active in the peace movement in the United States as well. All of this activity is based on the example of nonviolent resistance offered by Gandhi, and reflects the unyielding defiance of the group towards the international power structure. This kind of pacifism was not always characteristic of Fujii or his followers, however. There are indications that Fujii and his disciples were supportive of Japan's war effort earlier in this century, and it is to that issue that we now turn.

PRE-PACIFIST MYŌHŌJI

At the time of his second audience with Gandhi, Fujii entrusted the leader of the independence movement with a letter describing the purpose of his mission in India. Since this letter reveals the state of Fujii's thought on war and peace at that time, let me briefly summarize its contents.[10] Fujii begins by stating his belief that it is Indian Buddhism that is the true mother of Japanese civilization, and goes on to express his regret that this same Buddhism finds no followers in the land of its birth. Moving on to the issue of Japan's military activities in Manchuria, which had already begun to attract the condemnation of various countries throughout the world, Fujii acknowledges that Japan has been forced into a position of isolation because of its actions in China, but states that even if it should face the threat of armed coercion from the whole world Japan should not sway from the course that it believes is just. Fujii maintains that although Japan might be a country small in area, the fact that in its 2,600-year history it has not once suffered invasion from a foreign power indicates a strength out of proportion to its size. Furthermore, according to Fujii, aside from one or two wars that were fought to protect itself from destruction, in that 2,600-year history Japan for its part has not invaded any other country. Indeed, Fujii maintains that there is no other country in the world that can boast of such a peaceful history as Japan. Fujii goes on to state that it is religion, namely Buddhism, which has made Japan such a peaceful nation, and for that reason it is Japan's mission to spread that faith, so that other countries might enjoy the peace with which Japan has been blessed.

The contents of this letter clearly reflect the acceptance of some of the beliefs pertaining to Japanese ethnic or cultural superiority, connected in Fujii's case with belief in Buddhism as the foundation of its peace and stability. Furthermore, we have here a clear expression of belief in the national mission of spreading the benefits of civilization as the way to establish peace. The letter also clearly indicates that Fujii had not yet embraced pacifism when he met with Gandhi, for armed intervention in China is accepted as a matter of justice. Indeed, the activity of Fujii and his followers during the war years has occasionally come under criticism for being in contradiction with the pacifism that he claims was his belief even at that time. For example, Tokoro Shigemoto argues that the monks of Nipponzan Myōhōji participated in the Japanese invasion of China by performing functions comparable to that of army chaplains.[11] Specifically, there are reports that Myōhōji monks accompanied Japanese troops in their conquest of Nanking in 1937. Fujii does not deny the fact of their presence, and even boasts that it was the monks and their *daimoku* standard that were first to enter the city at the fall of Nanking. He points out, however, that the monks were unarmed and were there merely to offer prayers.[12] Fujii also admits that he himself made repeated trips to China during the war years and met with many of the top Japanese military personnel, but claims that these meetings had the religious purpose of handing over relics of the Buddha to these men, so that "Buddhism might tie the two people [Japanese and Chinese] together."[13] These meetings were not always for religious purposes, however, as Fujii himself once again admits. In his Japanese autobiography, Fujii states that he was invited to Tokyo to meet with members of the military general staff prior to the Japanese invasion of Burma. Furthermore, according to Fujii's account, the purpose of the meeting was clear from the time of the invitation: to provide information on the situation in India that might be helpful to the military planners. Although Fujii claims that he used the meeting to try to convince the general staff members of the folly of their plans,[14] the fact that he was invited to such a meeting could itself indicate that his past relationships with the general staff and other military leaders were such that they could expect his cooperation.

The evidence then does not support Fujii's postwar claims to have been a pacifist throughout the war years. There is one further incident that indicates that perhaps Fujii's claims to be a lifelong advocate of nonviolence are exaggerated, an incident connected with United States involvement in the Vietnam War that we will address shortly. There is little doubt, however, that Fujii and Nipponzan Myōhōji have been in the forefront in promoting nonviolent resistance as part of the peace movement in Japan, as well as internationally, in the postwar period. We turn next to an outline of those activities.

After Japan's defeat in the war Fujii returned to Kumamoto, the place of his birth, to contemplate what course of action he and Nipponzan Myōhōji should take. He once again entered a fast, and he says that it occurred to him then that Japan had been most at peace during the early years of its history, just after Buddhism was introduced to the country. Of that golden age he writes: "The prime mover to the establishment of peace in that age undoubtedly was Buddhism. I naturally became convinced that a peaceful cultural nation was formed and a moral and orderly society emerged in those days thanks to nothing but Buddhism."[15] He goes on to state his belief that the center of that Buddhist faith was the stupa, a memorial containing the relics of the Buddha. It is this belief that became the motivation for one of the major postwar activities of Nipponzan Myōhōji: the erection of stupas, or Peace Pagodas, throughout Japan and the rest of the world. Construction work on the first such stupa was begun in Kumamoto City that very year, supplementing the voluntary labor of the limited number of followers Fujii had in the area with that of war orphans picked up in the city and recruited for the task. Reliance on such amateurs, as well as the difficulty in obtaining construction materials in the immediate postwar period, led to long delays, and this Peace Pagoda was not completed until 1954. To commemorate the completion of the pagoda the second session of the World Conference of Pacifists was held in Japan that year, following a first session at the Gandhi ashram in Wardha in the early postwar period. The Nichiren sect headquartered at Mt. Minobu and Japanese Christian groups also participated in the session, as well as delegates from India, Ceylon, and Australia.

Following construction of Peace Pagodas in three other areas of Japan, the first pagoda outside the country was dedicated in 1969 in India, to mark the hundredth anniversary of the birth of Gandhi. This pagoda symbolizes the importance Nipponzan Myōhōji places on its relationship with India, not only because of connection with Gandhi, but also because the site chosen for the pagoda was close to where Śākyamuni is supposed to have preached the *Lotus Sutra*, the foundation of Nichiren Buddhism. In the same year a Peace Pagoda was dedicated on Mt. Kiyosumi in Japan, the place where Nichiren is supposed to have first chanted the *daimoku* in praise of the *Lotus Sutra*.

The Peace Pagoda in Leverett, Massachusetts.

The Peace Pagodas are meant to be both a symbol of peace and means for establishing that peace. As a symbol they are to inspire people to pray and work for peace. Members of Nipponzan Myōhōji also believe, however, that their very presence is efficacious towards the establishment of world peace, since the relics of the Buddha contained there should purify and pacify the surrounding area. To this aim, more than seventy pagodas have been erected, mostly in Japan but also in India, Ceylon, England, and the United States.

In addition to the propagation of peace through the construction of pagodas, Nipponzan Myōhōji has also been active since the mid-1950s in opposing American military bases in Japan and, later, in the United States as well. Following the end of the Allied Occupation of Japan in 1952, United States military forces were allowed continued use of bases throughout the country under the terms of the Mutual Defense Treaty signed by the two countries. The bases are a perennial source of contention, particularly in the far southern prefecture of Okinawa where the vast majority of these facilities are now located. What first occasioned Myōhōji's participation in these activities was the plan of the United

States military forces in Japan to extend the runway at the air force base in Tachikawa, west of Tokyo. Myōhōji monks decided to join students and laborers protesting alongside farmers whose land was to be taken for the expansion project. According to Fujii's description of the incident, the protestors, with the monks standing in the front line, were attacked by the police with clubs and over one thousand suffered injuries. After the mass protest was broken up the farmers built a hut for the Myōhōji monks at the end of the runway, where they could continue their opposition by maintaining a prayerful presence. In this way the protests at Tachikawa continued for more than thirteen years, until the United States Air Force decided to abandon the base.

Fujii has described the United States military presence in Japan as part of the continuing occupation of the country, as well as part of a plan "for her invasion of Asia."[16] Myōhōji's antibase campaign is not limited to Japan, however, but has also extended to bases on the American mainland. For example, in the 1980s Myōhōji monks joined other peace activists in the United States in protests at the Trident nuclear submarine base in Bangor, Washington. As an extension of these antibase activities, Myōhōji also joined students and farmers protesting against the construction of the New Tokyo International Airport at Narita in the 1970s, on the grounds that it could be used for military purposes.

Peace marches and peace demonstrations are also characteristic of the activities of this group. As an adaptation of *gyakku shōdai*, the practice of beating a drum and chanting the *daimoku* while walking, peace marches take on a special meaning for Myōhōji members. The group plans an annual peace march to Hiroshima and Nagasaki, coinciding with the anniversaries of the atomic bombing of these cities. In addition to the feelings of national mourning recalled every year on these anniversaries, Fujii also finds personal significance in the bombings, pointing out that the destruction of Hiroshima occurred on his sixtieth birthday. As part of its antinuclear activities, Myōhōji organized a peace march across the United States in 1981–1982, eventually joining in the massive antinuclear demonstration held in New York City on 12 June 1982.

Along with its antinuclear activities in the United States, Myōhōji has also cooperated with the American Indian Movement, participating, for example, in the Longest Walk organized by that group in 1978. This solidarity with native Americans was also expressed through the participation of the monks and nuns in the Walk Across the Americas in

1992, marking the five-hundredth anniversary of Columbus's arrival in the continents.

In the postwar period Fujii has generally advocated a strictly pacifist position that does not allow for the use of force, even in cases of self-defense. In his sermons he shows a full awareness of the implications of this choice. For example, a sermon given in 1950, just after the Cold War had gone hot on the Korean Peninsula, is representative of his position. There he calls for steadfast perseverance in the path of nonviolence, despite the consequences such practice will engender in a world divided into two armed camps.

> If disarmed Japan adheres to and practices persistent nonviolent resistance in light of the imminent international situation ruled by violence, the communist countries would seize the opportunity and give rise to a violent revolution and occupy Japan. At the same time, democratic countries would use Japan as their valuable strategic advanced base. At any rate, it is unlikely that we would be able to avoid being trampled, dishonored and killed at the will of today's violent civilization.[17]

Furthermore, the ultimate self-sacrifice in the face of violence is positively evaluated in the following way:

> Humanity's highest ideal of righteousness cannot be safeguarded if we are agitated by violence, profess fear and recede in its face. Only the self-sacrificing vows and practice of those who do not spare their bodies and lives, but who follow the supreme path, will make Japan a pure land and the world filled with celestial beings. They are those who do not spare their bodies and lives, aspiring to see the Buddha, the World-Honored One, who set an example of the highest ideal of humanity. They are the ones who follow the supreme path that brings deliverance to humanity.[18]

Fujii's followers in Nipponzan Myōhōji generally adhere to these pacifist principles, as reflected in the results of a questionnaire survey I conducted in late 1992–early 1993.[19] The survey included five items designed to measure the degree of consistency in the pacifist position of the respondents. Respondents were queried concerning their opinion on the Persian Gulf War, whether a nation has the right to an armed self-defense, the existence of the Japanese Self-Defense Force, the participation of Self-Defense Forces in United Nations peacekeeping operations, and their willingness to participate if Japan would become involved in a war in the future. Fully 58% of the Myōhōji respondents chose the pacifist response to all of these items, far and away the highest response rate of any of the seven new religious movements included in the survey.[20]

In the various collections of Fujii's sermons and other talks, however, we can find one glaring example of a judgment that casts doubt on the understanding of the pacifist position that he advocated. During the Vietnam War, Fujii sided with the Vietnamese nationalists fighting for an end to United States involvement in the war. Indeed, this was part of the motivation for Myōhōji protests against the New Tokyo International Airport to be built at Narita, for he believed that the airport would be used by United States forces to supply their troops in Vietnam. Several years after the United States had withdrawn from the war, following the final victory by the nationalists over the South Vietnam regime, Fujii gave a speech in the United States in celebration of that victory. In the speech, Fujii hails the war in Vietnam as a prime example of nonviolent pacifism in line with the Buddhist law of *fusesshō*, which prohibits the taking of life. Fujii argues as follows:

America became a violent, all-powerful devil-king, developing all kinds of barbarian, murderous, destructive weapons, and without any reason sent to Vietnam an army—a murderous band—of more than fifty thousand fully armed men, turning the full power of its land, sea, and air forces on the country; bombing, attacking, and shooting until everything that moved on the earth was destroyed. It was all-out war, worthy of the name "genocide." For that reason six hundred thousand young Vietnamese men and women; one million of the aged, women, and children; even the water buffalo and ducks were ruthlessly murdered. The soldiers of the Vietnamese Liberation Front, in order to save the lives of the people, took to the forests and caves and planned their defense. However, not one innocent American citizen—five times the population of Vietnam— was killed. And not one shot was fired at the American homeland, twenty-eight times the size of Vietnam. Not only that, when the American bombers, after dropping five thousand tons of bombs every day and killing or injuring tens of thousands of people, were shot down and the crew taken prisoner, the people avoided the word "prisoner" and instead, out of sympathy for them, created the new term: "pilot without a plane." To support these prisoners, the Vietnamese spent eight times what the normal person would use in one day in order to make their lives comfortable. This is unheard of in the bloody history of war.[21]

By allowing for armed resistance and the killing of military personnel, this statement of Fujii's is clearly in contradiction to his professed nonviolent beliefs, and would seem to limit the definition of pacifism to strictures against the taking of civilian life, which is, in fact, a tenet of the just war position. It is in its own way consistent, however, with some of the main themes of Nipponzan Myōhōji's beliefs and practices. It serves to indicate their preference to support peoples suffering oppression under Western colonialism, as seen in their support of the American Indian Movement and other native peoples of the Americas. It also illustrates the anti-American spirit that pervades Fujii's teachings, based on the development and use of nuclear weapons and the United States' continued military presence in Japan. I believe his position also illustrates one way that prewar notions of ethnic superiority and national mission, elements of the "civilizational" concept of peace, have been transformed in the postwar period, an issue that we will return to and treat at length in Chapter Six.

Nipponzan Myōhōji, as a small group primarily composed of monks and nuns who have renounced the world, provides us with the clearest example of a pacifist group among the new religious movements in Japan. By professing monastic vows, the core membership of this group have removed themselves from society, one way in which the absolute pacifist position can be maintained. We turn now to a very different group that illustrates another approach to pacifism.

BYAKKŌ SHINKŌKAI AND THE POWER OF PRAYER

Kimura Shintarō, a member of Byakkō Shinkōkai in his mid-forties, recounts the following episode from the months leading up to the Persian Gulf War.[22] Hundreds of foreigners, including a number of Japanese, were essentially held hostage in Baghdad as a kind of human shield against the threatened allied attack on Iraq. In an attempt to resolve the situation, Byakkō Shinkōkai took what Kimura believes to be decisive action.

> Masami-sensei,[23] our leader, drew a picture of Hussein's mind, and directed her power at the image. And the interesting thing is, the

Asahi Shinbun or some newspaper reported that Hussein had a dream, and in the dream—you know Hussein is a Muslim, so in the dream Mohammed appeared and said, "Stop this foolishness!" That's what the newspaper said. We believe it was our power, the power of our prayer that got Mohammed moving and stopped Hussein from doing something outrageous.

The main activity of Byakkō Shinkōkai, a group founded by Goi Masahisa (1916–1980) in 1955, is the promotion of the Prayer for World Peace.[24] The opening line of the prayer, "May peace prevail on earth," written on stickers and poles donated by Byakkō Shinkōkai members, can be seen on every continent. The group also stages Peace Ceremonies in Japan and abroad, in an effort to encourage as many people as possible to repeat the words of the prayer, for Byakkō Shinkōkai members are absolutely convinced of the efficacy of their prayer.

THE SEARCH FOR A POSTWAR SAVIOR

Goi Masahisa was born in Tokyo, the fourth son in a family of eight children. His father, of samurai stock, was sickly, and consequently his mother ran a candy store in order to support the family. Goi himself was also sickly from birth, and he recounts how the doctors who saw him frequently didn't expect him to survive childhood.[25] As a result of his weak constitution, Goi tells us that he was withdrawn as a youth, often thinking of death, attracted to books on philosophy and religion. After the Great Kanto Earthquake in 1923 that destroyed much of Tokyo, Goi was sent to live with his father's family in Niigata, northwest of Tokyo on the Japan Sea coast side of the country. The change in environment improved his health somewhat, and at the age of 13, once again in Tokyo, he was apprenticed to a textile merchant. It was about this time that he began meditating before retiring every evening, using a combination of yoga and breathing exercises that he had picked up from a source about which he was no longer clear.

Goi had long been interested in becoming a musician, and around the age of eighteen he quit his apprenticeship and opened his own business, studying music on the side. His business did not last long, and in 1940 he was employed by Hitachi, a major manufacturing firm, as a cultural officer. His work entailed directing a chorus and organizing movie screenings and other events for the employees. Although Goi avoided military service because of his weak constitution, as the war dragged on his work took on more and more the qualities of a morale officer, arranging for the playing of martial music and the reading of patriotic texts in the factory. It also fell to him to broadcast the emperor's speech announcing Japan's capitulation on 15 August 1945. Goi says that he was personally convinced of the righteousness of Japan's cause, as well as of its certain victory, and, consequently, the emperor's words came as a great shock to him. At the same time, Goi was also once again suffering physically, this time from a rather serious kidney disease.

Goi tells us that he had given up on conventional medicine by the time he was about eighteen years old. Instead he found healing in a mixture of religious practices and beliefs.

> Every summer, to escape the heat, I would go to my father's home in the mountains of Niigata. There I would spend several hours every day sitting in a Buddhist temple. I did this for my health rather than for the purpose of attaining enlightenment, but as the years passed it took on more and more the characteristics of a religious Zen practice, and I began to seek the attainment of emptiness or nothingness. In the meantime I was also reading the Bible and browsing through the sutras.... Although my practice of Zen at about the age of twenty was not useful to any great extent towards the attainment of enlightenment, it did have a great effect on my health. That was because first of all I was able to abandon any dependence on doctors, and secondly, as I was sitting in meditation, the breathing exercises I had learned as a musician sort of naturally blended with a religious breathing practice (that of yoga), and led to physical health. There was no doubt considerable help from the spirits of my ancestors in the mountains of my father's home as well.[26]

The breakdown in his health towards the end of the war did not lead Goi back to conventional medicine, but rather to more effective spiritual means of healing. Through a friend at the Hitachi factory, he became acquainted with the medical theories of Okada Mokichi (1882–1955), a former member of Ōmotokyō who was later to found his own religious group, Sekai Kyūseikyō. Influenced by Ōmoto's spiritualism, Okada, whose health, like Goi's, had been poor from infancy, developed a practice as a spiritual healer, work that eventually led to his separation from

Ōmoto as well as several run-ins with the law. He developed his healing principles in a work call *Myōnichi no ijutsu* [Medicine for Tomorrow], where he maintained that illness was caused by pollution arising from the bad effects of past actions, either by one's ancestors or by oneself in a previous life. This is combined with the toxic effects of the chemicals prescribed by modern medicine, increasing the pollution in the body, so that the body tries to combat these poisons naturally by burning them off, in the form of fevers. Taking medicine to control fevers, therefore, not only prevents the natural healing of the body but contributes to the buildup of additional toxins. In addition, the natural healing process of the body can be aided through the practice of *jōrei*, directing a healing light energy emitted from the palm of the hand to the affected parts of the body, thus aiding the purification of the spirit, which is the literal meaning of *jōrei*.[27]

Healed once through the practice of *jōrei* shortly before the end of the war, Goi continued to refuse conventional medicine when his kidney disease returned following Japan's defeat. After running a high fever for ten days he was apparently completely healed, confirming his trust in Okada's methods. More and more convinced of a reality beyond physical existence, Goi broadened his contacts with people active in spiritist circles, searching for a savior to deliver Japan from its postwar humiliation and confusion. Thinking that Okada might be that savior, Goi went to some lengths to arrange to be present at a meeting of Okada and some of his top disciples, only to be disappointed at what he saw. He described Okada as a politician and businessman rather than a person of religion, and says that the main thing he took away from the meeting was the dawning realization of the extent of his own powers.

It was about that time that Goi started his own healing ministry. Through the same friend that first introduced him to Okada's healing practice, Goi attended training sessions in the method, and through massage and *jōrei* was able to effect reported cures in a number of people. This experience not only increased his confidence in the method and his own ability to apply it, but also convinced him of the presence of spiritual powers, a presence that he began to pray to constantly when embarking on his healing missions. Goi recalls in particular one instance, when he had been called upon to help a young man in his twenties suffering from peritonitis. As he went on his way, he says that he was praying in his heart that he be used for the work of God when suddenly,

A voice echoed like a bolt of lightning: "God has received your life! Are you prepared?" It wasn't a voice inside my head, or a voice in my heart, but a voice from heaven. It was definitely a voice, definitely words. But it wasn't at all like the words from the spirits that I was later to hear morning and night, words that sound like human voices. Without any hesitation, I answered, "Yes!"[28]

Although increasingly aware of his own call, Goi continued his search for the savior that was to raise Japan from the depths of its destruction. About this time he became acquainted with a magazine published by Seichō no Ie, another group actively promoting spiritist thought, and started to experiment with spirit-medium practices. Goi became interested in the founder of Seichō no Ie, Taniguchi Masaharu, and was especially struck by the fact that they had been born on the same day and month, Taniguchi in 1893 and Goi in 1916. Goi went to hear Taniguchi speak, and was immediately taken up with the gospel that he heard preached there, the gospel of *seimei no jissō* "the truth of life." As Goi explained later:

There is a vertical and horizontal aspect to 'the truth of life.' The vertical aspect was what really moved me so deeply, that the reality of the human person is that of perfection and happiness; that there is no such thing as old age, illness, poverty, or pain; that this physical existence that seems so real in fact does not exist. Therefore, things like sickness and poverty can't exist; the belief that they do exist is an illusion. There is no physical body, there is no material existence. They only appear to exist as the shadow of our beliefs in them, when in fact all that exists is God. The horizontal aspect would be the Buddhist idea that the three worlds are the manifestation of the spirit, or the theory of Mental Science that thoughts are vibrations; that the spirit or mind is the creator of all things; that everything emerges as a result of the thoughts of humankind. The fact that people are now suffering is a result of the bad thoughts of humanity, the mistaken thoughts of humanity. If you think bad thoughts evil arises; if you think good thoughts then good appears. If you happen to be sick now, it is because there is a cause of that sickness in your thoughts or actions. You are responsible for everything that happens to you. It is all the result of the shadow of your own spirit.[29]

This absolute spiritualism became the foundation of Goi's religious belief, adapted and simplified by him as he continued his spiritual quest. In the meantime, however, the realities of the physical world were closing in on Goi. Having quit his job at Hitachi and refusing to accept any donations for his healing work, he was eventually forced to go looking for new employment. Without obvious talents in business or engineering, he faced repeated rejection, until he eventually found a job working on the publications of an institute dealing with labor-management relations. While there he became convinced of three things that contributed to a decision on his part to head off on his own spiritual path, to take up for himself the mantle of the messiah for whom he had been searching.

Goi's first realization while working for the labor relations institute regarded the power of the masses. In the immediate postwar period labor unions enjoyed the climax of their power and influence in Japanese society. Under the initial Occupation policy such movements were supported as expressions of the democratic development being nurtured by Gen. Douglas MacArthur and his staff. Fears of communist influence and social strife later led to a change in this policy, but Goi's account of his experiences while employed at the institute seem to reflect the social situation previous to this switch in policy. In particular, he recalls a May Day march in which he had to participate:

> To the dancing of red flags and the shouting of revolutionary songs, under the direction of revolutionary agitators, the working masses continued their march to Miyagi Square, just one step away from a riot.
>
> Not aware of the true human form and looking to materialism alone for the meaning of labor, the masses are like charcoal or kindling. Depending on how it is lit, it can serve the purposes of home and country. But if lit for the wrong purpose it can destroy the home, destroy the country, destroy the whole human race.
>
> If only the masses knew the true form of humanity, then they wouldn't let some foolish incendiary come near, and the incendiary himself would be reformed as well.
>
> ...While participating in the march I felt the power of the masses, the fearful power of the masses.
>
> If the masses aren't energized nothing will come of it. If the doctrine doesn't move the masses it is useless. If the doctrine and practice don't elevate at the same time the spirit and the lives of the masses they are useless.[30]

The second realization is already obvious from his wholehearted acceptance of Seichō no Ie's spiritist teachings, as reflected also in the above quote: the danger of materialist thought. Goi says that as part of his work he had to read the classics of both communist and capitalist thought, and that, indeed, this education was perhaps one reason why he had been led by God to this particular employment. His reading, as well as the discussions he participated in at the institute, convinced him of the meaninglessness, and danger, of such thought.

The final realization was both unexpected and, for that reason, the most important of the three for Goi. By this time Goi was a fervent, if not fanatic, missionary for Seichō no Ie. He tells us that his free time was almost exclusively devoted to spreading the gospel of Seichō no Ie, and that even at work his conversation focussed on the propagation of the teachings of Seichō no Ie. Gradually, however, Goi came to the conclusion that Seichō no Ie did not offer a doctrine that would move the masses. He eventually came to the realization that it was precisely Seichō no Ie's view of humanity, the vertical aspect of *seimei no jissō*, that was the source of the problem. By refusing to take account of the evil and suffering apparent for all to see, Seichō no Ie offered a view of reality that was too idealistic for the vast majority of people to find credible. Even at this point Goi says that he saw the solution to the problem in the second part of Seichō no Ie's teaching, the horizontal aspect. There we see that evil arises from improper thoughts, the "shadows" of our mistaken view of reality. Goi claims, however, that Seichō no Ie preachers were not sufficiently aware of this solution, and in their attempts to maintain the teaching of fundamental human perfection they were in effect preaching to those who had already attained perfection, if there are such creatures in this world, and missing completely the state of common humanity. For these reasons Goi left Seichō no Ie early in 1948 and embarked on a quest for a truth that would supplement the theoretical doctrine of that group with practical experience, and lead to a new and simpler teaching that could move the masses.

TRIAL BY SPIRITS

Turning once again to the acquaintance who had first introduced him to the teachings of Okada Mokichi, Goi became involved in a group that channeled spirits. After a session with the group when the spirit of someone who had lived more than 1,500 years ago spoke through a megaphone, as well as out of thin air—through the ectoplasm of the person acting as medium, in Goi's explanation—Goi returned home and engaged in his usual practice of meditation. Perhaps inspired by the experience earlier in the day, Goi started a conversation with a spirit that appeared to him, his first experience with spirits. In the course of the night it was revealed to him that there were five guardian spirits constantly behind him, and that he would act as the herald of some great activity of God.

These evening sessions continued, and Goi says that he was also often on the verge of falling into a trance at work as well. Occasionally he would reveal spiritual phenomena to his coworkers, or let them know of some prophecy he had received from a spirit, but these prophecies would inevitably miss the mark. Goi attributed this to the fact that he was making light of the new powers that were being revealed to him, using them as a form of entertainment.

Next, Goi began to experience automatic writing, the involuntary movement of the hand that produces writings or drawings with discernible meaning. In his first experience of this phenomenon he produced the name of a childhood friend who went missing in the war, supposedly in the handwriting of that friend, leading him to believe that this friend was among the war victims and he was being contacted by his spirit. He also produced a drawing of his brother Gorō's face. Gorō had died in New Guinea during the war, and along the side of the picture his hand wrote the words, "Hi Mom, this is Gorō. I'm doing fine. I'm healthy and working hard." After that, Goi says that his hand began to write almost constantly, either on paper or tracing out characters on his knee, to the point where he could no longer do any editing work because of interference from the automatic writing. Eventually he had to resign his job, and he points out that his letter of resignation was also written by the spirits who had taken over his hand.

The unemployed Goi moved in with the friend who had first introduced him to Okada Mokichi, and the two of them devoted themselves to developing their spiritual powers. Goi says that about this time he experienced levitation, as well as the ability to enter guarded buildings unnoticed. At this point he says that his body was already completely controlled by his contacts in the spirit world; that, in addition to the automatic writing, now all of his movements were in a sense involuntary, with the spirits showing him what steps to take next. In this state, Goi received a warning that now he was to undergo a further set of trials, but that if he so chose he could yet give up the quest and once again take up the life of a normal person. More than ever convinced now that he had a role to play in the salvation of Japan—indeed, all humanity—he chose to continue his training, and was told that the next step was to free his mind of all thought, even the involuntary thoughts that arise in the course of a normal day. He compares this to trying to maintain the emptiness of Zen meditation in the course of all one's activities, an almost impossible task. Walking around the city involuntarily, putting an end to all thought, Goi soon found that this also implied fasting, since asking for food involved thought. In this state he experienced a series of temptations from what he later assumed to be the devil. The first was a terrible sense of fear that his mission was over before it began, and that he would soon be taken up into heaven. The second was the temptation to buy a lottery ticket that was sure to win, thus ending his financial problems permanently. He did buy the ticket and it didn't win, convincing him that this was just another test.

To mark the end of this period of trial and training, one evening Goi was subjected to a series of questions from the spirit world, testing what he had learned. The questions began with the nature of the human being and led eventually to the content of his mission, in answer to which Goi said that he was to teach the world to pray for peace. The contents of this question and answer session are summarized as the kernel of Goi's and Byakkō Shinkōkai's teaching, reprinted in all publications of the group. Byakkō Shinkōkai renders this summary in English as follows.

Man is originally a spirit from God, and not a karmic existence.

He lives under the constant guidance and protection provided by his Guardian Deities and Guardian Spirits.

All of man's sufferings are caused when his wrong thoughts conceived during his past lives up to the present manifest in this world in the process of fading away.

Any affliction, once it has taken shape in this phenomenal world, is destined to vanish into nothingness. Therefore, you should be absolutely convinced that your sufferings will fade away and that from now on your life will be happier. Even in any difficulty, you should forgive yourself and forgive others; love yourself and love others. You should always perform the acts of love, sincerity and forgiveness and thank your Guardian Deities and Guardian Spirits for their protection and pray for the peace of the world. This will enable you as well as mankind to realize enlightenment.

Goi's personal spiritual quest is in many ways a summary of current spiritual activity that is labeled New Age in the West, or the Spirit World in Japan. Goi is eclectic in his practice, picking up elements from the religious traditions of Japan as well as contemporary religious teachers. Early on he develops his own practice, a mixture of yoga and Zen, that emphasizes the bodily nature of religious practice. Later he begins to channel spirits and divinities, and is provided answers to both mundane and transcendental questions. Goi is perhaps more extreme than most other participants in these contemporary movements in his denial of physical reality. But it is specifically the thoroughgoing nature of this denial that provides a consistent doctrine for Byakkō Shinkōkai's peace activities, to which we turn our attention next.

WORLD PEACE MOVEMENT THROUGH PRAYER

Goi married in 1950, and the following year a group of followers was organized in Ichikawa City, outside of Tokyo. It was this group that applied for status as a religious organization under the name of Byakkō Shinkōkai in 1955. The primary activity of this group, as mentioned earlier, is the promotion of the Prayer for World Peace. This prayer was supposedly revealed to Goi by God, and the prayer is thought to be effective in purifying the "atmospheric air surrounding us," itself creating an "area overflowing with peaceful energies."[31] In order to explain the means by which this is accomplished, recourse is made to the ideas that Goi picked up from Seichō no Ie concerning the primacy of thought or spiritual existence.

> What we refer to as the thoughts of each individual become vibrations and circulate around the universe. These thoughts gather together to form the destiny of mankind. Therefore, the thoughts of each and every one of us, without a doubt influence the destiny of the human world, in a greater or lesser way.[32]

The Prayer for World Peace, since it vibrates in harmony with the Divine World where it originated, is thus thought to be especially powerful in counteracting the disharmony brought about by evil intentions. Kimura

Shintarō, introduced earlier in this chapter, explains this process in the pedestrian terms undoubtedly used within the group.

> Let's say you're driving down the road and something happens, and you yell out, "Stupid jerk!" Right at that instant energy, bad energy, is released, and it's that bad energy that causes harm to the earth, and to other people as well. That energy goes around the world, and it not only affects me and the person I said it to, but everybody else, and the world itself as well.... Fortunately, if you say "May peace prevail on earth," then there is endless forgiveness.... Just say those words and they eat up the bad energy; that's what we have been taught.

Yet another believer has a considerably more dramatic explanation for the workings of this prayer. Terada Eiko, a middle-aged woman who experienced her body becoming a channel of light energy after reading Goi's books, testifies to the power of this prayer in the following way.

> My body has been switched on as a pillar of light for the sake of world peace. Therefore, I've made it my mission to walk throughout the world—so far I've walked in eleven countries.... Since I've been trained to be a pillar of light for God, and since I have come to pray with all my might and bring down the light, to purify that area, to make the earth clean, it's not good enough to just walk around absentmindedly. I have to walk with the intention of passing that light from heaven all the way down to the soles of my feet. Afterwards it's all right to walk as I please, but first of all I go with the intention of becoming a pillar of light.... When I pray, "May peace prevail on earth," and then, for example, if I'm in Germany, "May Germany's mission be accomplished," as soon as I say "May," it's like a switch has been turned on. After that the light just flows freely.

Although not all members have had the extraordinary experience that Terada describes here, it is believed that the prayer is also efficacious in purifying the person praying, extinguishing karmic thoughts and making one a more effective channel of the vibrations of peace.

> At the moment you direct your mind toward the Prayer for World Peace, no matter what karmic thoughts you might possess, your mind is open to the vast expanse of the whole of humanity; before you know it you have entered into the light of the Guardian Deities protecting all of existence.... Having received this light, the light

passes through the vessel of your body, radiating light to the rest of humanity in this physical world.[33]

It is perhaps for this reason that distinctions are made that indicate varying degrees of efficacy based on the experience of the person praying. For example, a special prayer meeting is held monthly at the headquarters in Ichikawa, where the peace of each nation and territory in the world is prayed for individually, in both Japanese and English. Members who have attended at least eight times are directed to point three fingers to heaven while praying, while those attending more than fifteen times are to use just the forefinger, the better to channel the energy of their prayer.

Although the use of light and vibration vocabulary testifies to the contemporary nature of the universe of belief modeled by this group, the idea that words have an almost mystical power is certainly not new to religion. In the Jewish tradition, for example, the name of God is not voiced, and in the Catholic Church traditionally much emphasis has been placed on the proper form, or words, used in the sacraments. In Japan, this particular belief is called *kotodama*, the spiritual power residing in words. The words used in Shinto prayers, or *norito*, for example, are carefully chosen to have a beneficial effect. In the Japanese Buddhist tradition as well, chants such as the *daimoku* used by Fujii Nichidatsu and other Nichiren Buddhists, or the *nenbutsu* in the Pure Land sects, are thought to be particularly efficacious as a form of prayer. Other new religious groups, notably the two Mahikari groups that also share roots in Sekai Kyūseikyō, make more explicit use of *kotodama* belief, while still others—Shūyōdan Hōseikai treated in Chapter Five, for example—exhibit a more indirect acceptance of this particular Japanese religious form. Goi's innovation consists in the fact that the power of words is given a position of absolute prominence, on the basis of his spiritist belief that peace will only be established through the rectification of disharmonious vibrations effected by repeating the divine words of the Prayer for World Peace. This was the simple teaching sought by Goi that was to empower the masses in postwar Japan.

SPIRITISM AND PACIFISM

Goi advocates the Prayer for World Peace as a means for the common person to become involved in directing his or her own destiny, especially

Peace Pole on the grounds of a Shinto shrine in Hiroshima.

in the face of the nuclear standoff that characterized the postwar period until recently. He believed that the masses would never have much success in persuading the superpowers to disarm through normal means; that, in fact, such activity as demonstrations and petitions just serve to increase the disharmony in the world through the disruptive power of

69

their words. He believed that only by the spiritual agency of the Prayer for World Peace could the evil thoughts contributing to the accumulation of arms be erased.

In this way, the members of Byakkō Shinkōkai have removed themselves from the world, but in a totally different way from that of the monks and nuns of Nipponzan Myōhōji. For Goi's followers, ultimately, the world does not exist; it is but the passing shadow of the accumulated wrong or evil thoughts of humankind. Believers with this kind of an outlook cannot be bothered with questions of self-defense, or war guilt, or anything beyond the need to pray. They would also obviously not be very interested in answering a questionnaire about those mundane issues. When I distributed my questionnaire at a local meeting of believers in a suburb outside of Tokyo, I unwittingly opened myself up to a long explanation of how the issues I was raising were of a "lower dimension," to be avoided by one seeking harmony with the Divine World. Needless to say, no valid responses were gathered from that particular group. On an official level as well, Byakkō Shinkōkai declined to help with the survey, and it was primarily through the good offices of a certain member of the group, who assisted in distributing the questionnaire to members returning from the special prayer meeting at the headquarters for several consecutive months, that I was able to obtain any valid responses at all. For this reason, the sample obtained from Byakkō Shinkōkai was exceedingly low, as was also the case with Nipponzan Myōhōji, and as a result we can make, at best, only the most tentative of conclusions from answers to the questionnaire. The results would seem to confirm, however, that Byakkō Shinkōkai approaches Nipponzan Myōhōji in the degree to which the absolute pacifist position is maintained.

Three of the five questions on pacifism included in the survey offer the clearest indication in this area, namely, the questions on the Persian Gulf War, on the need for an armed defense, and on what one would do in the event that Japan becomes involved in another war. On the issues of the Persian Gulf War and the need for an armed defense, Byakkō Shinkōkai was second only to Myōhōji in the percentage of its believers who chose the pacifist response. In answer to the third question, only 23% said they would actively oppose any war, much fewer than Sōka Gakkai's 91% or Myōhōji's 84%. This would be in line with Goi's views on the harm that such demonstrations cause, and, indeed, nearly 70% of Byakkō Shinkōkai followers said that they would quietly pray for peace, far and away the highest percentage for this response of any group included in the survey.

The other two questions included in the pacifist measure, those on the existence of the Self-Defense Forces and participation of those forces in United Nations peacekeeping operations, yielded less clear results, perhaps reflecting the confused terms of debate on these issues in Japan. The main activity of the Self-Defense Forces has been disaster relief, and consequently many people see them as an emergency service rather than an army. Therefore, almost 90% of Byakkō Shinkōkai respondents gave conditional support to the existence of these forces, with the stipulation that their activities and size be strictly limited. This was in line with the overall average response to this question, with only Myōhōji clearly rejecting any justification for their existence. Finally, Self-Defense Force participation in United Nations operations in Cambodia, the only implementation of the Peacekeeping Operations Law at the time of my survey, was billed as restricted to unarmed support activities, such as building roads. Given those conditions, just over half of Byakkō Shinkōkai respondents supported those operations, slightly less than the overall average of 58%. Perhaps more illustrative of the fundamental stance of this group is the fact that nearly 20% declined to answer the question at all.

As one final testimony to the position of this group, a detachment from the world based on its spiritist beliefs, let me introduce the opinion of one more member, a man in his mid-forties by the name of Inoue Yūji. Inoue describes himself as a borderline schizophrenic, troubled by the voices of spirits and the dark thoughts of writers such as Dostoyevsky, saved by contact with the Prayer for World Peace, which serves to calm his mind and help him lead a somewhat normal life. When asked about issues of war and peace, or Japan's possible participation in a future war, he answered with these words:

> I don't think there is any special need to protest, saying, "It's against the constitution!" If it isn't necessary it will fade away by itself.... We are taught that war is just a fading image, and I believe that is true. The violence that lies in the hearts of men and women takes shape and appears in the world in order to fade away. God has to let it take shape as war so that it can fade away. And that helps to purify the world. I agree entirely with that kind of thinking, and so when war occurs there really is no need to oppose it, or to support

it. I wouldn't take either of those actions. I would just pray, "Make it fade away quickly!"

●◇   ●◇   ●◇

Although both model the pacifist position, Nipponzan Myōhōji and Byakkō Shinkōkai could not be further apart in their attitudes and actions. As a nonviolent activist sect Nipponzan Myōhōji is keen to be in the forefront of antiwar demonstrations and peace marches, while Byakkō Shinkōkai shuns such activity as harmful to the establishment of the divine harmony that it hopes to assist through its prayer. Although they take no vows and do not live apart from society, Byakkō Shinkōkai believers' separation from the world is the more complete for their spiritist disregard of events in this "lower dimension" of reality. Many people who see the stickers and poles emblazoned with the words of the Prayer for World Peace, "May Peace Prevail on Earth," will agree wholeheartedly with the sentiment, and even find it inspiring. However, one must wonder how many would be convinced by the spiritist worldview behind the propagation of the prayer.

These two groups have been able to maintain a pacifist position because of their separation from the world, either through monastic vows or a spiritist worldview. In the following two chapters we turn to some of the more mainstream new religious groups, to explore what happens to the pacifist ideal when the choice is made to actively participate in society. We turn first to a group that is important not only for its size and the level of its participation in Japanese society, but also because it perhaps best illustrates the problems with pacifism as a majority position.

THREE

Compromised Pacifism

While conducting my research on Nipponzan Myōhōji, I had the opportunity to talk extensively with a young man from the United States who, while not officially a member of the religion, had over the course of several years worked together with the monks and nuns on their various projects. As we took leave on the occasion of our last meeting together, looking back on the years of his association with the group he allowed as to how he would really like to be a convinced pacifist, like the people he knew from Myōhōji. However, if a situation ever arose where he would have to choose between the ideal of complete nonviolence and defense of his family, for example, he knew that he would choose the latter. His wistfulness in revealing this choice certainly indicates the gravity with which it was taken.

I am reminded of this young man when I contemplate Sōka Gakkai's position. Sōka Gakkai often uses pacifist rhetoric in its literature, and I believe it is fair to say that the vast majority of members would describe themselves as *heiwashugi-sha*, or pacifists. However, the obligations of the path they have chosen in Japanese society have forced them to compromise that decision. In contrast to the young American, though, they do not seem to be aware of the choice they have made, and as a consequence, their stance both reflects and contributes to the confusion in Japanese society regarding the implications of the pacifist option.

Like Nipponzan Myōhōji, Sōka Gakkai is a religious group within the Nichiren Buddhist tradition. Until its excommunication in November 1991, it was officially a lay movement within the Nichiren Shōshū sect, and since that time it continues to function as a lay Buddhist movement.[1] With as many as eight million members in Japan, it is the largest of the new religious movements in that country, and a prime example of the mass lay Buddhist movements that began to attract attention in the early postwar period. Furthermore, through its international branch, Sōka Gakkai International, it has members in more than 120 countries and territories worldwide, and claims over a million members outside of Japan.

Sōka Gakkai and its leader, Ikeda Daisaku, a former president of the organization who now holds the titles of Honorary President of Sōka Gakkai and President of Sōka Gakkai International, have been controversial throughout the postwar period, initially as a result of the group's aggressive proselytization and, later, because of its political involvement. Its involvement in politics, culminating in the formation of its own political party, now nominally independent of Sōka Gakkai, is particularly indicative of an active involvement in society that I have argued is incompatible with the absolute demands of the pacifist position. The history of that involvement, therefore, will be of special interest as we look at the development of this group and examine its concept of peace and its peace activities.

VALUE-CREATING EDUCATION AND SŌKA GAKKAI

Sōka Gakkai was founded by Makiguchi Tsunesaburō (1871–1944), an educator who stressed the role of creativity and personal experience in his educational philosophy. Its original name, Sōka Kyōiku Gakkai, or Academic Society for Value-Creating Education, indicates that in its origins the group was primarily composed of educators interested in Makiguchi's philosophy. Indeed, Sōka Gakkai traces its foundation to the publishing of the first volume of Makiguchi's opus *Sōka kyōikugaku taikei* [Outline of Value-Creating Education] on 18 November 1930, where the Academic Society for Value-Creating Education is listed as the publisher. It was only in 1937, however, that an inaugural meeting of the society was held, and already at that time the group had taken on a decidedly religious character.

Makiguchi was born in a fishing village in Niigata Prefecture, on the Japan Sea coast. His father left the family when he was three years old, and the resulting financial problems necessitated his adoption into a relative's family. At the age of fourteen he left to live with yet another relative, an uncle in Otaru on the northern island of Hokkaido. Since the financial situation of his uncle did not allow him to continue in school, he soon got a job with the police department, where his hard work and seriousness caught the eye of the station chief. For that reason, he moved to Sapporo at the age of eighteen when the chief was transferred there, and two years later Makiguchi was accepted into the Hokkaido Normal School. After graduation he was employed at the elementary school affiliated with that institution.

Makiguchi is described as a hardheaded rebel in official Sōka Gakkai biographical accounts as well as in outside scholarship.[2] Clearly his educational philosophy, emphasizing creative thought and personal experience, did not conform to educational practice in Japan, where repetitious practice and the rote memorization of facts continue to be valued. For this reason, it seems that Makiguchi's career was one of continuous clashes with his immediate superiors and the educational system in general. In 1901 a dispute over discipline led to the termination of his employment in Sapporo, and he moved to Tokyo with his wife and two children.

In Tokyo, Makiguchi initially tried to support himself as a scholar, publishing his first book, *Jinsei chirigaku* [Life Geography], in 1903. This book, drawing connections between geography and everyday life and advocating the study of geography through field trips and other hands-on experiences, seems to have been well received, and through its publication he became acquainted with other scholars such as Nitobe Inazō and Yanagita Kunio, the founder of Japanese folklore studies. Makiguchi took on editing work to support his family, and even started his own correspondence school, but when that enterprise failed in 1909 he was forced to find employment once again as an elementary school teacher in the Tokyo school system. Periodic clashes with authorities characterized a twenty-year career there, until finally he was made principal of a school already slated for closure, leading to his early retirement. It was about the time of his retirement that Makiguchi became involved in the Nichiren Shōshū faith through an acquaintance at the school where he was principal. Nichiren Shōshū is an early offshoot of the Nichiren movement, founded by a disciple of Nichiren, Nikkō, who moved from the Nichiren establishment at Mt. Minobu to Taisekiji at the foot of Mt. Fuji in 1289. Nichiren Buddhism in general enjoyed an upsurge in popularity during the late nineteenth and early twentieth centuries, largely due to the popularization of nationalist ideas associated with the sect by Tanaka Chigaku and others. Nichiren Shōshū is perhaps the most militantly exclusivist of the Nichiren sects, its very name proclaiming its belief that it is the True Religion.

There are several reasons that might explain Makiguchi's turn to religion at this time. By the time that he reentered the teaching profession in Tokyo he had fathered five children, but four of these children had been lost to disease before he became a Nichiren Shōshū believer, giving us reason to believe that this personal misfortune might have been one motivation for his religious faith. Furthermore, he was having no obvious success in promoting his ideas of transforming society through education, and may have felt that religion could be a more effective vehicle to accomplish his aims. Finally, with his own highly-principled, some might say stubborn, personality he might have felt at home in the militant atmosphere of this particular religious group. The gradual shift to an increasingly religious concern in Makiguchi's writing and activities in the 1930s might indicate that personal misfortune first brought him to religion, and that it was only later that he came to see religion as important for fulfilling his broader social aims. At any rate, it is clear that by 1936 educational and religious "revolution" had become fused in his thought, for in that year the small group of educators that had gathered around Makiguchi started regular meetings with the title *Kyōiku shūkyō kakumei shōhō kenkyūkai*, or "Study Group for True Law Educational and Religious Revolution." The following year Makiguchi published a pamphlet titled *Sōka kyōikuhō no kagakuteki chōshūkyōteki jikken shōmei* [Practical Experimentation in Value-Creating Education Methods through Science and Supreme Religion], further indicating the increasing emphasis placed on religion as a means of social reform.

In 1938 Makiguchi's followers were organized into the Sōka Kyōiku Gakkai with an inaugural meeting held at a Tokyo restaurant. Sixty people were in attendance at this meeting, a number that had risen more than fivefold by the time a second meeting was held three years later. From the time of the first meeting it seems that the main activity of this group was missionary work for Nichiren Shōshū. A primary method of this activity was the *zadankai*, literally meaning a forum or roundtable discussion, held in the believers' homes. These were largely testimonial gatherings, where the believers shared their experiences of the concrete benefits obtained by faith and thus sought to attract newcomers to the religion.[3] This emphasis on personal experience is a characteristic of many of the Japanese New Religions, especially those that emerged around this time, as well as a reflection of Makiguchi's educational theories. Testimonials were also prominent in a periodical begun by the group in 1941, *Kachi sōzō* [Value Creation].

It seems that Makiguchi and his activities began to attract the attention of the authorities shortly after the first publication of *Kachi Sōzō*, for the magazine was closed down after only nine issues by order of the government. The group claimed more than three thousand members nationwide at that time, a significant movement within the relatively small Nichiren Shōshū sect, and their refusal to bend to the wartime government policy on religious groups was no doubt causing some irritation with the authorities. The official policy of the government since the passing of a Religious Organizations Law in 1939 had been to consolidate religious groups, in order to enhance government control over the groups and enlist their help in the war movement. As part of this policy, the various Nichiren sects were coerced into forming one body, which in fact would have entailed the absorption of Nichiren Shōshū by the much larger Nichiren Shū. Reportedly, some of the Nichiren Shōshū priests were themselves in favor of the merger, a move opposed by Makiguchi as compromising the true faith held by that group alone. The merger was rejected at a meeting of lay and clerical Nichiren Shōshū believers in April 1943, and the group was subsequently able to receive government approval to remain independent.

One other issue included in the government's religious policy proved to be Makiguchi's downfall, however. Since the launching of Japan's drive to become a modern nation-state in the mid-nineteenth century, State Shinto had been created as a complex of beliefs and rituals centering on the emperor in order to serve as a kind of civil religion, integrating and mobilizing the people to carry out the policies of the state. By the 1890s, State Shinto had been defined as a matter of national custom and patriotism, the duty of every loyal citizen that transcended religious belief or practice—a duty that was increasingly emphasized as the country went to war. As a concrete expression of this loyalty, every family was required to accept into their homes a talisman from the central Shinto shrine at Ise, a requirement that once again the priests at Taisekiji were willing to accept but at which Makiguchi balked. His refusal led to his arrest on charges of *lèse majesté* and violation of the Peace Preservation Law on 6 July 1943, along with twenty other leaders of the Sōka Kyōiku Gakkai. Makiguchi was already seventy-one at the time of his arrest, and he died from malnutrition in prison on 18 November of the following year.

SŌKA GAKKAI AS A MASS MOVEMENT

Toda Jōsei (1900–1958) had been an associate and disciple of Makiguchi since 1920, when he joined the staff at Nishimachi Elementary School, where Makiguchi was principal. Toda was born on 11 February 1900, the eleventh son of a fisherman in Ishikawa Prefecture, also on the Japan Sea coast. At the age of four his family moved to Hokkaido, where he eventually found employment as a youth in Sapporo, studying part time in order to qualify as a substitute primary school teacher at the age of seventeen. The following year he was employed at a school in a remote mining town, where he remained until he moved to Tokyo in 1920 and was hired by Makiguchi.

Toda left the school system three years later and started his own college preparation course, where he is supposed to have attempted to implement Makiguchi's educational philosophy. The school apparently had little success, for Bethel reports that throughout much of the 1920s he was in dire poverty, and his financial state might have contributed to the death of his infant daughter, the loss of his wife to tuberculosis, and his own contraction of that disease. The next decade saw a dramatic turn in his fortunes, however, as a mathematics text published by Toda in 1930 became a runaway bestseller and served as the foundation of a business empire that extended to seventeen companies and a personal fortune of over one million dollars at the time of his arrest with Makiguchi in 1943.[4]

Toda survived his experience in jail, and even claims to have had an intense religious experience while there, as a result of his reading the *Lotus Sutra* and incessant chanting of the *daimoku*. Toda says that after agonizing for a long time over the meaning of the sutra, finally one day he had a vision of the word *seimei*, or Life-Force, flashing in his mind, as well as a mystical experience of seeing himself in attendance in the assembly of the Buddha. This experience was apparently the foundation of Toda's unique contribution to the development of Sōka Gakkai doctrine, the theory of Life-Force.[5] This Life-Force is thought to permeate the universe, and it is through connection with the Great Life-Force that we can ensure health, prosperity, good relationships with others, and happiness. In Sōka Gakkai practice, these benefits are obtained through faith in Nichiren as the greatest and final manifestation of the Buddha, worship of the *gohonzon*, or mandala inscribed by Nichiren, and the chanting of the *daimoku*. Such practice should lead to benefits in this life, and even greater happiness in an unending series of future lives in this world. In this way, Toda laid out a very practical faith of immediate benefits, a classical example of what has been called the "vitalistic" conception of salvation frequently encountered in Japanese new religious movements.[6]

Toda spent the first years after the war trying to rebuild his business empire, as well as the organization destroyed by Makiguchi's arrest. At a memorial service held on the first anniversary of Makiguchi's death only some twenty people were in attendance, but the following year Toda started offering courses on the *Lotus Sutra* out of his office in Tokyo. At the end of the first set of courses on 28 March 1946 Toda changed the name of the organization to Sōka Gakkai, dropping the last vestige of the group's roots as an organization of educators. Toda's business went bankrupt in 1950, a turning point in his life that led him to devote himself exclusively to the religious organization, and on 3 May of the following year he took over formally as the second President of Sōka Gakkai. In his inaugural speech he announced the "great march of *shakubuku*," with the concrete goal of winning 750,000 families to Sōka Gakkai before his death.

Shakubuku is one of two methods of proselytization found in Buddhist canonical sources, the other being *shōju*. *Shōju*, meaning to "embrace and accept" is a mild method of leading others gradually to the truth without criticizing their previous position. *Shakubuku*, on the other hand, means to "break and subdue," and it involves the use of a rather fierce polemic in order to get the subject to reject his or her previous beliefs. In his writings, Nichiren allows that both methods have their appropriate time and place, but insists that *shakubuku* is to be used in the Japan of his own time in order to rebuke the enemies of true Buddhism and bring the country to faith. Throughout its history there have been arguments within the Nichiren sect as to which method is proper for the contemporary situation, with Sōka Kyōiku Gakkai and Nichiren Shōshū advocating the use of *shakubuku* in the prewar period.[7] Indeed, it was the employment of this method that led to the charges against Makiguchi and his lieutenants for violating the Peace Preservation Law.

The drive for membership, carried out under the banner of *shakubuku*, was marked by aggressive, confrontational tactics and, occasionally, military rhetoric. The *Shakubuku kyōten* [Manual of *shakubuku*] was published in 1951, and in addition to laying out the essentials of Sōka Gakkai teaching on the *Lotus Sutra* and the writings of Nichiren, it also provided sample arguments to be used against the objections of prospective converts. Sōka Gakkai youth divisions were organized in the early 1950s to spearhead the proselytization drive, and Murata reports that overtly military language was employed.[8] For example, the young members were organized into *butai* (corps), complete with *butaichō* (corps commanders) and *butaiki* (corps flags), and the central organization was called the *sanbōshitsu* (general staff office). At a rally on 31 October 1954 Toda even mounted a white horse as he addressed the assembled columns with the following words.

> In our attempt at *kōsen rufu* [propagation of Buddhism], we are without an ally. We must consider all religions our enemies, and we must destroy them. Ladies and gentlemen, it is obvious that the road ahead is full of obstacles. Therefore, you must worship the *gohonzon*, take the Soka Gakkai spirit to your heart, and cultivate the strength of youth. I expect you to rise to the occasion to meet the many challenges that lie ahead.[9]

As Jacqueline Stone points out, this policy was changed in the 1970s to one of at least implicit tolerance more in keeping with the peace activities we will be looking at shortly,[10] and although the word *shakubuku* is still used within the group, it seems to have become more synonymous with general proselytization, at least on the official level. Although the militant, even militaristic, stance naturally attracted a considerable amount of bad press and was decisive in forming public opinion about Sōka Gakkai that endures in many quarters of Japanese society until the present, it was also effective in laying the foundations for the phenomenal growth of the organization, making it the premier example of a postwar new religion as a mass movement. Toda's goal of 750,000 families was apparently reached in 1957, before his own death on 2 April 1958.

SŌKA GAKKAI AND POLITICS

One more legacy of Toda's leadership is Sōka Gakkai's active participation in Japanese politics. Sōka Gakkai is not unique among religious groups, in Japan or elsewhere, in seeking to advance its goals—normally seen as religious by their members—through political means. This activity has taken several different forms in postwar Japan. A Tenrikyō official, for example, was a candidate for a seat in the Lower House of parliament in 1946, while Risshō Kōseikai lent its support to a conservative candidate in the 1947 Tokyo gubernatorial elections. Seichō no Ie has been much more active in conservative politics, forming a Political Policy Committee in 1953 to coordinate its activities, joining right wing members of the ruling Liberal Democratic Party in organizing a National Self-Defense Conference in 1958, and reorganizing its political organization into the Seichō no Ie Political Alliance in 1964. What sets Sōka Gakkai apart from these other groups, however, is the formation of its own political party, Kōmeitō (often referred to as the Clean Government Party in Western publications), in 1964.

Sōka Gakkai's political activities began in 1955, when the group sponsored more than fifty of its own candidates in local elections, resulting in the election of forty-seven Sōka Gakkai members to two prefectural assemblies and more than twenty city councils around the country. In national elections held for the Upper House of parliament the following year, three of six candidates sponsored by Sōka Gakkai were successful in their bids, garnering more than one million votes nationwide. In 1959, a further six candidates were elected, followed by the reelection of the original three members plus an additional six in 1962, making the Sōka Gakkai councilors the third largest group in the Upper House. On the basis of this success, a decision was made in 1964 to sponsor candidates for the more powerful Lower House, and at the same time Kōmeitō was formed. In the general election in 1967, the first held after the establishment of Kōmeitō, the party won twenty-five seats in the Lower House, attracting almost two and one-half million votes. Two years later these totals were almost doubled to forty-seven seats and over five million votes. However, an attempt in that same year to stop the publication of a book critical of Sōka Gakkai and its political activities caused a controversy focusing on freedom of the press, and led Sōka Gakkai to officially disassociate itself from Kōmeitō in May of 1970. What this means in practice is that parliamentary members of Kōmeitō will resign from any official posts in Sōka Gakkai, but Sōka Gakkai's activities in support of Kōmeitō, as well as its influence over Kōmeitō policy, are no secret.

On one level, Sōka Gakkai's political activity could be attributed to the legacy of its founder, Makiguchi Tsunesaburō, who apparently saw his religious activity as a means to effect social reform. There is also a doctrinal foundation within Nichiren Buddhism for such activity. Nichiren himself was convinced that the salvation of the nation depended on its conversion to the true faith of Buddhism, and for that reason he was especially critical of other religions, in particular the Pure Land sects, as dangerous to the survival of the nation. The fusion of true religion and politics that would result from this conversion is called *ōbutsumyōgo*, and it was to be represented in the establishment of a *Kokuritsu kaidan*, or National Hall of Worship, to be built at the foot of Mt. Fuji. Throughout the 1950s this was presented as the final aim of Sōka Gakkai's proselytization, called *kōsen rufu* in Nichiren terminology. Critics of Sōka Gakkai's political activity maintain that *ōbutsumyōgo* and the related concept of the establishment of the *Kokuritsu kaidan* call for the establishment of a state religion, explicitly prohibited by the postwar constitution. Perhaps in an effort to defuse these critics, the completion of a massive worship hall at the Nichiren Shōshū headquarters in Taisekiji in 1972 was identified by Sōka Gakkai as the establishment of the *Kokuritsu kaidan*, indicating that *ōbutsumyōgo* in fact signifies a broader influence of Buddhist principles in society and that it does not necessarily rely on the conversion of the whole nation and the adopting of Nichiren Shōshū as an official religion.[11]

Although Kōmeitō seats in the Lower House fell to twenty-nine in elections held after the controversy mentioned above, in subsequent elections the party has consistently polled more than five million votes and its seat count has generally remained in the mid-fifties. This representation made it the third largest party in Parliament, following the Liberal Democratic Party and the socialist group, now called the Social Democratic Party of Japan. Following a splintering in the LDP and their loss in elections held in 1993, Kōmeitō joined with all non-LDP parties save the Communist Party of Japan in forming a coalition government—the first time the LDP had to relinquish power in the thirty-eight years of its existence. Since that loss the political situation in Japan has remained fluid, and the controversy surrounding Kōmeitō as a political party with obvious connections to Sōka Gakkai has helped considerably to muddy the waters.[12]

Our interest here is how this political activity has influenced Sōka Gakkai's stance regarding war and peace. Although Kōmeitō did not formally join a government until formation of the coalition that ended the postwar conservative monopoly in 1993, it had often been the power-broker in the national Parliament, reflecting its role as the third largest national party and the fact that it has staked out for itself a centralist position, with the conservative Liberal Democrats and liberal socialists on its flanks. Indeed, from its foundation it has taken as its aim the establishment of world peace based on a "global nationalism" and "human socialism," offered as a way to resolve the conflict between capitalism and socialism, a fusion of opposites that aptly reflects its centralism. As part of its attempt to serve as a centralist power broker, Kōmeitō has adopted positions that clearly are not pacifist. Since the 1980s Kōmeitō has been on record as supporting Japan's military alliance with the United States, and after a defeat of the ruling conservative party in Upper House parliamentary elections in 1989 Kōmeitō formed an unofficial coalition with the conservatives, offering their support on key measures. It was in this context that Kōmeitō support of the Peacekeeping Operations Law, allowing for the overseas deployment of Self-Defense Forces in UN-sponsored activities, became crucial for the enactment of this controversial law. In response to these developments, Sōka Gakkai members are wont to point out that as an independent political party Kōmeitō does not necessarily reflect the position of Sōka Gakkai, and, indeed, at least one observer has pointed out that "some Sōka Gakkai members were outraged" by the decision of Kōmeitō to support the Peacekeeping Operations Law.[13] Be that as it may, in their support of Kōmeitō, Sōka Gakkai has indicated that it is not pacifist, to the extent that it endorses a party with nonpacifist policies. This situation illustrates poignantly the difficulty of maintaining the pacifist position without abandoning all political engagement with society.

SŌKA GAKKAI'S PEACE ACTIVITIES

To say that Sōka Gakkai is not pacifist is not to deny that it is very active in trying to establish the basis for world peace. As in the case of its political activity, Sōka Gakkai's peace activities can also be traced back to Toda Jōsei, the second president of the group. At an athletic meeting held in Yokohama in September of 1957 Toda called for a complete ban on nuclear weapons, adding his voice to the popular movement in Japan to ban such weapons, especially in the wake of the accident at Bikini Atoll three years previously.[14] Petition drives against these weapons organized by the Sōka Gakkai youth group garnered more than ten million signatures and were handed over to the United Nations in 1975. In 1973 the youth division further adopted a resolution for the "preservation of the right to life," and in response to that resolution undertook to raise money for Vietnamese refugees and the starving in Africa, as well as the publication of antiwar books. These books, an activity later also adopted by the women's division of Sōka Gakkai, amount to more than one hundred volumes at present and are collections of accounts of survivors of the Second World War. They are meant to educate the postwar generations on the horrors of war, as recounted by those who have lived through the experience.

Such a contribution to peace education is perhaps especially appropriate to a group whose roots lie in an association of educators, and indeed peace education is one of the characteristics of Sōka Gakkai's participation in this field. In addition to the antiwar book series, Sōka Gakkai International has been active in organizing peace exhibits, beginning with "Nuclear Arms: Threat to Our World," which made the rounds of sixteen countries between 1982 and 1988. A second exhibit,

84

"War and Peace: From a Century of War to a Century of Hope," was opened in the lobby of the United Nations Headquarters in New York in 1989, followed by an exhibit on environmental issues and peace opened to coincide with the United Nations Conference on Environment and Development held in Rio de Janeiro in 1992.

Cooperation with United Nations projects is another characteristic of Sōka Gakkai's peace activities. Sōka Gakkai has been registered as a Non-Governmental Organization with the United Nations' High Commissioner for Refugees since 1981, and two years later the SGI was recognized as an NGO with consultative status in the United Nations Economic and Social Council.

Ikeda Daisaku (1928–), Toda's successor as the third president of Sōka Gakkai, was himself a recipient of the United Nations Peace Prize in 1983. Ikeda was born in Tokyo on 2 January 1928, the fifth son in a large family of nine children. His father processed and sold dried seaweed, a job with which he was barely able to support the family. Ikeda was apparently sickly from an early age, and while attending high school during the war years he was also stricken with tuberculosis and pleurisy. After the war he found a job working in a factory, and around the age of nineteen he began to attend Sōka Gakkai *zadankai* at the invitation of a childhood friend. He soon joined the group, quickly became a protégé of Toda, and, in 1952, was appointed as leader of Sōka Gakkai's youth division. Ikeda's formal education ended in 1949, when he briefly attended night classes at a junior college. After that he is said to have been tutored in various subjects by Toda.

Despite this lack of formal higher education, Ikeda has been prominent in international peace forums, addressing the United Nations General Assembly and keeping a high profile in his frequent exchanges with prominent statesmen and academics. In his numerous proposals on peace and disarmament, Ikeda makes continued reference to the ideal of universal disarmament and resolution of conflict through negotiation. At home, any change to the postwar Japanese constitution, which renounces war as a sovereign right, is opposed by Ikeda, and the constitution is held up as a model for all nations.[15] He decries the lack of a Supreme Court decision on the constitutionality of the Japanese Self-Defense Forces,[16] and, in seeming contradiction to the position taken by Kōmeitō, he also opposes overseas deployment of those forces as part of the UN's Peacekeeping Operations.[17] Furthermore, he criticizes the

Japanese government for seeking protection under the United States nuclear umbrella.[18] All of these positions are in keeping with the absolute proscription on armed means to conflict resolution that is at the core of the pacifist position.

A further look at Ikeda's stated positions, however, leads to the conclusion that his fundamental position should more accurately be described as one of multinationalism rather than pacifism, for he does not absolutely rule out the use of force. He recognizes the occasional need for the application of force in order to maintain order, although he would shift responsibility for the deployment of such force from the nation-state to an international body such as the United Nations. For example, although he disallows permanent membership for Japan on the UN Security Council, because of a perceived obligation for such members to participate in collective security activities—a requirement whose fulfillment he maintains is prohibited by the Japanese constitution—this prohibition is apparently considered to be unique to Japan.[19] Specifically, the necessary use of force for the maintenance of collective security is recognized in the case of the Persian Gulf War.[20] The combination of Japanese pacifism with multinational armed intervention is also reflected in the position of the general membership of Sōka Gakkai, an issue we turn to next.

THE BELIEVERS: ARE THEY PACIFIST?

The concept of peace offered by Sōka Gakkai is based on Toda's theory of Life-Force. In the *Sōka Gakkai nyūmon* [Introduction to Sōka Gakkai's Faith], which replaced the *Shakubuku kyōten* as the basic text of Sōka Gakkai doctrine in 1970, this Life-Force theory is developed along the following lines: Life is not created, but rather it subsists in all existing things.[21] Therefore, life has no beginning and no end, and all of existence is united in this one all-encompassing Life.[22] As one part of this Life that permeates the whole universe, every single human being has immutable, all-surpassing value. Any attempt to relativize the value of human life, any attempt to make it subordinate to any other value, will only harm human welfare and peace.[23]

It would seem that this kind of concept, with the absolute value that it gives to human life, would lead Sōka Gakkai believers to embrace the pacifist position. Indeed, it is just such a position that is advocated by Ban Kyōko, a Sōka Gakkai housewife in her forties.[24] When asked about the issues that I used to measure adherence to the pacifist position—that is, the handling of the Gulf War, the existence of a right to national self-defense, and Japanese participation in United Nations peacekeeping operations—Ban consistently gave a pacifist response. She explained her basic position in this way.

> Everyone is equal, because we are all the same as human beings. It is an equality that goes beyond differences in color, a fundamental view of life. And until that idea has been firmly established, there will be continuous ethnic wars and wars between nations. If we continue to have this category called "human," and decide for ourselves who fits in that category and who doesn't, then I think there will be no end to war. Therefore, we have to keep insisting that all human beings are equal, all human beings are the same.... Even President Hussein. A lot has been said about him, but in the end he was also born of a woman, and he has the same feelings as any other human child would.

The fundamental equality advocated here comes off as a simplistic, almost sentimental attitude when applied as Ban does to Saddam Hussein. Her point is perhaps more convincingly presented by Kirihara Tetsuko, a professional in her mid-thirties who explains the problem with popular perceptions of Hussein in the following way, on the basis of a lecture she once attended.

> The speaker said, "It is easy to start a war." This was just after the Persian Gulf War. "All you have to do is make the people hate your enemy." For example, convince the American people that Hussein is another Hitler. Or, on the other hand, convince Hussein and the Iraqi people that the Americans are invaders. All you have to do is instill hate like that, and from hate war will begin. Therefore, if the leaders want to start a war, it is a simple matter.

Kirihara's point here is that perceptions are important, and those perceptions can be easily manipulated by political leaders or other opinion makers. The propagation of a strong philosophical or religious view of fundamental equality, as contained in Sōka Gakkai's Life-Force theory, would then be an important protection against such manipulation.

Others would point out, however, that the recognition of the ideal of fundamental equality must be tempered by the realization that not all people are yet prepared to accept that presupposition. Ichikawa Yūsuke, a man in his mid-thirties, represents this position. Like Ban and Kirihara, he believes that dialogue, based on an attitude of equality, should be the first response to any problem. He is somewhat less sanguine about the possibilities of that dialogue in every circumstance, however.

> In fact, there are a lot of people who are just not prepared to dialogue. So how do you bring these people into the dialogue? You just have to handle it case by case, and use all of your wisdom [to try and make it work]. The Buddhist spirit will hold out until the end, trying right up until the end to create a place for dialogue. It won't reach for the guns until the end, even though there are some times when you might want to go for the guns right away. But that's really the last option.

Ichikawa believes that dialogue will work in ninety-nine percent of the cases, but he also thinks that the world should be prepared for the occasions when it fails. Furthermore, he is of the opinion that Japan should play a role in establishing a process to deal with cases where coercion by force becomes necessary, and participate in that process, even if this involves amending Japan's constitution to make such participation possible. In our conversation he mentioned the proposal of the then Secretary General of the United Nations, Boutros Boutros Ghali, for the establishment of a United Nations Peacekeeping Force and expressed his agreement with the idea.

> Deployment in a Peacekeeping Force should be allowed, for Japan's army as well. I don't think that would violate Japan's constitution, but if some people want to argue that it does, then we should amend the constitution. We can make a proposal for the first amendment of the constitution, to revise Article 9 that is. Or we can just add one more line to Article 9, something like: In the case of United Nations activities Self-Defense Forces can be deployed [outside of Japan].

Nakamura Takeshi, a journalist and Sōka Gakkai member, amplifies Ichikawa's remarks. Starting from the premise that even in a relatively peaceful country like Japan an armed police force is necessary to maintain law and order, he maintains that a nonviolent approach is not always effective in resolving conflicts. Like Ichikawa, he would turn to the United Nations to act as the world's policeman, and he voices regret that Chapter 7 of the United Nations Charter, allowing for the establishment of United Nations Forces, has not been implemented, leaving it to individual nations or alliances to provide for their own defense as provided for in Chapter 8 of the Charter. He would advocate a standing multinational force, and his reasoning for this echoes the idea of fundamental universal unity that we have seen in Sōka Gakkai's theory of Life-Force.

> We believe Buddhism teaches that you can't think in terms of the sovereignty of one nation, but rather in terms of humanity, or the earth, the global or universal. Therefore, the nation-state is not an absolute, but rather we need to work towards the realization of an international alliance as a superior organization that transcends national sovereignty.

In this way, Nakamura advocates the creation of an international system that will have the ability to resolve conflict wherever it emerges in the world. With a hint of an admonition from the Jewish and Christian scriptures (Jer 6:14),[25] he also criticizes those who think in terms of what he would describe as a more simplistic means to the establishment of peace, what he calls *heiwa nenbutsu shugi*, or peace *nenbutsu*-ism, so named after the belief in the Pure Land sects of Buddhism that one can reach salvation by just calling on the name of the Amida Buddha.

> [What we need is] an active "pacifism." It's not enough to just pray. It's just nonsense to believe that if we keep saying "Peace, peace," that peace will come.

Results from the questionnaire survey on the items designed to measure the degree to which the pacifist position is maintained reflect some of the above issues, and offer a rather confused picture regarding Sōka Gakkai believers' opinion on this issue.[26] Fully 75% of the respondents maintain that the Persian Gulf War should have been resolved by nonviolent means, a result roughly equal to Byakkō Shinkōkai's 77% and second only to Nipponzan Myōhōji. This is ten percent higher than the average of all the groups surveyed in reaction to this item. However, 92% of Sōka Gakkai respondents support Japanese involvement in United Nations peacekeeping operations, far and away the highest rate of support from any of the groups surveyed. We may suppose that this result was influenced by Kōmeitō's role in ensuring passage of the law, as well as by the common perception that such involvement would be limited to unarmed ancillary work, as was mentioned in the previous chapter. It might also indicate that Sōka Gakkai believers would be more receptive to activities involving military force in cases where the United Nations is clearly in charge, reflective of the multinationalism advocated by the group.

A clear majority of the Sōka Gakkai respondents do, however, offer recognition of a right to armed self-defense. The 52% that responded positively to this question mirrors the average for the survey overall, and is clearly not in line with the responses of the two groups that I identified as pacifist in the previous chapter. In light of this result, we must say that the most puzzling result is the fact that more than 90% of the Sōka Gakkai respondents said that, although they generally agree with the right to national self-defense, they would actively oppose Japan's participation in any future war. This response rate was even higher than Nipponzan Myōhōji's, and begs further clarification.

It would seem that Sōka Gakkai believers are willing to accept a theoretical right to armed self-defense, but in practice are reluctant to grant this right to their own country, Japan. I would offer two possible explanations for this position. The first has to do with the multinationalism espoused by Sōka Gakkai, evident in Ikeda's speeches and given religious approbation, as seen in Nakamura's remarks above, as an extension of Sōka Gakkai's Life-Force theory. The right to self-defense can therefore be seen as a means of preserving the sanctity of life, but in practice it is not to be applied at the national level, but rather by some international mechanism yet to be created. This attitude exhibits a healthy fear of the passions that nationalism and patriotism can arouse.

A further explanation focuses more directly on Sōka Gakkai members' attitudes towards their own country. I would argue that these believers harbor a suspicion regarding the aims of their country, a suspicion that is founded in the history of their religious group. Sōka Gakkai is the only group included in this study that suffered persecution at the hands of the authorities in wartime Japan. Sōka Gakkai literature often claims that this persecution was the result of an antimilitary stance taken by Makiguchi.[27] Although my reading of the situation indicates that Makiguchi's opposition was more narrowly focused on the religious policy of the government, Sōka Gakkai's view of its own history highlights their role as victims during the war and serves as a warning of the dangers of nationalism. Such an attitude could be behind the decision not to fight for their country in any case.

This victim-consciousness might also serve to absolve Sōka Gakkai believers of any direct responsibility for what Japan did during the war, making it easier for them to accept the notion of war guilt than for the other groups included in this survey. It is to that question that we now turn.

THE LEGACY OF JAPAN'S WAR GUILT

Three questions were included in the survey to measure the extent to which the respondents were willing to acknowledge guilt for the war or for the activities of their country during the war. The first question dealt with Japan's military exploits in China and queried whether this should be called an invasion, or whether some circumstances may have been present that made military intervention in China necessary. More than 90% of the Sōka Gakkai respondents were unequivocal in calling this action an invasion, a figure almost twenty-five points higher than the average for all the respondents.

A second question asked whether the Japanese were the aggressors or the victims during the war, an effort to measure just how much the awareness of having been the only country to suffer an atomic bombing has influenced attitudes towards the war. The vast majority of respondents, 85% overall, chose a middle option that described the Japanese as both aggressors and victims, and Sōka Gakkai respondents fall precisely in this mean; 13% of the Sōka Gakkai members chose to describe the Japanese as the aggressors, a figure slightly higher than the overall average of 11%, and along with Shūyōdan Hōseikai this figure ranks second behind Nipponzan Myōhōji's 19%.

The third question concerned the issue of the so-called "Comfort Women," reportedly over two hundred thousand women in some of the countries occupied by the Japanese who were forced to serve as sexual slaves for Japanese troops. It was an issue that had resurfaced just at the time I was conducting my research, as military documents were uncovered that proved Japanese Imperial Army complicity in the setting up and running of the brothels. Until then, the Japanese government had claimed that the women were recruited by private brothel operators and no coercion was involved. Following this revelation women in several countries began to press anew their claims for redress, and although the Japanese government issued an apology to the women in August 1993, it has resisted pressure to provide financial compensation, saying that reparation treaties signed in the 1960s settled all war claims issues. In lieu of that, a private fund has been established by the government to compensate the women.[28]

The question included in the survey offered three options: recognizing official complicity and maintaining that the government should offer both an apology and financial compensation to the women, recognizing complicity but maintaining that any necessary apology and compensation had already been taken care of, or denying that official complicity had been established. Once again, Sōka Gakkai members were far and away the strongest in condemning the actions of their own government during the war, with 90% calling for an official apology and financial compensation for the victims. This compares to an overall average of 68%, and the second highest group in this category was Nipponzan Myōhōji with 84%.

Although the evidence seems to suggest that Nipponzan Myōhōji was active in supporting Japan's wartime activities, as were nearly all religious groups in Japan at that time, its postwar denial of such activity and strong antiwar, nonviolent stance would encourage its members to be critical of what are now widely recognized as Japan's crimes during the war. The other pacifist group included in this survey, Byakkō Shinkōkai, continued its pattern of giving ambiguous responses, in line with its belief that such questions only serve to cause disharmony and bind us to this lower dimension where such issues are thought to be of some importance: on the first and third question Byakkō Shinkōkai respondents offered the highest no-response rate, and on the second question they offered the highest response rate for the middle-of-the-road choice of the Japanese being both aggressors and victims in the war.

We may assume that Sōka Gakkai's sense of having themselves been victims of their own government's policies during the war helps the members of this group to sympathize with other victims, making them more likely to be critical of the government's wartime activities. Perhaps equally importantly, the status of victim absolves them personally of any responsibility for what was done, and thus makes it easier to be critical of their government's action in Asia. At any rate, responsibility for World

War II continues to be a matter of considerable controversy in Japan, and it is an issue we will return to in evaluating the peace activities of these groups in the Conclusion of this book.

◦◇   ◦◇   ◦◇

In the Introduction I referred to the unreflective "pacifism" of Christian groups in England and the United States in the interwar years. In David Martin's study of British pacifism, he points out that some who espoused a pacifist position after World War I were among the most vociferous in calling for a holy war against the German forces once Hitler's aims in Europe became clear.[29] Martin Marty likewise details a similar phenomenon among Jewish and Christian groups in the United States, where "pacifism" had become the mainstream position in the years between the two world wars. Such studies offer historical evidence to back up what is presented here as a logical argument, that the absolute prohibition on the taking of life characteristic of the true pacifist position is available only to those who choose not to recognize conflicting claims, or that protecting life might itself involve the taking of life. In order to maintain this absolute position, the pacifist must remove himself or herself somewhat from active participation in the governance of society, where the validity of those conflicting claims is acknowledged in order to protect life and property in a world not yet made perfect. Indeed, Ikeda himself seems to acknowledge this logic, for in a published dialogue with Linus Pauling, Nobel Chemistry and Peace Prize winner, Ikeda indicates that the "absolute pacifist" position is only available on the individual level and not as a political option.[30]

Martin and Marty's studies suggest that those who take up the "pacifist" position without adequately reflecting on its implications will easily abandon it when other fundamental values are threatened, perhaps all the more fervently for their inclination to absolute positions. This leads us to question what might happen to Sōka Gakkai and its members if Japanese society were to find itself under threat. Could we expect the same reaction displayed by pacifists in interwar Britain and the United States? Although this group's evident rejection of nationalistic rhetoric and sentiment might temper the shift from pacifism to holy war in defense of the nation, in the right situation the same dynamic could be expressed under the banner of multinationalism—support of a holy crusade against a common enemy of the United Nations, or of humanity itself. While we might, in fact, laud such a move when it comes, a serious consideration of the implications of the pacifist stance in the absence of an immediate threat would certainly be preferred to wild changes in policy once a threat emerges. That is why I believe that religious groups, as moral teachers, have a crucial role to play in helping to clarify peace discourse in Japan, rather than contributing to its greater confusion. I will return to this issue in the Conclusion, but first we turn to a consideration of the doctrine and practice of two more groups, Risshō Kōseikai and Shōroku Shintō Yamatoyama, in the context of contemporary problems with the just war theory.

FOUR

The Just War and Its Discontents

Sōka Gakkai is a clear example of how it is impossible to maintain the absolute pacifist position unless a group is somehow removed from full participation in society. In Sōka Gakkai's case it becomes necessary to compromise the ideal of pacifism because of its direct political activity in its support of Kōmeitō and the multinationalism advocated by its leader, Ikeda Daisaku. The peace doctrine and practice of the two groups we will look at in this chapter differ from Sōka Gakkai's in two ways. Although both of these groups also hold up pacifism and nonviolence as the ideal, they are less hesitant to recognize the need for the use of force in a world not yet made perfect. And, as a means towards establishing a peaceful world they have chosen a more strictly religious, rather than political, strategy.

Since these groups more readily recognize the occasional need for the use of force, we will want to look at what criteria, if any, they offer for judging when the application of force is justified. In Western, Christian discourse these criteria have generally been offered as part of the just war theory, and we saw in Chapter One how just war rhetoric was used by the Meiji Christians, in addition to pacifist rhetoric. The just war theory is not without its problems, especially in light of military and political developments in the last century or so.

Since at least the 1960s the just war theory has come under attack even within the organization that has traditionally been perhaps its greatest defender, the Catholic Church.[1] The greatest impetus for this contemporary questioning of the theory's usefulness is the development of nuclear weapons, and their proliferation during the years of the Cold War—for the total destruction that these weapons promise[2] clearly violates the principles of proportionality and discrimination upon which the just war theory has been developed.[3] Official documents of the Catholic Church have shown an ambivalence toward the possibility of a just war in the nuclear age since the time of Pope John XXIII,[4] with the pastoral letter on war and peace adopted by the United States bishops in 1983, *The Challenge of Peace: God's Promise and Our Response*, the most poignant example of this ambivalence. The bishops go to some length to explain, in terms of the military and political realities of the Cold War, how any use of nuclear weapons must be condemned,[5] but the continued possession of such weapons, under the doctrine of deterrence, is given conditional approval.[6]

The indiscriminate destructive potential of nuclear weapons is not the only problem that contemporary critics find with the just war theory. For example, the applicability of the criterion that war be fought for a just cause, the foundation of the just war theory, is questioned in an age when many people are aware that the justice of the cause they are called upon to defend is itself, in many cases, relative. Is it just to defend the boundaries of nation-states drawn up by colonial powers, or, on the other hand, would it be just to invite the chaos, and bloodshed, that an open season on redrawing borders might entail? Is it just to defend the value of democracy in a state that is hardly democratic, against a threat from a state that is even less so? Or does the presence of other, perhaps less noble, motivations, such as economic advantage or the preservation of spheres of influence, outweigh the purported reason for the war? Indeed, this growing awareness of the relativity of just causes in the real world has led some to include the criterion of "relative justice" to the list of those traditionally found in just war theories.[7]

Others argue that the complexity of the moral judgments called for in evaluating whether a war might be just, including the criteria of relative justice, undermines the whole enterprise. This would be the position of the Quakers, for example, who hold that some people might be morally convinced of the justice of a certain cause, and in that case they should follow their conscience in defense of that cause, but given the moral complexities involved it is, in the end, more prudent to err on the side of peace in all cases.[8] This argument is also concerned with the criterion of competent authority, one of the traditional elements of the just war theory. Competent authority refers to who is allowed to make the judgment to go to war. Up until modern times such authority would be the king or sovereign, but with the rise of the democratic state this competency has been shifted to the citizenry, through their elected representatives. The moral obligation to pass judgment on the justice of a particular cause is further individualized through the recognition in the modern period of conscientious objection. Opponents of the just war theory thus argue that each individual person is now responsible for making the complex moral judgments required for a valid use of this theory, and given all the variables—and the mass amounts of information, often not available to ordinary citizens—the vast majority of people are not equal to the task.

One more contemporary challenge to the just war theory argues more broadly that, in fact, history has shown that the theory is not effective in its putative aim, limiting conflict. Rather than causing nations to pause and question before embarking on armed conflict, the theory has instead normally been used as a means to justify a course already taken. And as a justification of war, it has also encouraged the escalation of conflict since, in practice, an argument can be made for the use of almost any method, including the "carpet-bombing" of urban centers and the use of atomic weapons, in defending the cause of justice. The use of such tactics and weapons in this century is offered as proof that the just war theory has failed in one of its fundamental aims, that is, to limit the destruction caused by armed conflict.

Finally, others point out that in allowing for even a single instance when the use of force might be justified we have opened a Pandora's Box that will lead to endless conflict. John Howard Yoder, a Mennonite and leading contemporary critic of the just war theory, calls this the "sliding scale": that once one allows for the taking of life as an exception to the general rule against killing, the need for ever "lower" levels of exceptions can be recognized.[9]

Peace discourse in Japan indicates some familiarity with the just war theory. As mentioned above, the material presented in Chapter One indicates how the theory was a major element of Western discourse introduced to Japan in the Meiji period. With the emphasis on pacifism in the postwar period the just war theory is generally dismissed. Criticism, at least on the popular level, often seems to ignore the finer points of the criteria outlined by the theory, or dismiss them as casuistry, and concentrate on the broader claim that the theory is more often used to justify rather than limit war. We have seen an example of this argument already in Uchimura Kanzō's "Justification for the Korean War," where he argues that in the West "justice" has been replaced by "lusts." In the postwar period we can imagine that this argument resonates well with the older, wartime generation who were exposed to the rhetoric of just war in their youth, and have thus become suspicious of "just causes."

We will see traces of this widespread rejection of just war rhetoric in the groups examined in this chapter, Risshō Kōseikai and Shōroku Shintō Yamatoyama. In the first case the rejection of the just war theory is explicit, whereas in Yamatoyama the avoidance of any mention of the theory is itself noteworthy, in light of the emphasis placed on justice in the doctrine of this group. As we look at the doctrine and practice of these groups, therefore, we will want to question what moral guidance is given to help evaluate when force might be necessary, in lieu of the just war theory.

NIWANO NIKKYŌ AND RISSHŌ KŌSEIKAI

Risshō Kōseikai, which claims a membership of six and one half million, rivals Sōka Gakkai as a mass religious movement within the Buddhist tradition. Kōseikai was also founded in the 1930s and enjoyed spectacular success in attracting members in postwar, urban Japan. Although following a path in some ways radically different from Sōka Gakkai—remaining independent of any traditional Buddhist sect and pursuing a policy of cooperation with other religious groups—the rivalry between these two groups has, at times, been very public and very intense.

Risshō Kōseikai was founded by Niwano Nikkyō (1906–) and Naganuma Myōkō (1889–1957) in March 1938 and continued under their joint leadership until Naganuma's death twenty years later. While Niwano himself experimented with various folk religious practices, some of which were incorporated into Risshō Kōseikai's faith, it was Naganuma who possessed certain charismatic powers that allowed her to enjoy considerable influence over the direction of Kōseikai's early development. After her death in 1957, authority was concentrated in Niwano's hands, and under his direction Kōseikai has become a leader in the movement towards interreligious dialogue and cooperative activities to promote peace.

Niwano was born into a large family in a farming village in northern Japan, an environment that by all accounts was a determining influence on his character and religious beliefs.[10] He finished his schooling at the age of twelve; proceeding any further would have required living away from home, an expense his family apparently could not bear. After working on the family farm for several years, he left at the age of sixteen to work on a hydroelectric project near his village. The following year, like many of his generation, he left to seek his fortune in Tokyo.

Niwano did not have much time to fulfill his dream on this first trip to Tokyo, however, since he arrived in the city just three days prior to the Great Kanto Earthquake that devastated the city in 1923. Burned out of the retail rice store where he had found employment, Niwano returned to his village to await the city's reconstruction. During the interval at home he suffered his mother's death, and it was not until November of the following year that he was able to return to Tokyo. In his early years there he was engaged in a number of jobs: gardening, coal and charcoal delivery, and a pickled vegetable dealership. It was at this time that he also developed an interest in fortune telling, primarily through one of his employers, and learned several methods of divination.

Niwano was conscripted into the navy in 1926, and, by his own account, his military service had a profound influence on his life. A naval assignment was a rather elite position in the years of disarmament following the Washington Conference of 1922.[11] He apparently excelled during his three years of service, finishing highest in his class of 196 at the end of the six-month training period, despite his limited formal education. Niwano recalls the experience as a time that offered him self-confidence and a growing recognition of his own abilities.

Before I entered the navy I was a country bumpkin from Niigata living in Tokyo who hadn't even finished school, and I had a terrible inferiority complex. That was completely gone after I returned from the navy, however. By then I had become confident, saying, "Given an equal chance, I can do as well as anyone!"[12]

In his autobiography Niwano claims that "one of the greatest harvests from my military experience was the reinforcement of my philosophy of nonviolence."[13] As an example of this nonviolence, he says he refused to use corporal punishment on his subordinates, suffering himself instead at the hands of his superiors when the men under his leadership fell short. Overall, however, he evaluates the experience positively, and is even nostalgic about the pomp and pageantry, as indicated in his recollection of a full naval review, when his ship, *The Haruna*, was selected as the imperial flagship.

The full review of the fleet held in November, 1928, was a sight none of us will ever forget. There were two hundred large and small craft in Tokyo Bay, all with full crews and all in the finest trim. The present emperor [Hirohito], who was still a young man then, came aboard the Haruna for the review. As the band played the Navy March and the imperial salute boomed, the Haruna sailed smoothly past the ships waiting in review. Setting aside all thought of militarism and war, I still enjoy the recollection of that magnificent pageant, the likes of which will never be seen in Japan again.[14]

Shortly after being discharged from the navy at the end of 1929, Niwano married a cousin from his hometown in Niigata and the two of them settled in Tokyo. By the end of 1931 a daughter had been born, and, borrowing money from his uncle, Niwano set up his own pickled vegetable business. Within a month after his daughter's birth, however, she developed a severe ear infection, and Niwano was told that an operation would have to be performed. As one often sees in the accounts of the founders of the Japanese new religions, it was as a result of this misfortune that Niwano turned to religion in a serious way.

Advised by a friend to try prayers to Tengu Fudō,[15] Niwano visited the house of a local shamaness who incorporated worship of the Buddhist Fudō deity with Shugendo practices of strict austerity and faith healing. Visits to pray at the house of this shamaness became part of his daily routine, and following the recovery of his daughter he decided to take up himself the ascetic training, rising to the rank of the shamaness's assistant and performing the healing rites on his own. He was taken aback, however, when the shamaness insisted that he give up his pickle business and work with her full time, and left the group to become involved in yet another form of divination, a form of onomancy based on the number of strokes used in writing the characters comprising a person's name. Niwano says that he found this system more rational, and thus more appealing than the acquisition of "mysterious spiritual abilities" that the leader of the Fudō sect had been encouraging.[16] Rational faith is a recurring theme in Niwano's writings and speeches, and belies the reliance on divination and direct revelation that was particularly strong in Risshō Kōseikai's early years, as we shall see in a moment. Onomancy in particular has retained its importance in Risshō Kōseikai's beliefs, and it is normal practice for converts to be given a new, more auspicious, name based on this system.

LAY BUDDHISM

Niwano's last, and definitive, formative religious experience began in the summer of 1934. At that time he was visited by a missionary of Reiyūkai who warned him that if he failed to convert to the group he would shortly suffer some misfortune. His second daughter fell ill with a high fever exactly one week later, convincing him to join Reiyūkai at once.

Reiyūkai was a new religious group that had been founded just nine years earlier by Kubo Kakutarō and Kotani Kimi. Kubo had been influenced by the nationalist Nichirenist ideas of Tanaka Chigaku, and the coincidence of his birth in the same town that Nichiren had come from, Kominato in Chiba Prefecture, northeast of Tokyo, helped to convince him that he had a special mission to carry the mantle of the thirteenth-century Buddhist priest in the modern era. Kubo's preaching was decidedly anticlerical, however, proclaiming that personal and social ills were the result of the inadequate veneration of the ancestor spirits, a task traditionally left to the Buddhist clergy. These spirits could not attain buddhahood and become guardian spirits until the proper rites had been performed, and the clergy were more concerned with earning money through such practices as the selling of *kaimyō* (posthumous names) than performing the proper rites.[17] Kubo's genius was that he offered the urban migrants, who had broken contact with the ancestral graves set in temples in the countryside, a means to perform the veneration rites themselves in the home, without relying on the Buddhist clergy.[18] To this he added the practice of spirit-mediumship and faith healing, having his sister-in-law, Kotani Kimi, undergo cold water ablutions until she was able to perform such rites herself.

Reiyūkai was a rapidly growing movement in the 1930s among the immigrants to the city, perhaps especially among the lower class of the *burakumin*, traditionally discriminated against in Japan.[19] Niwano became a disciple of Arai Sukenobu, a Reiyūkai teacher who was apparently well known within the group for his learning and his lectures on the *Lotus Sutra*. Niwano says that his daughter was cured within a week of his joining the group, and he gradually became more and more involved in Reiyūkai missionary activities under the direction of Arai, to the extent that his business began to suffer. In order to devote more time to his religious work, Niwano decided to give up the pickle business and took up milk delivery, since he could limit his work to the early morning and evening, devoting the rest of his time to Reiyūkai. One of his customers in this new business was a woman by the name of Naganuma Myōkō.

Naganuma Myōkō was born in Saitama Prefecture, directly north of Tokyo, in December of 1889. Losing her mother at the age of six, she had to start work to support the family. Married at the age of sixteen, she divorced her husband, who was famous for his drinking and womanizing, just before she turned forty, following the death of her infant daughter. She then left on her own for Tokyo, where she remarried and opened an ice and sweet potato shop with her husband. Always sickly, Naganuma had sought salvation through several religions, including Tenrikyō and Ontakekyō. After her meeting with Niwano she was won over to Reiyūkai, eventually becoming, along with Niwano, one of Arai's most fervent disciples. She was trained by Arai's wife in the Reiyūkai practice of *hatsuon*, or spirit mediumship in a semitrance state. By 1936 both Niwano and Naganuma had become leaders of their own *hōza*, a group of followers that they had recruited themselves.[20]

On 5 March 1938, Niwano and Naganuma jointly started their own religious group, Dai Nippon Risshō Kōseikai, joining the growing number of groups that had split off from Reiyūkai.[21] Niwano offers as reasons for this split the pressure from Reiyūkai headquarters to ensure a steady increase in membership, as well as the fact that Arai and his lectures on the *Lotus Sutra* were not sufficiently appreciated by the leaders of the group. About thirty Reiyūkai members followed them, and Risshō Kōseikai's membership grew steadily, if not overly impressively, to somewhat over one thousand by 1941.

During the war years it is clear that Kōseikai did not take a stance in opposition to the nation's militarist aims, but neither does it seem that they were called upon to take any extraordinary action in support of the war. For this the group can probably be grateful for the fact that they were still a minor religious movement, more concerned with their own internal affairs than the state of the nation. On the part of the nation as well, they were insignificant enough to avoid the heavy hand of control and oppression under which others suffered. They were perhaps also aided here by the fact that they were identified with Nichiren nationalism, a view Niwano himself gives voice to in the Japanese edition of his autobiography.

> Dai Nippon Risshō Kōseikai was founded in 1938. The previous year the war between China and Japan had begun, and the month after we founded our group an order to complete national mobilization was issued, meaning the whole country was entering a war footing.... At that time, the whole country was under pressure from the military, and the religious world felt its effects rather severely. What is now known as Ishinkai, at that time Myōdōkai, was ordered to disband, and then the precursor of Jinrui Zen'aikai, Ōmotokyō, was suppressed for the second time and destroyed. Honmichi was also suppressed, and the late Okada Mokichi of Nihon Kannonkyō, the precursor of Sekai Kyūseikyō, was arrested. Hito no Michi Kyōdan, the precursor of the present PL Kyōdan, was also disbanded.
>
> In that respect, groups that venerated the *Lotus Sutra* found themselves in a better position. Because certain Nichirenist groups supported an ultranationalist position, the military also interpreted the *Lotus Sutra* in such a superficial way. But in fact, the *Lotus Sutra* teaches the exact opposite of the idea of "power."
>
> ...In the eyes of the state at that time, the life of the ordinary citizen was nothing. Teaching as we did the value of even the smallest

person's life, we also should have been suppressed by the government. But we were saved by the mistaken beliefs of the military, and of people in general, concerning the *Lotus Sutra*.[22]

On the other hand, Kōseikai was also not critical of Japanese nationalist policies during the war. In 1940 the group adopted as its official standard a banner with the words *Tenjō mukyū*—meaning "without end," but, as Tokoro Shigemoto points out, at that time indicating the unending reign of the imperialist state.[23] Niwano also tells us, again in the Japanese version of his autobiography, that he received a draft notice in 1941, and that he had determined to accept his responsibilities with courage. He failed to pass the physical, however, a development he attributes to the mysterious intervention of the Buddha, since his speedy return to the group had been foretold to Naganuma in a trance.[24] Finally, Niwano reveals that until he quit his milk delivery business in 1942 and devoted himself full-time to his religious activities, any donations given to him by members of the group were taken to the local police station and handled as contributions to the war effort. The evidence would seem to indicate, therefore, that although he and his group avoided the ultranationalism of other elements within the Nichiren movement at that time, they exhibited a normal level of patriotism and cooperation with the war effort during these years.

POSTWAR DEVELOPMENT

For the first twenty years of Risshō Kōseikai's existence, Niwano and Naganuma shared responsibility for its leadership. Naganuma, as the conduit of divine revelations, seems to have had a larger role in guiding the group and directing the training of leaders, including, to a certain extent, her cofounder. Early on Niwano was directed to devote himself exclusively to the study of the *Lotus Sutra*, and so the reading of extraneous material, including newspapers, was banned. Later on he was allowed to expand his interests to the writings of Nichiren and studies in early Buddhism, and it was through this effort that he was able to eventually take the dominant role in developing Kōseikai's doctrine.

Naganuma's influence contributed to a series of conflicts with society, most directly in the first instance, when she and Niwano were briefly arrested in 1943. It seems that Niwano's wife was not entirely in favor of his religious activity, especially after he abandoned his business in order to devote all his energies to the group. Naganuma for her part had been ordering Niwano to give up his family so that he would be undistracted in following his calling, a demand that he had managed to put off. Niwano tells us that his wife, jealous of the influence Naganuma was exerting over their lives, joined with the Fudō shamaness that he had abandoned years earlier to put pressure on the police to have the two arrested for violation of the Peace Preservation Law. The specific charge was that they were disturbing the peace with their missionary activities, similar to one of the charges made against Makiguchi of Sōka Gakkai and his lieutenants, as we saw in the previous chapter. In the end, Niwano was released without charge after two weeks, and Naganuma a week later. As an aside, Niwano attributes their release to the fact that he had been leaving the members' contributions with the police for several years.[25] In the end, Niwano's family was evacuated to his hometown in Niigata as the situation in Tokyo became worse with the start of the American bombing of the cities, and they remained separated from him for almost a decade after the war.

Risshō Kōseikai was unable to match Sōka Gakkai's phenomenal growth rate after the war, but nevertheless it did expand quickly, growing from 32,000 families in 1947 to ten times that amount in 1955. In the mid-1950s, however, it was the target of a number of controversies that temporarily halted its growth. In 1952 the national broadcasting agency, NHK, linked Risshō Kōseikai's practice of onomancy to the suicide of a woman and her twelve-year-old son in the city of Zōshiki, west of Tokyo, a report that was subsequently picked up and expanded upon by other media organs.[26] This incident set the stage for further attacks on Risshō Kōseikai, including legal action involving the purchase of land in Tokyo where the present headquarter complex can be found, as well as criticism of the group for their use of divination, including onomancy. Also, early in 1954 legal action was started by Shiraishi Shigeru, a former newspaper reporter and recent convert to the group, to disband the organization in accord with the provisions of the Religious Corporations Law. The lawsuit charged Kōseikai with misrepresenting the teachings of the *Lotus Sutra* and Nichiren Buddhism, employing prophesy and divination to influence its believers, and accumulating wealth from its members. The whole affair culminated in hearings before committees of parliament where Niwano was called to testify, and, finally, in an out-of-court settlement with Shiraishi that set him up as the head of a task force to monitor Kōseikai activities. Niwano's acquiescence to the terms of the agreement led to an internal rift within the religion, and a movement to appoint Naganuma the sole head of the group. This was only finally resolved when she fell sick early in 1957 and died in September of that year.

MANIFESTATION OF THE TRUTH

Early in the following year, Risshō Kōseikai made a dramatic change in direction. The first twenty years of the group's history were called the *Hōben* Period, or Period of Skillful Means, which had now come to an end with the initiation of the Manifestation of the Truth. These titles come from the Mahayana Buddhist, particularly *Lotus Sutra*, belief that less than explicit means may be used to bring people to the truth, and that ultimately the full truth will be revealed. In Risshō Kōseikai's case it meant specifically that the age marked by divination and prophecy based on Naganuma's leadership was over, and the group would now be engaged in the development of their doctrine, under Niwano's leadership. Courses in doctrine, focusing on the *Lotus Sutra* and early Buddhism, were held for the leadership and the Kōseikai Youth Association, with a definitive textbook being developed in 1963.

Under Niwano's leadership the group also became involved in civic and interreligious activities with the aim of addressing various social ills. In 1969, for example, the Movement for a Bright Society was founded to promote volunteerism, educational and cultural activities, grassroots peace activities, and other civic movements. Although nominally independent from Risshō Kōseikai, both its local branches and national organization often make use of Kōseikai facilities and personnel. Risshō Kōseikai began a course for the training of volunteers to work in local social welfare institutions in 1971, and started sponsoring boat trips for its Youth Association in 1973, to visit Hong Kong, Manila, and Okinawa for the purpose of praying for the war dead of all the countries in Asia and to promote personal exchanges. In 1970 Niwano was also instrumental in organizing the First World Conference on Religion and Peace in Kyoto, and on both the national and international level Risshō Kōseikai remains a central figure in the work of this interreligious body. The World Conference on Religion and Peace, or WCRP, meets every four or five years, drawing together religious leaders from around the world and all major traditions to discuss the role of religion in promoting peace. Local conferences have also been established, and the Asian Conference on Religion and Peace, once again organized under the leadership of Niwano and Risshō Kōseikai, was especially instrumental in promoting a regional response to the plight of the Boat People refugees from Vietnam in the late 1970s. In 1978, on the fortieth anniversary of the founding of Risshō Kōseikai, the Niwano Peace Foundation was established to provide funding for development projects, primarily in Asia, and to promote peace research. That same year Niwano was also invited to address the United Nations General Assembly First Special Session on Disarmament.

KŌSEIKAI'S CONCEPT OF PEACE

The concept of peace that motivates these activities is, in its broad strokes, similar to that of Sōka Gakkai, based as they both are on faith in the *Lotus Sutra*. Using Niwano's words, it can be summarized as follows.

> There is a single, invisible entity that is embodied in all things existing in our universe. This is the great life force of the universe. All things in this world fundamentally are of this one entity. Therefore, though phenomena appear in infinite variety, essentially they are equal in their existence.
> ...[I]f the real embodiment of all things is a single entity, it becomes understandable that all mankind, over four billion people, each with a unique appearance, fundamentally forms one single existence. When one can fully realize this, then fraternal love, the feeling that all human beings are brothers and sisters, will spring up in one's heart. One will be filled with a sense of harmony and cooperation. This sentiment of fraternity is the benevolence or compassion taught in Buddhism. Friendship based on this great sense of oneness with others is the very essence of benevolence.[27]

Although he also claims that the teaching of the *Lotus Sutra* is fundamentally one of nonviolence,[28] it is clear that Niwano and Risshō Kōseikai do not advocate a strictly pacifist position. In his writings Niwano makes a distinction between the ideal aimed at and the reality with which we are faced, and, for example, the necessity of a Self-Defense Force is explained by means of the analogy of public safety.[29]

Niwano points out that although we would all like to live in a society where it is not necessary to lock your door or to maintain a police department, humanity has not yet reached the stage where that is possible. The challenge for humanity, and especially for people of religion, is to make reality reflect the ideal, to create a world where force or the threat of force is no longer necessary. Until that ideal is achieved, however, the necessity of force is recognized.

However, Niwano displays a distrust of the concept of justice, the ethical basis normally given as the criterion for judging when force is necessary. The concept is criticized as lacking tolerance, and specifically devoid of meaning in the age of nuclear weapons.

> It is a fact that in the past there was a tenet of Christian theology that taught that it was all right to go to war for the sake of upholding justice. However, although there might be a moral duty to correct injustice, because of Christianity's monotheism and the resultant inability to recognize other religions or allow them to exist, when there was a war it would commit terrible atrocities, because of its intolerance.... In this age when people possess the awful power of nuclear weapons is it even possible to speak of a just war any more? Now is not the time to speak of justice, but rather our first consideration must be of peace.[30]

Here, in addition to the argument that the existence of nuclear weapons make the just war position untenable, we can also see a particular development of the "sliding scale" argument that just war theories are not, in fact, effective in limiting war. Niwano attributes the proliferation of war in the West to the rather common view in Japan that monotheistic religions are inherently intolerant, as opposed to the attitude of tolerance engendered by the religiously pluralistic situation of Japan. Niwano's acceptance of these commonly held assumptions is an important part of Risshō Kōseikai's concept of peace, a question we will return to in Chapter Six.

While Niwano's arguments reflect broadly held contemporary doubts regarding these theories, substitute criteria for judging when force needs to be applied are not provided. The result of this lack of moral direction is aptly illustrated by interviews I conducted with two Risshō Kōseikai members engaged full time in the group's various peace activities.[31]

Fukamoto Keiji, in his early 30s, is somewhat of an expert in this field, having engaged in formal peace research as part of his education. When asked for his opinion regarding the Persian Gulf War, he is critical of all the participants: President Hussein and the Iraqis for invading Kuwait, the American-led multinational force for attacking Iraq, and the United Nations for not preventing the whole mess to begin with.

> What we really need to think about, concretely, is a system that won't let a situation like that develop. For example, maybe a stronger United Nations, but not in a military sense.... We have to think about the stage before something like the Hussein administration gets started. Right now the United Nations can't interfere in the internal affairs of a country. Therefore, once an administration like that gets established, there's nothing more that the United Nations can do. So we need to think about a United Nations system that can interfere, that can stop such an administration from getting started. I really don't have any concrete image of how it can be done, though.

Undoubtedly, many people, not only members of Risshō Kōseikai, can sympathize with Fukamoto's efforts to find some kind of concrete means of policing the world without resorting to the use of arms, but the untenability of the position soon becomes apparent. Fukamoto ends up describing himself as a "flexible pacifist," caught between the ideal of a world without arms and the reality of the situations that humanity has to face.

Andō Ken is old enough to have participated in the student protests of the 1960s, and recalls being impressed by the communists among the student leaders at that time. They were always ready with an answer regarding the kind of society that they were out to build. Andō didn't much agree with the answers that they offered, but admired them for at least thinking through their positions and offering clear, concrete aims—an opinion, by the way, that many people in Japan voice when speaking of the Japan Communist Party in comparison to other political parties in the country. As opposed to these student leaders, Andō says that all he felt was frustration towards Risshō Kōseikai and its leaders, and he recalls one incident when his frustration boiled over and he shouted at a Kōseikai teacher, "You have absolutely no policy about how to institute this 'peaceful society' that we all talk about!"

Thirty years later, however, Andō admits that if someone were to come to him now with the same complaint that he would be at a loss for an answer.

> Even now I don't have an answer to that question. I'd probably end up giving the same answers that were given to me. From a Buddhist standpoint, the present social structure, the social system, is just a passing thing, it isn't the true reality. But that doesn't mean that we can just get rid of the whole thing, but rather the efforts that we make within that structure are important. That's about the extent of it. But I wanted something more concrete then, and that kind of an answer just didn't make it.... Buddhism just isn't very good at taking the lead and giving concrete ideas about what kind of social structure, what kind of system, what kind of political system we should have.

Andō speaks here of Buddhism, because that is the position represented by Risshō Kōseikai, and one that had left him disappointed and frustrated as a youth. However, his frustration is no longer limited to Buddhism, as illustrated by an episode from the time of the Gulf War. Andō recalls an international forum of religious leaders dealing with the war, where the issue of the justice of the war was discussed. In the end it became apparent that no agreement could be reached, and the conference broke up without offering any concrete guidance, or hint of a "policy," such as Andō had craved in his student days. Andō says the incident brought home to him once again the impotence of religious leadership when faced with the question of war.

The survey results on the pacifist questions also reflect the lack of a clear position. Kōseikai members were less willing to admit the need for armed defense (46%) or to support Self-Defense Force participation in UN peacekeeping activities (48%) than respondents to the survey overall (56% and 58%). However, while 58% said that they would actively oppose Japan's participation in any war, this percentage is considerably lower than that of Nipponzan Myōhōji (84%) and Sōka Gakkai (91%), and only slightly higher that the overall overage of 56%. Risshō Kōseikai members, therefore, are only marginally more opposed to any war on principle than the overall sample that we are working with here, but considerably less inclined to allow for an armed defense or Japanese participation in international peacekeeping operations. Although on an official doctrinal level Risshō Kōseikai recognizes the need for arms in a world not yet made perfect, the reluctance to speak of situations where the use of force might be necessary, to offer criteria, or a "policy" for its use, seems to have left the members confused as to what position to take on the concrete matters of war and peace.

In the case of this group, a visceral distrust of the concept of justice leads to a lack of guidance on the question of war and peace, a situation reflected broadly in Japanese society today. We turn now to yet another group whose doctrine is even more amenable to the recognition that, at times, force may be necessary to defend common values of life and good order, to see how the issue of the just war is dealt with there.

SHŌROKU SHINTŌ YAMATOYAMA

Shōroku Shintō Yamatoyama provides an interesting contrast to Risshō Kōseikai and the other Nichiren Buddhist groups we have looked at in this study. Yamatoyama draws its religious resources primarily from the folk-religious tradition of Japan, and it is the only group included in this survey that has its headquarters outside of the greater Tokyo metropolitan area. Despite these rural, folk-religious foundations, however, in doctrine and outlook it has clearly been influenced by contemporary trends in the broader religious world, through the training of the founder's son and second leader of the group as a professional religious researcher. On the issues of pacifism and just war as well, it provides somewhat of a contrast to Risshō Kōseikai and the previous groups we have looked at, since it possesses a somewhat less optimistic view of human nature than that presented by the Japanese New Religions in general.

Shōroku Shintō Yamatoyama was founded in 1919 by Tazawa Seishirō (1884–1966) and has over sixty thousand members, largely in the rural areas of Hokkaido and northern Honshu.[32] Seishirō was born in Aomori City, a provincial capital in the north of Japan, the son of a wood and charcoal dealer. Abandoned by his mother at the age of seven, Seishirō lived alone with his father until the age of sixteen, when he ran off to Tokyo, presumably to escape his strict and taciturn father, who had forced him to abandon his plans for further education in order to help with the family business. Following arrest as a runaway, Seishirō was able to persuade his father to allow him to return to Tokyo, where he

111

was apprenticed to a wood and charcoal dealer licensed to the Imperial Household. At the age of twenty Seishirō was drafted into the infantry, but, because he had suffered from rheumatism as a youth, his legs were somewhat impaired and he was discharged after only five months. After his discharge he returned to Aomori to help with his father's business, applying what he had learned in Tokyo to improve its product line and forming a trade association of local businessmen. He broke with his father at the age of thirty-three, moving back to Tokyo with his family, which now included five children. He tried without success for two years to establish himself independently in Tokyo before moving back to Aomori to work for his father yet again in 1918.

By this time Seishirō had already lost a son to sickness, and his youngest daughter was also gravely ill. His stepmother, convinced by an Inari practitioner[33] that Seishirō's misfortune could be transmitted to others, would not let him move into the family house, and he was forced to take up residence in a small office near the company logging site on Mt. Soto-dōji. Although the forests on the mountain had been exploited since the eighteenth century, access to the mountain was still difficult, and in the lonely atmosphere of his hut Seishirō began to experience the presence of a divinity. While still an apprentice in Tokyo, Seishirō had adopted practices associated with *fudō shinkō,* a popular form of belief already seen in the account of Niwano Nikkyō's religious development. One night in the dead of winter, unable to sleep because of the cold, despite being covered by every piece of clothing he had, empty rice bags, and even the straw matting, he began to chant the "Fudō Sutra" that he had learned while in Tokyo. While chanting he began to feel warm, and thinking this was strange he opened his eyes to see an image of Fudō Myōō with sword in hand, standing in the midst of flames that were reaching up to the roof of the hut. Just as soon as he saw it, the image disappeared and cold returned to the hut. Seishirō records this as his first experience of seeing God face-to-face.

Hearing that a local youth working on the mountain had also had a vision of God, Seishirō set off the following spring to erect a shrine on the spot, after first receiving a prayer from the local Shinto priest to chant on the occasion. From that time on Seishirō began to sense that he had been given a special mission by God, and started performing cold water ablutions in a river near his mountain hut. One night in the fall of that year, upon retiring he suddenly heard the voice of a god identifying

Organic farms at the headquarters of Shōroku Shintō Yamatoyama, in the mountains of Aomori Prefecture in the north of Japan.

itself as the Moon, asking for his worship the following evening. Rain the next day made it unlikely that the moon would appear, however, so Seishirō addressed the following words to the god:

> Great god of the moon! This is the twenty-third, the day I've been told is the memorial day for the god of the moon. As you can see, however, it's cloudy and drizzly, and it's going to be difficult to worship the moon tonight. Not only that, I don't know what time the god of the moon will make an appearance, and I have to think about my work tomorrow, so I'm going to go to bed. If the clouds clear up and it is possible to worship the moon later on, would you mind waking me?[34]

Later that night he awoke to find the skies clear and the moon shining brightly in his hut. Looking up he saw the mountain bathed in light, and a single star coming up to join the moon. He heard a voice saying, "This star is the god called the Ninth-day Star, the god who serves God. I will be your protector god throughout life."[35] It was this event that led

113

Seishirō to the decision to devote his life to the service of God, and it is taken as the occasion of Shōroku Shintō Yamatoyama's birth.

The above account of Seishirō's early revelations already indicates the incorporation of various Japanese folk beliefs and practices in this new religion: *fudō shinkō*, Shinto prayers, gods identified with heavenly objects, cold water ablutions, an innocent closeness to the divine. Following his call, Seishirō adopted Yamato Shōfū as his name, appropriating the traditional name for Japan, Yamato, as his own. He set off as an itinerant healer, moving throughout the northern tip of Honshu as well as the island of Hokkaido. With the death of his father in 1922 Seishirō entered a period of seclusion that lasted nine years, during which his daughter began to act as a conduit for revelation, seeing ideographs one by one before her eyes that were written down, eventually comprising five volumes that are considered Yamatoyama's sacred scriptures.

During this period of seclusion Seishirō moved to Mt. Soto-dōji and began work on what would become the headquarters of his new religion. In September 1924 five small buildings were constructed on the mountain, including a small hut to house the founder. The headquarters complex displays several unique features, reflecting perhaps the temperament and religious experiences of the founder. Shrines were erected on the four corners of the property, and later three additional shrines were added: the Shōkijō to symbolize prayer for world peace, the Shinshūjō for mutual understanding and cooperation among religions, and the Sume-mioya-no-miya for peace in Japan. Seishirō also constructed a rock garden at the back of his hut as a model of what this "Divine Capital" would eventually look like. Finally, rather than adopting one of the gods from the Japanese Shinto or Buddhist pantheon, or carving his own image of the divinity as other religious founders have done, during his cold water ablutions in the river on the mountain Seishirō gathered seven rocks in which he saw images of the divine and erected them as the Seven Rock Statues. These statues are now taken as a sign of religious diversity, indicating the many images of the divine that can aid humanity towards salvation.

In 1931 Seishirō resumed his activity as an itinerant healer, attracting a following of several hundred believers. Increasingly discouraged with the limited focus and selfish desires of those who came to him for healing, and troubled by apocalyptic visions of a world facing judgment from God—all this as Japan increasingly set itself on a course towards war in Asia—Seishirō once again retired to Mt. Soto-dōji in 1937, and did not leave the mountain until 1955.

GOD'S JUDGMENT

From the material available on the life of Seishirō it is difficult to get a clear reading of his position on the war.[36] His official biography relates that he made periodic statements during the war that were taken as prophecies by his followers, often after the fact, due to the obscure nature of his pronouncements. The believers say there were prophecies, for example, of Hitler's advance into the Sudetenland as well as the Japanese attack on Pearl Harbor. His followers were also able to find a reference to the date on which Japan surrendered, 15 August 1945, hidden in a poem written by Seishirō three years previous to that date.

Whether one puts stock in these prophecies or not, a clear apocalyptic theme can be found in Seishirō's teaching. He believed in a God who acted in history, often as judge, in order to establish an ideal order. For this reason he apparently felt that God's judgment might come at any time, as a violent cleansing of the current unjust order. This is expressed positively by Yamatoyama in the following way.

> One important characteristic of the founder's idea of God was the hope-filled belief that this all-powerful God directs history in order to create a world into which all people would be grateful that they had been born.... People are aware of and constantly distressed by the fact of how powerless they are in the cause of justice and truth, and how prevalent is ill will and corruption. But God, who sees all, will reward justice and right without fail; God assures the ultimate victory of justice, and God will likewise pass judgment without fail on the unjust.[37]

Seishirō's son Yasusaburō tells us that this sense of impending judgment was so strong that he was not allowed to participate in school field trips or athletic meets, nor was he allowed to attend movies or even the town festival, because the congregation of people in one place made it more likely that God's judgment would strike in the form of some disaster.[38] The war and the destruction that it caused was no doubt interpreted in terms of this cleansing action of God in history. Seishirō did offer prayers for the safe return of the troops sent off to war, expressing a concern for the individuals caught up in the misery of the war, in Yamatoyama's explanation.[39] The group also claims that the founder himself had caught the eye of the authorities, primarily because of the apocalyptic teaching outlined above. Although Seishirō, secluded on Mt. Soto-dōji, was not himself harassed by the police, some of his followers apparently were.[40]

In the postwar years Seishirō's son Yasusaburō took over leadership of Yamatoyama, a role he filled until his death early in 1997. Yasusaburō was born in 1914 and, after graduating from the local junior high school in Aomori, he went on to high school in Hirosaki, finally matriculating into Tokyo Imperial University. At the university in Tokyo he entered the Religious Studies Department, where he remained until returning to Mt. Soto-dōji in the immediate postwar period. While in Tokyo, Yasusaburō tells us that he was accustomed to attend Sunday services at a Mukyōkai congregation, the Japanese indigenous Christian group founded by Uchimura Kanzō. He also allows how he was greatly influenced in his religious outlook not only by his experiences with this congregation but also by his reading of Uchimura's works.[41]

"EVIL LURKS IN THE HUMAN HEART"

Seishirō's eschatological beliefs and Yasusaburō's contact with Christian theology, as taught by Uchimura Kanzō, greatly influenced Yamatoyama's doctrine, codified in the writings of Yasusaburō in the postwar period. The less than optimistic—one could say Augustinian—view of human nature alluded to above gives us a clear example of these influences. Yamatoyama, like many of the Japanese New Religions, teaches that each individual life comes from God, and for that reason it is possessed of a surpassing dignity. However, people are careless with this gift of life from God, and soil it with their unjust and selfish deeds. While this idea of "sin" can be found in other new religious movements as well, Yamatoyama places more emphasis on the weight and pervasiveness of this reality. For example, Tenrikyō speaks of eight "dusts" that accumulate on the human heart—miserliness, covetousness, hatred, self-love, grudge-bearing, anger, greed, and arrogance. However, the emphasis here is on the fact that with a little daily attention, a daily "dusting" of the heart, we can prevent their accumulation and preserve ourselves in our original, pure form. In Yamatoyama this is presented as a far graver task.

The search for truth in life will be accompanied by suffering. Are you going to reject the search for truth out of fear of suffering? Defending justice in life is not always easy. Will you be blinded by your own interest and not dare to challenge injustice? Life comes from God. Those who know that they should accept life every day [as a gift] from God will count as joy even the suffering they endure to protect the truth of life.[42]

This view of human nature obviously affects Yamatoyama's outlook on war and peace. Yamatoyama believers in general have less trouble accepting the fact that violence is sometimes needed to "defend justice." Taguchi Maki, a young lady in her twenties, is, I think, illustrative of the position taken by many of the members of this group.[43] She expresses her beliefs in the following words.

Evil still lurks in the human heart. It is only when we finally get rid of that evil heart that we will no longer need armies, that weapons will no longer be necessary. But unfortunately the way things are right now we need a force to control that evil.

While acknowledging the need for a force to defend justice, however, Taguchi also has her problems with talk of a "just war." Her reservations are based on the suspicion that justice could, in fact, merely be a pretext to cover other motives, a result of her experience during the Persian Gulf War. Taguchi was studying in the United States at that time and she remembers the way the war was presented in the media. Here is how she evaluates American participation in the war, on the basis of what she saw and heard.

America entered the war on the pretext of defending right and justice, but in fact it seems that economic concerns were actually more important. Should we say that they used the situation skillfully, or maybe it could be called an example of a new imperialism.... At any rate, it left me thinking, "What a dangerous country!"

Taguchi's criticism of the use of the concept of justice here is based on the perception of mixed motives, a part of the contemporary critique of the just war theory that emphasizes the relativity of justice. Significantly, her comment was the only direct criticism of this concept that I came across in my study of Yamatoyama's literature or in my interviews with members of the group. Justice would seem to be an important part of Yamatoyama's belief; it is described as something to be established by

God, something to be sought after, something for which it is worth suffering. Yet the content of this justice is still unclear. Let us take a look at what some elements of this concept might be, by examining the results of the questionnaire survey.

SELF-DEFENSE AND CULTURAL IDENTITY

Results from the questionnaire survey confirm that Yamatoyama believers are much more accepting of the need for an armed defense than the other groups covered in this research. Fully 80% of Yamatoyama respondents to the survey acknowledge the need for such a defense, a result considerably higher than that seen in any other group. Notwithstanding objections such as those seen above, Yamatoyama believers were also markedly higher in their support of the Gulf War, with 43% recognizing the need to resolve that conflict militarily, against an overall average of 25%. Although only 15% expressed unqualified support of the Japanese Self-Defense Forces, this was almost three times the overall average for this item, and, significantly, not one Yamatoyama respondent expressed the opinion that the forces should be disbanded, opting instead for the overwhelmingly popular response of a constitutionally limited force. Yamatoyama respondents were also second only to those of Sōka Gakkai in expressing support for SDF participation in United Nations peace-keeping operations, with almost two-thirds adopting this position. Finally, in answer to the question as to whether they would participate in a possible future war in which Japan might be involved, fully one-quarter of the respondents answered positively. While a slightly higher 27% said that they would actively oppose such a war, the positive responses were significantly higher, and the negative significantly lower, than the overall averages for this question (8% and 56% respectively).

In addition to the doctrinal justification of such a view—the idea that evil is a reality that must be grappled with, even actively opposed—one can offer other possible explanations for these results. Yamatoyama believers in general are overwhelmingly rural, and perhaps more conservative than their fellow citizens in the urban areas. The Self-Defense Forces seem to recruit more heavily from Hokkaido and the other northern provinces where these believers are concentrated, perhaps because these areas are less economically advantaged than much of the rest of the country. This could mean that a higher percentage of Yamatoyama believers, or their acquaintances, have themselves been members of the Self-Defense Forces, raising the level of acceptance of these forces as well as the recognition of a need for an armed defense. Yamatoyama respondents were also much younger than the overall sample, with two-thirds in their 20s and 30s. This generation, without the experience of war, may be less inclined to reject all war out of hand. One final explanation could be the unabashed patriotism that has been cultivated by Tazawa Yasusaburō in the postwar years.

In his account of why he abandoned his research in Tokyo and returned to Mt. Soto-dōji after the war, Yasusaburō recalls that his mentor, Kishimoto Hideo, an advisor to the Occupation Forces, called the students in the Religious Studies Department together one day to discuss what he had learned from his meetings with the Americans. In his retelling of the incident, Yasusaburō says that Kishimoto expected a much longer occupation than the five to ten years that had been rumored at the time, even suggesting that thirty years might be more realistic. During that time he feared that the Japanese people, already reeling from their first experience of defeat in war, might completely lose their cultural identity in the face of the inevitable Americanization of society. Kishimoto thus urged his students to be prepared for the day when they would be needed to help revive the unique Japanese cultural identity, especially as it is preserved and expressed in the religion of the people. It was with this mission in mind that Yasusaburō determined to return to the religious community founded by his father and take up a leadership role in that group.[44]

The cultural identity that Yasusaburō sought to protect through his religious activities reflects overall a healthy national and ethnic self-awareness, shorn of the excesses of wartime rhetoric. He tells us, for example, that the belief in Japan's unique position as the Land of the Gods has been replaced by one that emphasizes Japan's role within the community of nations.[45] Reverence towards the emperor is also expressed as part of the Japanese cultural identity. However, in Yamatoyama's teaching this is apparently not in the prewar sense of a divine entity but rather in conformity with the postwar constitutional term of the "symbol of the State and of the unity of the people."[46]

Kihara Ichirō, a recent graduate of the high school at Yamatoyama headquarters, offers us an example of these beliefs in his interview with me. In answer to my question he did not hesitate to declare his willingness to fight for the defense of the country. However, in terms that echo the sentiment often attributed to members of the Japanese military during the war, he offers that, in fact, he would be fighting in defense of the emperor rather than the country, for the following reasons.

> In Japanese history there has only been one dynasty, a single line, a symbol representing all of history until now. In addition, the Shōwa Emperor was the one who did the most to save Japan. When he had his interview with General MacArthur, the Shōwa Emperor said something like, "It doesn't matter what happens to me, to my life, please do something for the people, feed the people. I don't care what happens to me, but don't starve the people!" And MacArthur thought, "Here's the most important person in Japan. Has there ever been a case where a person in that position would say something like this?" And because of that Japan escaped from the worst of the American occupation, and somehow managed to remain the way it is today.

I was a bit surprised by this response, and decided to pursue the question of how this young person views the emperor. I asked about the divinity of the emperor, as well as his status in the present constitution, and Kihara's replies can be summarized as follows.

> What we mean by the word *kami* in Japan is a sign of respect, or a great person. So *kami* doesn't really mean god, but rather a person who's worshipped, or revered, something like that. That's what *kami* has meant from way back.... And the line of the emperor has continued from way back, so he's like a symbol of that history. In Yamatoyama I guess it also has some deeper meanings than that. I guess you could also add that the emperor is the person who protects Japan.... The emperor is also revered as the symbol of the unity of the Japanese people, and that's as it should be, the symbol of the Japanese people.

Perhaps because of his youth, and the fact that he has not yet had the time to reflect on the sentiments he might have learned at the Yamatoyama high school, Kihara is not able to present a coherent explanation of the group's reverence for the emperor. There are echoes of prewar beliefs in the unbroken imperial line and uniquely Japanese concepts of divinity, but these are overlaid with sentiments of gratitude towards the Shōwa Emperor's postwar role, perhaps seen as a more rational way to express this particular cultural element that Yamatoyama seeks to promote as part of the Japanese identity.

An item was included in the questionnaire survey regarding the revision of the postwar constitution, and those responding positively to the question were further asked their opinion regarding the status of the emperor and Article 9, renouncing war as a sovereign right of the nation; 53% of the Yamatoyama respondents favored revising the constitution, the highest percentage of any of the groups included in the survey, and a full sixteen points higher than the overall average. Only 11% of these favored the abolition of Article 9, but, compared to the other groups in the survey, this was also the highest percentage, well above the 5% overall response.

Likewise, only 16% favored making the emperor the sovereign, rather than only a symbol of the nation, but, while this was well ahead of the 11% overall average, in this case Yamatoyama believers came behind Risshō Kōseikai respondents, 18% of whom favored the emperor as sovereign. Only 3% of Yamatoyama believers favored abolishing the emperor system altogether, well below the 10% overall rate, while 77% favored the present interpretation of his role.

What we see here is a reinterpretation of prewar beliefs regarding the imperial institution in line with postwar developments. The emperor is identified as one important element in the Japanese cultural identity, and an effort is made to preserve the emperor's position by reinterpreting it in line with current constitutional understandings. Whether this attempt is ultimately successful is unclear, a result that is reflected in the rather vague notion of "deeper meanings" expressed in the interview with Kihara.

The right to self-defense is offered as one criterion for judging when the use of force is justified. This understanding would be basic to mainstream theories regarding war and peace in any other country in the world, but the postwar atmosphere in Japan, with its emphasis on pacifist rhetoric, has made it difficult to press even this most basic claim. The advocacy of this position is made possible to Yamatoyama believers by the strong cultural identity and unabashed patriotism that is promoted within the group. However, it would seem that these traits in no way stymie, and may even promote, the development of an international concern.

RURAL RELIGION ON THE INTERNATIONAL STAGE

In the postwar period, Yasusaburō and Yamatoyama have done an impressive job of incorporating the emphasis on national identity with an international outlook, a rural livelihood with such broad issues as peace and development. In 1969 Yasusaburō arranged for the purchase of the whole mountain where the group's headquarters can be found. On the mountain, long denuded by the timber industry, they have engaged in a reforestation program that is often offered as a sign of their religious concern for the environment. Today several hundred Yamatoyama believers, including students at the group's own high school, lead a commune-type lifestyle on Mt. Soto-dōji. They participate in prayers offered for the ancestors in the morning and evening, work on the organic farm on the mountain, eat together in a large dining hall, bathe in the hot spring dug from the mountain, and participate in cold water ablutions either in the river running through the headquarter complex or at a waterfall found further up the mountain.

Under Yasusaburō's direction Yamatoyama has also been active in promoting religious cooperation both within Japan and internationally. They have been involved in the New Japan Federation of Religious Organizations, an ecumenical group of Japanese new religions established in 1951, and are also active members of the World Conference on Religion and Peace.

The melding of such international concerns with action on the local level is characteristic of Yamatoyama's peace activities. A major annual function of the group is a bazaar held early in September featuring produce from the farm at the headquarters, as well as from members' farms throughout northern Honshu and Hokkaido. Annual proceeds from the bazaar, amounting to well over one hundred thousand dollars, are contributed to Yamatoyama's Peace Fund. Money from this fund is used for the construction of orphanages and hospitals throughout Korea and China, in reparation for Japan's activities during the war. Students at Yamatoyama's high school visit these facilities in Korea every year, to encourage the patients as well as to increase their own awareness of Japan's responsibility for the war.[47]

Yasusaburō's most important contribution to popular peace activities in Japan has been the One-Meal Campaign. Eager to promote a means for the common believer to become active in efforts to secure

Poster promoting the One-Meal Campaign at Yamatoyama's annual bazaar.

world peace, Yasusaburō proposed this campaign on returning from the Second World Conference on Religion and Peace held in Leuven in 1974. As a sign of repentance and sacrifice, the believers are called upon to forgo one meal a month, and the money saved through this practice is then contributed to the Yamatoyama Peace Fund. In this way work for peace is linked with personal sacrifice, in line with Yamatoyama's doctrine that the establishment of a just world will not be accomplished easily. This campaign is not limited to Yamatoyama believers, but has been adopted by other groups in Japan active in the peace movement. Among the religions included in this survey, it is especially popular with members of Risshō Kōseikai, 93% of whose respondents say they have participated in the campaign. This is even higher than Yamatoyama's 91%.

In this way a relatively small, rural religion, incorporating many of the common themes and practices of Japanese religiosity, has established for itself a rather significant role in contemporary international interreligious circles. The combination of a strong sense of cultural and ethnic identity—rooted spiritually in folk beliefs and physically in the Japanese countryside—with an international outlook offers a promising example of the positive role that religion can play in contemporary Japanese society.

◦◇   ◦◇   ◦◇

Both Risshō Kōseikai and Shōroku Shintō Yamatoyama acknowledge self-defense as a legitimate reason to resort to the use of arms. However, Risshō Kōseikai explicitly rejects the use of the term "justice," at least as it is used in the West, while Yamatoyama embraces the term. In general, Yamatoyama is clearer in recognizing the implications of the stance it has taken in favor of self-defense, while Risshō Kōseikai seems more confused. Several factors can be raised in order to attempt an explanation of this difference. Religious tradition might play a part in it; a folk-religious group, especially one that has consciously chosen to emphasize cultural identity, might be better prepared to argue for self-defense than a Buddhist group. The results of my research on Shūyōdan Hōseikai presented in the following chapter would tend to support this hypothesis. Perhaps more importantly, Yamatoyama's relatively small size and the homogeneous makeup of its believers might make it less susceptible to the pressures of public opinion, which favors pacifist rhetoric. Risshō Kōseikai represents mainstream Japanese society here—recognizing in some vague sense the need for self-defense but refusing to think about what that might imply in the real world. I think many people in Japan would be comfortable with the appellation "flexible pacifist" that the Risshō Kōseikai believer takes for himself in the interview presented earlier in this chapter. Perhaps, in the end, every situation has to be judged on its own merits, "case-by-case," to use an English expression that has entered the Japanese language in reflection of its popularity. One would hope, however, that such decisions are not made ad-hoc but rather that they rely on some principle, or "policy," as the other Risshō Kōseikai interviewee demanded. This brings us again to the question of moral leadership that I raised at the end of the preceding chapter, an issue to be taken up again in my concluding remarks at the end of this volume.

In the past three chapters we have considered the question of postwar Japanese pacifism. Although pacifist rhetoric dominates the public debate, there is little awareness of the implications of this position. As an absolute prohibition on the taking of human life, in any situation, it is an option available only to those who would separate themselves in some way from responsibility for society, as Nipponzan Myōhōji has done through its monastic vows and Byakkō Shinkōkai through its spiritist dualism. Sōka Gakkai would like to maintain Japanese pacifism, but acknowledges the need for force on an international level to deal with security issues. As a result of its active role in politics it has even had to compromise on Japanese pacifism, in its support of a political party that has accepted the postwar national security arrangements. Risshō Kōseikai acknowledges the right of self-defense and the need for an armed force to protect that right, but shies away from developing the implications of that right, leading to a level of confusion among its own believers as to what concrete stands they should take. Shōroku Shintō Yamatoyama displays considerably more clarity in its position, by removing itself somewhat from the mainstream of Japanese society and its unexamined pacifism. That a level of clarity can only be achieved by placing some distance between oneself and the rhetoric of mainstream society itself indicates the confused nature of this debate in contemporary Japan.

FIVE

Peace through Moral Cultivation

In this and the following chapter we take up the issue of the civilizational idea of peace, which I propose as the distinctively Japanese concept of peace. As I argued in the introduction to this book, this concept has two aspects, an emphasis on individual moral cultivation as the key to peace, as well as the idea that peace can be obtained through the spread of the benefits of a peaceful civilization, often identified as that offered by one's own cultural or ethnic group.

The emphasis on moral cultivation runs deep in Japanese society, supported traditionally by Buddhist and Confucian religious elements, formulated into an official ideology of state in the Tokugawa period, and promoted as part of a popular ethic, among the warrior and ruling classes through tracts on bushido and among the common folk by Ninomiya Sontoku and other popular preachers in the immediate early modern period. In this period it took the form of a popular "philosophy of the heart," the belief that internal changes could effect a transformation in the surrounding environment, especially through the practice of virtues codified into a "conventional morality." In contemporary Japan this emphasis is especially characteristic of the new religious movements, to the extent that many observers would agree with Helen Hardacre, who sees these groups as concerned almost exclusively with the "question of individuals improving themselves individually and collectively through self-cultivation."[1]

As a group that explicitly identifies itself with this tradition of moral cultivation (*shūyō* in Japanese), Shūyōdan Hōseikai offers us the best example of how this is incorporated in the concept of peace. Before we consider the teaching and activities of this group, however, let us go back and see how this idea is developed in the postwar period by the other groups that we have already looked at, in order to illustrate both its pervasive presence as well as the various forms that it takes. We begin with our two pacifist groups, Nipponzan Myōhōji and Byakkō Shinkōkai.

MORAL CULTIVATION IN A SPIRITUALIST GROUP

As we have already seen, Byakkō Shinkōkai's peace activities begin and end with the Prayer for World Peace, the words that bring all of existence into harmony with the spiritual energies of the divine world. Such a concept of peace naturally lends itself more to a concern with one's inner state than outward-directed activity, and thus would seem to be conducive to an emphasis on self-cultivation. However, what is emphasized is not the cultivation of certain virtues such as loyalty, filial piety, industriousness, or harmony—the normal content of Japanese popular morality. At least their direct cultivation is not the focus of the believers' practice. Rather, they are seen as results that flow naturally from Byakkō Shinkōkai's practice. The intermediate step, that is, the direct aim of the practice, is the extinguishing of karma, and the way to achieve this goal is, of course, the recitation of the Prayer for World Peace.

Karma is a common religious element in Japan, often used to explain the cause of misfortune in terms of the lingering effects of actions taken previously in this life, in a personal former life, or by one's ancestors. Karma can also be used in a positive sense, to explain one's present favorable status or some fortunate occurrence, and, perhaps especially in contemporary religions, one can find various interpretations of karma that attempt to free it from fatalistic implications.[2] Various words are used to refer to the concept in Japanese, and in Byakkō Shinkōkai both the phoneticization *karuma* and the more traditional Japanese Buddhist term *gō* are employed. Karma is given a particular interpretation by this group, in accordance with its fundamentally spiritist view of the world. Here karma is described as the result of misguided thinking, based ultimately on the mistaken belief that the material world enjoys an independent existence outside of our minds. Consequently, the cultivation of correct thoughts will erase karma, and this individual, inner activity will eventually affect the whole universe.

> It is the selfish desires of nations and peoples that have put the world in a precarious situation. However, these selfish desires of nations and peoples are no more than the accumulated desires of each individual person. The thoughts of each individual become vibrations and circulate throughout the whole universe. These thoughts accumulate and determine the fate of the human race. Therefore the thoughts of each person, no matter how insignificant, have an effect on the fate of the whole human race.... Normally we think that the human person is a physical reality, but in fact this human person is just the accumulation of the vibrations of each individual thought. The physical body is nothing more than the place where these thoughts accumulate. Likewise, when these individual "accumulations" (bodies) congregate we get the nation, and finally the world.[3]

These "accumulations" give us the illusion of a material world, beginning with our physical selves, and therefore it is freedom from these accumulations, the erasing of karma, that will save both the individual and the world. The means offered for the eradication of karma is recourse to the light of God, obtained through the recitation of the Prayer for World Peace.

> In order to save the individual, as well as the human race, more than calling for an end to arms we need to devote ourselves to freeing the human race from karmic thought vibrations, the most basic form of cancer on the human race. While caught in these karmic vibrations, no politician, no matter how great he or she might be, can prevent world war.... Unless we melt, through the power of light, these vibrations of karmic thought—the dark thoughts separated from the light of God, a light that envelops the earth—no matter what political policy you adopt the human race will not be brought to peace.... If we want to avoid the destruction of humanity, if we

want to prevent a Third World War, then each one of us must erase the karmic thought vibrations of the human race, each one of us must reflect to the world the light of God, each one of us must participate in the Prayer for World Peace Movement.[4]

Here we see the doctrinal explanation of Byakkō Shinkōkai's refusal to deal with the concrete issues of life on a "lower dimension." Such efforts are in the end useless, for no change can be brought about until the underlying karmic vibrations are removed, through the recitation of the prayer revealed to Byakkō Shinkōkai's founder.

The efficacy of the Prayer for World Peace is explained in terms that rely on the worldview of Byakkō Shinkōkai. Beyond the three-dimensional world of forms that is normally present to the senses lie other levels of reality, inhabited by spiritual forces actively pursuing humanity's salvation. The cultivation of right thought, through the recitation of the Prayer for World Peace, will make available to the individual the power of those spiritual forces, extinguishing karma and thus contributing to the salvation of all humankind.

> Everything that exists in the universe is an echo. It could be the echo of light, or it could be the echo of karmic thought vibrations, or undeveloped light. Since the world is inhabited by undeveloped humanity, it is a world of mixed light and karmic thoughts. It would be no problem if light and darkness could be clearly distinguished in this world of forms, but here they are mixed together, just as light (the mind of God) and darkness (karma) are mixed together in the thoughts and actions of the people of the world. In this situation it is difficult for a harmonious world, a peaceful world, to emerge. Prayer is the means by which we can distinguish light (truth) from darkness (lies), and shine light onto darkness in order to extinguish the darkness.... Put simply, the Prayer for World Peace emerges from the great light of the congregation of Guardian Spirits, and so if one devotes one's thoughts to the Prayer for World Peace, one obtains the power to extinguish one's own karmic thoughts, as well as the karmic thoughts (darkness) of all humanity.[5]

Kimura Shintarō, introduced in Chapter Two, gives us an idea of how the believers see this process. Kimura was a member of Sekai Kyūseikyō, a group that was instrumental in Goi's own religious formation, before he joined Byakkō Shinkōkai. He tells us that he entered Kyūseikyō seeking healing for his mother, a benefit that was obtained through the activity of that group, but he became dissatisfied when they could not offer him psychological healing as well. Although Kimura did not reveal the exact nature of the psychological difficulty that he was experiencing, we can make a fair guess that it had something to do with the fact that he faced discrimination as a child, since one of his parents was not Japanese. Kimura is the person who used the example of a kind of "road rage," seen in Chapter Two, to illustrate the power of words, and as the following example also illustrates, overcoming anger seems to be one of the themes of his life.

> Let's say there is a fight. No matter how much a third person tries to stop it, saying, "Okay, cut it out!" it really won't have much of an effect. Because there is always a reason for the fight, and that reason lies in a world that can't be seen, the Astral World. That's where all the energy comes from.... Unless you extinguish that energy first, there is no way we can stop fighting and get along. With our face we might be smiling, but in our gut we're saying, "Stupid jerk!" That's what our Astral Bodies are doing, in the Astral World. And that's why there are so many fights. Until we extinguish that energy there is no way that we can live in peace. That's why religion teaches us the importance of prayer. So it's not a matter of finding a solution in this three-dimensional world.

Another example describes this process perhaps more concretely. Hattori Eriko is a woman of about fifty who says that she was deeply wounded in a relationship, an experience that led her to search for some kind of spiritual healing. Not knowing where to turn, she went to the local bookstore and started looking through the books in the religion section, where she came upon one of Goi's books. Opening the book, she was immediately taken by a phrase in the "Summary of the teaching of Master Goi" found in all of Byakkō Shinkōkai's publications.

> It says there, "You should forgive yourself and forgive others; love yourself and love others." You don't really notice it at first, but people usually say to forgive others and then forgive yourself. Or love others and then love yourself. But here it is just the opposite. I read those words, "Forgive yourself and forgive others; love yourself and love others," and I was taken by them, wondering, "What could this mean?"

Hattori bought the book and read it immediately, after which she wanted to talk to the author herself. She tried calling the number given in the book, only to find out that Goi had died years before, or, as she was told over the phone, that he had returned to the Divine World and was now at work there. Dejected at the news, and wondering what to do, she was told to pray the prayer found in the book, the Prayer for World Peace. After praying the prayer continuously for two weeks, Hattori says that she had a kind of mystical experience, where a ball of light entered through her "third eye," located between the eyebrows, and in an instant her anguish disappeared. Seeking to give some meaning to this experience, she explains it as follows.

> To pray means that the good vibrations that you give off are transmitted to the other person. As long as you have good vibrations, even if the other person is giving off bad vibrations those can be wrapped up in your own openness, and suddenly it is possible to forgive.... By giving off good vibrations, even if the whole world isn't saved, at least the people around you can be saved, they can be changed.

Hattori's vision of light energy entering her body and thus making forgiveness possible is a dramatic illustration of the belief in the intervention of spiritual forces in order to induce the personal transformation prescribed by Byakkō Shinkōkai as the content of individual moral transformation. Such beliefs are overlaid on the preexisting "philosophy of the heart" and its conception of concentric circles of change, beginning within oneself, extending to "the people around you," and eventually reaching the whole of existence.

However, not all members of the group make use of explanations that employ a direct recourse to spiritual forces. Inoue Yūji, also introduced in Chapter Two, prefers the following, perhaps more rational, psychological reasoning to explain the efficacy of the Prayer for World Peace.

> Just like it says [in the Bible], "The Word was God," [John 1:1] the Prayer for World Peace works through the power of the word on people's brains, on people's consciences, and in that way brings about world peace. Also, it opens your own eyes up to [the presence of] God. Therefore, the Prayer for World Peace has two effects. First, it wakes up people's consciences, and secondly it wakes you up to God.

The moral cultivation urged by Byakkō Shinkōkai, as in the case of its peace activities and all other aspects of its faith, is founded in the practice of the Prayer for World Peace. By attuning oneself with the perfect harmonies of the spiritual world through the recitation of this prayer, the believer eliminates the effects of mistaken words, thoughts, and actions—both his or her own as well as humanity's—and will come naturally to a state of forgiveness, acceptance, and love. While different from the direct cultivation of these and other virtues advocated by many of the other Japanese New Religions, Byakkō Shinkōkai's complete reliance on spiritual agencies makes it all the more inner-directed and individualistic. Furthermore, although Byakkō Shinkōkai's development of the concept of moral cultivation in the postwar period is certainly not reflective of the mainstream understanding of this emphasis, it is common to the worldview of the latest group of New Religions that have become popular since the 1970s. As such, it could be a harbinger of future developments in this concept, a further internalization and individualization of the "philosophy of the heart."

INNER CONVERSION AND NONVIOLENT ACTION

The Peace Pagodas established by Nipponzan Myōhōji throughout the world are thought to have an effect similar to that of Byakkō Shinkōkai's Prayer for World Peace. I have already pointed out, in Chapter Two, the significance of these pagodas as both a source of spiritual energy efficacious in purifying and pacifying the area surrounding them, as well as a reminder to those who see and visit them, to turn their hearts towards peace. We can see employed here much the same kind of logic, calling upon both spiritual and psychological reasoning, as that expressed by Byakkō Shinkōkai in explaining the efficacy of the Prayer for World Peace. Unlike Byakkō Shinkōkai's reliance on this one method to establish peace, however, Myōhōji does not limit itself to the establishment of Peace Pagodas but engages in a variety of direct nonviolent actions for the establishment of world peace. In this way it provides an interesting contrast with Byakkō Shinkōkai, and leads us to question just what role moral cultivation plays in these activities.

Whereas Byakkō Shinkōkai emphasizes the virtues of harmony and forgiveness as the core of the individual moral transformation needed to establish a peaceful world, Nipponzan Myōhōji's founder Fujii Nichidatsu identifies trust as the content and goal of the conversion to which humanity is called. Fujii says that modern people have lost the capacity to trust, giving rise to doubt, fear, and, finally, war.

> All the measures adopted in anticipation of possible future conflicts and wars cannot establish genuine peace. If we want to establish genuine peace we must first solve the problem of eliminating fear and distrust among opposing modern states. The elimination of fear and distrust is a purely spiritual matter, a lesson that religion has taught repeatedly from ancient times. If you believe in God all-knowing and all-powerful, then fear will be removed. In order to eliminate fear, believe in God. We fear others because we suspect that they are evil. If we believe others are good, we have no reason to fear them. It isn't because you have seen God's omnipotence that you believe in God, but because you believe in God that you see God's omnipotence. Likewise, it isn't because you see that others are good that you believe in their goodness, but by believing that they are good you can eliminate your fear and be on friendly terms with them. Belief in the unseen power of God teaches us to believe in the unseen goodness of others.[6]

Fujii identifies the problem of trust as a modern problem, and places the blame on science. This is because science is based on the assumption that all accepted truths must be questioned, and that nothing can be taken on faith. Fujii's argument here introduces an oppositional schema of scientific civilization and religious or spiritual civilization that is central to his concept of peace, a point we will take up at length in the following chapter. In terms of the cultivation of trust advocated here, let me point out that there are problems with Fujii's position, problems that arise, I believe, specifically because of the oppositional schema out of which he operates. Such a schema, with its blunt distinctions, enables Fujii to conflate religious belief in God, conceived as absolute—all-knowing and all-powerful—with trust in the human person, normally seen as a less certain quality. If one can only be either religious or scientific, trusting or skeptical, then all beings must be equally worthy of trust—a problematic conclusion.

Fujii's argument that trust is the foundation of peace is, nevertheless, well taken, as seen in the emphasis placed on trust-building measures in ending the states of conflict in, for example, Northern Ireland or the

Middle East. Significantly, however, these are predominantly measures in the political, rather than personal, realm, a fact that calls into question the efficacy of moral cultivation as a means to peace. Indeed, Fujii himself voices this concern, as we will see in a moment.

An additional virtue to be cultivated by Myōhōji believers is that of faith, leading to a reliance on a power beyond one's natural abilities. This is seen as central to the fulfillment of the demands of nonviolent action, particularly the ultimate demand of martyrdom. Katō Hiromichi, the monk whose story was introduced in Chapter Two, spoke of a fellow monk who had been killed in Sri Lanka in 1984. Yokotsuka Nobuyuki, age thirty-two, was shot dead on a street in Jaffna, evidently a victim of the ethnic strife in the country where he had lived for most of his six years as a Myōhōji monk. Katō allows as to how right now he would find it impossible to make the same sacrifice, saying,

> If it would be possible in that moment of death to give myself up completely, like the young monk in Sri Lanka, it wouldn't be by my own strength. It would be Buddhist compassion, not my own strength. It would be the strength of the Buddha, the compassion of the Buddha that would make such sacrifice possible, in that moment.

It would appear, then, that the object of moral cultivation in Myōhōji is the traditional religious virtues of faith, trust, and love, and similar emphases can be found in most, if not all, of the major religious traditions. We would further expect that the tendency towards internal cultivation identified as a characteristic of Japanese religion, especially the New Religions, would be tempered somewhat by Myōhōji's strong social orientation. Indeed, Fujii explicitly rejects moral cultivation as a sufficient means to the establishment of peace, in the following words.

> In the beginning I also thought that religion, as something concerned with the inner human spirit, should have no say about politics or concern itself with social problems, but should stick to giving spiritual guidance to each individual person. However, these days the problems we need to be concerned with necessarily involve the large social structure of the state, or even further, the world. Until the world itself changes even individual moral cultivation is impossible.[7]

However, Fujii's shift to an emphasis on changing social structures, described in the above quote as a prerequisite to individual moral cultivation, is apparently not fully reflected in the attitudes of his followers. A question concerning the most necessary means to establishing peace was included in the survey distributed to the members of Myōhōji and the other groups treated here. Sixty-one percent of Myōhōji respondents chose individual internal attitudes, equaling the overall average for all of the groups. Where they differed from the other religious groups was in choosing civic action over interstate relations in an organization such as the United Nations, with 16% stating that preference, more than double the overall average of 7%, a position that probably reflects their own participation with other civic groups in joint peace activities. It would seem that even in this group dedicated to nonviolent social action the emphasis on internal moral cultivation prevalent in Japan is hard to escape.

CREATING THE NEW HUMAN PERSON

Byakkō Shinkōkai and Nipponzan Myōhōji present somewhat idiosyncratic developments of the emphasis on self-cultivation, in line with the positions they have staked out on the fringes of Japanese society. Byakkō Shinkōkai has overlaid the preexisting emphasis on moral cultivation with its own spiritist worldview, and Nipponzan Myōhōji advocates structural change over inner cultivation, at least in its doctrine and practice, if not in the attitudes of its believers.

As mainstream groups that have attracted a considerable following in the postwar period, we would expect that Sōka Gakkai and Risshō Kōseikai are more reflective of the emphasis given moral cultivation in Japanese society in general. We have already seen how these two groups present a similar worldview based on the Buddhist concept of the fundamental unity of all existence. They also offer similar slogans to express the emphasis placed on individual development: Sōka Gakkai's Human Revolution (*ningen kakumei*) and Risshō Kōseikai's Creating the Human Person (*hito zukuri*).

Kirihara Tetsuko is the young lady in her mid-thirties who spoke in Chapter Three of the need for a philosophical or religious view of fundamental equality to counteract the manipulation of the masses by political leaders with the rhetoric of hate. The spread of such a philosophy is, for her, the foundation of a peaceful society, as she elaborates in the following comment.

> It comes down to each individual person possessing a solid philosophy, because this personal philosophy, personal ideology, is the basis of each person's thoughts and opinions. So we need to think about how to go about constructing that kind of a spiritual foundation in each individual person.

Kirihara goes on to explain that this is what is meant by Sōka Gakkai's Human Revolution, and, further, that it is precisely this individual transformation that will change nations, echoing the image of concentric circles of action and influence that has become the common morality of many of the Japanese New Religions. Kirihara's reasons for joining Sōka Gakkai at the age of nineteen centered on her feelings towards her father, who she blamed for the troubled relationship between her parents as she was growing up, something that she alludes to in the following remarks.

> Honorary President Ikeda talks about a Human Revolution, and says that this great revolution in even a single person can change a country, even the world. I believe that very deeply. Therefore, how can we make this Human Revolution possible for each individual, how can each individual overcome his or her egoism and live for the happiness of others? It is only when that happens that we will have real peace in the country, or real peace in the world. When I was a university student I felt that I wanted to make some kind of contribution to world peace. But then I thought of my own family. We certainly didn't have peace at home. And I felt that if I couldn't change that situation, no matter what kind of grand ideals I had, if I couldn't make peace in my own backyard how could I hope to make peace in the world? Therefore if, through faith, I couldn't come to respect my own father, and if I couldn't make peace in my own family, then I would just be speaking empty words, or dealing in abstractions, and I didn't want to be that kind of a peace activist.... I am convinced that any great transformation begins with a single person.

The heart of this revolution, as Kirihara alludes to it, is the overcoming of individual greed, anger, and foolishness, the vices and failings that muddy the Life-Force.[8] Therefore, it is believed that the elimination of these vices and the cultivation of virtue by each individual contributes towards the unimpaired appearance of this universal Life-Force, ushering in a new age for humanity.

The elimination of these common vices is also the focus of Risshō Kōseikai's creation of the human person, called alternatively "perfection of character" (*jinkaku no kansei*)[9] or "reconstruction of the spirit" (*kokoro no kaizō*).[10] This is, likewise, also attained through internal cultivation and change. It is a fundamental tenet of Risshō Kōseikai that the spirit leads the material world; that a change of "heart" (spirit) will change any situation. This is expressed by Niwano as follows.

> If humanity is to be saved, if the human race is to find true happiness, we must wake up to the fact that "a change of heart will change any situation"; we must accomplish the conversion to a way of life that puts mind over matter.[11]

This is not just a matter of positive thinking, but involves looking first within oneself to find the causes of personal misfortune or strife, leading to a conversion from judgmental or narrow attitudes to more accepting and nourishing attitudes. In the realm of personal relations, a common expression of this belief is that other people act as mirrors, reflecting back at us either the meanness or the openness of our own hearts, an explanation that has become commonplace in the New Religions, as Helen Hardacre notes in her work on the worldview of these groups.[12] The acceptance of complete responsibility for one's circumstances that this implies can be a heavy burden to bear for those already suffering at the hands of others' cruelty or betrayal, but it also offers the individual a chance to reform often unnoticed harmful behaviors. Ichikawa Rie, a Risshō Kōseikai believer and young mother of three in her thirties, offers us an example of the latter.

Ichikawa met me at a Risshō Kōseikai church where she is active as a leader of the Youth Division—perhaps too active, as her story reveals. About a year previous to our meeting she had begun to have problems with her son, an early teen who had taken to dyeing his hair and modifying his school uniform so that it was no longer in line with the dress code—actions that are becoming a more and more common form of youthful rebellion in Japan today, but in the early 1990s were still rather shocking, especially for Ichikawa in her role as a church youth director. In our conversation she expressed her shame and frustration in the following way.

> When I saw him like that, I was really hurt. I tried to talk with him, about his uniform and his hair, and all he would say is, "Right now this is what I want to do!"

Ichikawa went to see the leader of her local church to ask for advice on how to deal with his rebelliousness. The church leader's advise was not what she had expected.

> When I asked him for guidance he said, "Leave your son alone! You should think about yourself instead. Think about how much motherly love you've shown your son since he was born." That's the advice he gave me. Ever since my son had been born—I have three children all together—I had this impression that practicing the faith meant coming to church [and working there].... The church leader said, "If you change, the other person will also change. What you're doing is trying to change your son, isn't it? Where is your faith in that?" When he said that, I realized that all I was thinking about was changing my son, changing his appearance, without even trying to change my own behavior.

Realizing that she had been more concerned with church affairs than with her own family, Ichikawa started paying more attention to her son, and the effect was almost immediate. Although he still refused to wear his school uniform properly, he had his hair cut and his attitude had changed—enough of a success to convince this young mother that Risshō Kōseikai is right in emphasizing individual conversion in the face of difficult situations.

Risshō Kōseikai and Sōka Gakkai have apparently taken the popular ethic developed in early modern Japan and delivered it intact as a pattern for life in the postwar period. They teach that any change must begin with the individual person, that it is the individual human heart that ultimately directs history. This view is presented as the foundation of their peace activity; the reconstructing of the human person or the Human Revolution through the self-cultivation of each individual leading to the establishment of true peace.

The teaching of Shōroku Shintō Yamatoyama, while also reflective of this fundamental worldview, introduces an interesting innovation through the emphasis it places on personal sin. Let us take a brief look at Yamatoyama's own particular twist to the "philosophy of the heart" and then return to a consideration of how this mainstream emphasis on individual moral cultivation is reflected in the peace activities of all three of these groups.

We saw in the previous chapter how Shōroku Shintō Yamatoyama has a somewhat less optimistic view of human nature than that found in many of the other Japanese New Religions. Many of these groups take the position that the human person is fundamentally pure and perfect, sharing in divine nature. Although this purity can be clouded by sin—primarily the sin of forgetting this divine nature and the debt of gratitude owed it—removing this sin and returning to a pure and perfect state is usually conceived as a rather simple task, for example, Tenrikyō's "dusting" of the heart, as previously mentioned.[13] In contrast to this view, Yamatoyama places somewhat more emphasis on the dark side of human nature, as illustrated by their founder secluding himself for a number of years out of disappointment with his followers' narrow-minded search for immediate benefits, as well as his apocalyptic view of history. The road to salvation is consequently seen as more difficult and fraught with suffering, a worldview that encourages such ascetic practices as cold water ablutions and fasting for peace—the One-Meal Campaign promoted by this group. Kihara Ichirō, the young Yamatoyama believer whose views on the emperor we looked at in the previous chapter, expresses this outlook in the following way:

> By experiencing hunger yourself, you are able to cultivate a sense of compassion for those who are suffering from hunger throughout the world. At the same time, you reflect on your own life, control your desires, and try to make yourself a better person.

In this way, Yamatoyama teaches moral cultivation through penance and self-restraint. Ultimately, however, this is not a task that the human person can achieve alone. Taguchi Maki, the other Yamatoyama believer who spoke of evil lurking in the human heart, tells us that it was the reliance on both works and grace emphasized by Yamatoyama that attracted her to the group.

> Reliance on works and grace, that means you can't just rely on God and do nothing yourself, and, on the other hand, you won't be saved by your own efforts. It's you and God working together. You

give one hundred percent of your effort, and God will lend a hand. This teaching on works and grace—more than anything else that's what attracted me here.

In its greater emphasis on the effects of sin, seen as well in the belief that divine help must accompany moral cultivation in order to overcome sin, Shōroku Shintō Yamatoyama is somewhat removed from the mainstream of both the New Religions as well as Japanese society in general. Although this less optimistic view of human nature contributes to a concept of peace somewhat different from the other groups in this survey, in analyzing its peace activities certain characteristics common to those of the mainstream groups of Sōka Gakkai and Rissho Kōseikai can be pointed out.

The emphasis on personal conversion seen in these three groups expresses itself in two ways in their peace activities. The first is through the development of activities that highlight individual commitment to the promotion of peace. Chief among these, at least for the believers of Risshō Kōseikai and Yamatoyama, is the One-Meal Campaign, which, as we saw in the previous chapter, draws attention to individual sacrifice as a means to peace. Another activity that funnels the energies of a large number of people are the bazaars that are held, primarily by members of these three groups, to raise money for their various peace funds while at the same time raising the consciousness of the members. In answer to the survey question on participation in various activities to work toward peace, 87% of Yamatoyama respondents, 66% of Kōseikai believers, and 37% of Sōka Gakkai respondents said that they had helped with a bazaar, all higher than the levels of participation by the members of other groups included in the survey. Both the One-Meal Campaign and work at bazaars call for personal commitment, in terms of time and personal sacrifice, and illustrate to the believers how such personal commitment by many individuals can result in a significant contribution to the cause of peace.

A second way that the emphasis on individual cultivation is expressed in the typical peace activities of these groups is through the extensive use of people-to-people exchanges. Ichikawa Rie spoke of her participation in a "One-Meal Campaign Study Tour" to the Philippines, sponsored by Risshō Kōseikai. The purpose of the tour was to promote actual contact with some of the people who are being helped by the group's peace fund activities. The Peace Boat sponsored by Kōseikai for its Youth Division likewise is an attempt to "personalize" the Asian countries that suffered as a result of Japanese military activity during the war, as is the annual excursion of Yamatoyama high school students to South Korea. Likewise Kirihara Tetsuko emphasizes the personal exchanges among Sōka Gakkai believers of the many countries where branches have been established as an important means to promote peace, instilling in people an awareness of being "citizens of the earth" rather than their own various nations.[14] We might question whether Kirihara's belief that such contact inevitably will lead to dialogue and understanding—rather than a confirmation of mutual mistrust and dislike—is naive, or perhaps based on the commonality of faith and practice already shared by these intra-Gakkai exchanges.[15] Criticism can also be leveled at the depth of the exchange—how much can one learn in a week in a foreign country?—and the use of considerable sums of money for "donor tourism." Nevertheless, these programs seem to be effective at promoting some level of international understanding at a truly grass-roots level. We could take the example of Ichikawa Rie as indicative of this result; how many other housewives with three young children have had the opportunity to meet their counterparts in Manila, and how might the upbringing of their own children have been changed because of it? And once again here, the emphasis is on the individual—changed through an encounter with another individual.

In this way, the emphasis on moral cultivation as the means to establish world peace is not necessarily passive, but can rather encourage a commendable amount of activity at a truly grass-roots level. At its best it can empower people who would not otherwise be personally involved in social action, providing proof that the smallest individual effort, when combined with those of others, can yield impressive results. Before offering a more comprehensive evaluation of this means to peace, however, we turn to Shūyōdan Hōseikai, the quintessential expression of this emphasis in the civilizational concept of peace that we are looking at here.

IDEI SEITARŌ AND SHŪYŌDAN HŌSEIKAI

Shūyōdan Hōseikai is a relatively small new religious group, comprised of approximately 12,000 members. Its faith and practices reflect both the folk religious traditions and popular morality of Japan, as expressed by its founder, Idei Seitarō (1899–1983). The membership is, on average, considerably older than the other groups included in this survey. Sixty percent of the respondents to my questionnaire, for example, were over sixty years old, with thirty-one percent older than seventy.[16] Ninety-one percent of the respondents to my survey also indicated that they had been members of Hōseikai for more than ten years. Considering the relatively small size and intimate nature of the group we can therefore assume that most of the members have had some personal contact with the founder, and consequently his personality and charisma continue to play a determining role in the faith of the group. Indeed, we may wonder whether the group will yet be able to institutionalize this charisma and find some way to attract, and keep, people who have had no contact with the founder.

Idei Seitarō was born at the turn of the century in a poor farming community north of Tokyo.[17] Idei's father, while apparently popular with the other people of the village, was fond of drink and women, and for that reason he was not allowed to inherit the family property. He died when Seitarō was thirteen. Seitarō's mother seems to have been a woman of some learning, as it is related that she composed poetry and supported the family by offering classes in *soroban*, or abacus. Seitarō had two older brothers, one of whom died in infancy, and an older sister. Popular stories within Hōseikai claim that both his mother and sister were prone to have mystical experiences, having visions, for example, of Fudō or Kōbō Daishi.[18]

The already poor soil of the area where Idei was born was made largely unusable due to pollution from local mining operations, perhaps the first well-known modern case of industrial pollution. The cause of the farmers was championed by a national politician from the area, Tanaka Shōzō, and there seems little doubt that in his youth Idei himself met Tanaka, perhaps on several occasions, and we may assume that Tanaka's influence contributed in some degree to Idei's own critical stance towards society in the prewar years. Idei was apprenticed to a rice shop in a neighboring town immediately after completing elementary school, and from there he left for Tokyo at the age of 16. He spent the next several years shining shoes, delivering papers, working in the post office, and supporting himself with other odd jobs, until he was drafted in 1920.

Reports of his military service are nonexistent, so we have no reliable sources regarding Idei's reaction to military service. Idei himself claims that he had serious doubts about the Japanese incursions into China (1915) and Siberia (1918), but given the unreliable nature of the sources we have no way of confirming his position at that time. At any rate, he says that as a lowly enlisted man he kept his opinions to himself during his military service.[19] Interestingly, however, Idei says that he was personally taken with the ideals expressed in the imperial rescripts on education and to soldiers and sailors. The Rescript to Soldiers and Sailors, while not as well known as the one on education, also served as a codification of the traditional Japanese morality combined with the imperial emphases that we saw in the education rescript in Chapter One. Idei claims that both of these documents became for him a standard for criticizing the social reality of the times:

> The more I came to understand the real intent of the imperial rescripts on education and to soldiers and sailors I couldn't help but notice the discrepancy between them and the reality.[20]

At any rate, he credits his military service with opening his eyes to the broader social reality.[21] After finishing his compulsory military service he returned briefly to his hometown, and then left once again for Tokyo, arriving in 1923, just before the Great Kanto Earthquake. In the wake of the earthquake, he was pressed into service collecting and disposing of the corpses, an experience that obviously affected him greatly. Idei had joined Tenrikyō during his first stint in Tokyo, through the influence of an acquaintance he had met while working in the post office. It seems that he had experienced an illness at the time that led him gradually to deeper involvement in the faith.[22] However, it was his experiences in the wake of the earthquake that became formative for his religious life. In his autobiography, for example, he recounts an incident in which a young girl approached his crew just as they were going to dispose of the corpse of the girl's mother, a coincidence that he attributes to the spirit of the mother calling to her daughter, and says he came to believe in the existence of human spirits through this experience.[23]

Following his experiences in the aftermath of the earthquake, Idei became more deeply involved in Tenrikyō, becoming a kind of itinerant missionary for the group. In his autobiography he recalls several instances of revelation while on these journeys. Among these revelations

143

The altar at Hōseikai's Niigata meeting hall, where pictures of the
founder and his wife flank the altar.

he reports hearing a voice tell him that he was the "Pillar of the
Nation"—a title appropriated by Nichiren. He also reports that he heard
the voice of Nichiren himself encouraging perseverance in his missionary
work, and finally that through these revelations he came to the realization
that he was one with God.[24] Idei's recollections, with their references to
Fudō, Kōbō Daishi, Nichiren, and other religious figures indicate how
broadly he drew from the popular Japanese religious tradition in forming his own "universe of faith." In fact, in his autobiography there is no
mention of affiliation with Tenrikyō, the institutional religious form
within which he was apparently operating at this time, a curious omis-
sion that can perhaps be explained by subsequent events.

PROTEST AND MORAL EXHORTATION

In the latter half of the 1920s Idei joined the acquaintance who originally introduced him to Tenrikyō in breaking off into a splinter group,

Tenri Kenkyūkai,[25] founded by Ōnishi Aijirō. Ōnishi was a Tenrikyō missionary and local leader who, in 1913, declared that he himself was the living *kanrodai*, the symbol of salvation.[26] Ōnishi was excommunicated for his doctrinal innovation—and challenge to church authority—but it took a dozen years before he was able to gather his own following and found Tenri Kenkyūkai.

As the international situation worsened, Ōnishi, already convinced of his role as savior, began to teach that he should take the emperor's place in order to lead the nation through the difficult times. In 1928, a leaflet to that effect was prepared and distributed by Ōnishi's followers nationwide. As a result, Idei was arrested, along with five hundred other members of Tenri Kenkyūkai, and convicted of the charge of *lèse majesté*.

Idei was released from prison after about a year, and soon married Imaizumi Kikuno, also a native of the farm country north of Tokyo. Idei maintained some contact with his former religious companions, but largely ceased his religious activities and found employment in a munitions factory. A daughter was born early on in the marriage, but died shortly after birth, and the couple subsequently had no other children. In 1934, however, he quit his job and returned to religious work, a development that, in his autobiography, is attributed to the fact that he had fallen off a truck at work and had to be hospitalized for a time. Idei says that the accident woke him from his lethargy and reinstilled in him a sense of his mission.[27] This time, however, he did not return to his activities for Tenri Kenkyūkai, but instead started acting independently as a kind of miraculous healer and preacher. He had begun to attract a number of followers when he was arrested again in 1935, also on charges of *lèse majesté*. It seems that in one of his sermons he offered support to a contemporary theory maintaining that the emperor was merely an organ of the State, a theory that had recently been banned as contrary to the official state doctrine exalting the emperor's position above the state. Idei spent much of the next three years in prison.

Meanwhile, the group that had begun to gather around Idei was held together by his wife, and even grew somewhat as former members of Ōmotokyō, which had been disbanded by the government in 1935, joined the ranks of Idei's followers. Upon his release from prison in 1938 Idei returned to his religious work, traveling frequently to the cities around Tokyo, even as far as Niigata on the Japan Sea side of the country. He was arrested and held briefly again in 1939, this time for violation of the medical practices law, because of his spiritual healing activities.

Throughout his life, Idei enjoyed the ability to attract the elite of society to himself, a rather surprising development that can only be attributed to his personal charisma, for, as we have already seen, he himself was from the lower ranks of society and had little formal education. He could be quite critical of the status quo, a trait that would not naturally endear him to those who enjoyed an advantageous position in society. In the postwar period Idei first attracted the attention of some officers in the occupying American army, and later some of the major politicians in Japan seemed to take more interest in Idei and Shūyōdan Hōseikai than the size of its membership would warrant as a source of votes. This ability to attract powerful people had aided the group from the beginning, since Shūyōdan Hōseikai was established as a juridical foundation in 1941 with the help of two retired army and navy officers who had become followers of Idei.

Idei's teaching during the war years reflects the ambiguity of his position, namely a person with an arrest record for political crimes who nonetheless was able to obtain official permission to found a religious group in the most repressive of climates.[28] Within the collection of teachings from this period, one can find admonitions to love and respect all people, specifically including one's enemies,[29] as well as comments that seem to acknowledge the necessity of the war and call for renewed efforts to win the war.[30] Significantly here, in one instance when he apparently offered support for the war effort, Idei uses a play on words, a favorite rhetorical device used especially in Japanese humor, particularly because of the language's many homophones, or near homophones.[31] In this particular instance, the play is on the words *sensō*, meaning war, and *senzo*, or ancestor.

> When you say, "*sensō*" it immediately conjures up bad images, but if you realize the *kotodama* of "*sensō*" then you see that it bears a connection with "*senzo*." The belief that ancestors are to be reverenced is a noble thing, from ancient times until the present. Likewise, war is something that has continued from ancient times, without end. Nobody wants war, but without war people won't mend their ways, humanity will not progress, and for that reason war is inevitable.[32]

In his wartime sermons Idei also actively employs concepts such as the "Land of the Gods," but frequently this is used as a standard to condemn injustice and corruption in society, calling for moral cultivation commensurate with this exalted position, rather than as an expression of cultural superiority. In doing this he criticizes the arguments he himself presented above, contributing to the confusion as to what his real stand on the war might have been.

> Although we have been born in this Land of the Gods, created by God, and are allowed to live as children of God, people cannot live in harmony with each other, and they start meddling in each others' affairs and attacking each other.... As children of God shouldn't we be embarrassed to say that unless we attack with weapons they won't mend their ways, or unless we interfere they won't understand?[33]

Although his position on the war remains ambiguous, the circumstances under which he was speaking, and his own history of arrests for opposing the emperor system, lend weight to even the limited or veiled criticism that appears in his wartime teachings.[34] His use of concepts usually identified with nationalist causes—such as the Land of the Gods or those propounded in the rescripts on education and to soldiers and sailors—as a standard to criticize the social reality and a call to moral cultivation presents us with an interesting example of the attempted retrieval of such concepts and symbols, an effort that became one of the identifying marks of Hōseikai activity in the postwar period.

MAKING PEACE

Idei also actively used symbols of wartime nationalism in the immediate postwar period, in an effort to preserve the national spirit and identity—a concern also reflected, as we have seen in the preceding chapter, in the activity of Tazawa Yasusaburō of Shōroku Shintō Yamatoyama. For example, at the new year's meeting of the group in 1946 Idei directed that the Japanese national flag be raised at Hōseikai's headquarters in Tokyo, something unheard of in the early Occupation period.[35] In his immediate postwar preaching he also seems to have made frequent use of the title "Land of the Gods" for Japan, usually in the context of moral exhortations to accept defeat peacefully, but with pride intact. An address entitled "World Peace," delivered on 21 August 1945, less than a week after Japan's surrender, introduces many of the themes of Idei's postwar teaching. In this address Japan's activities in the war are placed in the context of the long history of human conflict, resulting in the statement that

> armed conflict is a crime on the part of both parties. War is a grave crime, and there is nothing more fearful. Although nobody desires war, if you strike you will be struck, if you kill you will be killed, if you are trampled upon you will in turn trample upon, if you are tempted you will in turn tempt, you go astray and make others go astray, and in this way war is piled on top of war without end.[36]

Idei goes on to say that the seeds of the war were planted in mistakes made in Japan's modernization, resulting in unjust social conditions, which remain unnamed in this address. He calls on his followers to humbly reflect on these mistakes, and dedicate themselves now to the cause of peace. To this end, he teaches that one should neither be proud in victory nor despondent in defeat, but should seek only to follow the will of God.

> In war, as in business and in life, if you realize the will of God, both victor and vanquished must trust each other, live in peace with each other, help each other, and be united in spirit. An attitude of "I'll show you!" or, "We may have been defeated but we can still strike back!" or displaying the hatred of the defeated towards the victor either in your heart or in your countenance is against the will of God. Winning cleanly, winning justly and nobly, as well as losing cleanly, justly, and nobly is the only true way to build peace.[37]

He concludes the address with an exhortation to moral cultivation, through an appeal to what he proposes as the true meaning of the appellation "Land of the Gods," and "Japanese spirit."[38]

> It is now the people of our nation who are called upon to follow the will of God; to increase their virtue and spread this virtue throughout the world; to follow the path of goodness and sincerity; to guide and live in peace with all people, whoever they might be; to put into practice the light of virtue that the world awaits. Herein lies the dignity of the Japanese as people of the Land of the Gods. Cultivating the "Japanese spirit" (*yamato damashii*), making your own spirit clean, just, and noble, is the sincere following of God's will.[39]

The Peace Stone Monument erected by Hōseikai in Sydney.

This address has several important elements. Its ambivalence regarding Japan's role in the war reflects accurately the predominant view of Japanese society, or at least Japanese politics, in the postwar period. The war is justified, after a fashion, as one more instance of humanity's failing—a crime, certainly, but one of which all people are guilty. Along these lines, vague references are made to Japan's own "mistakes," issuing in a call for self-examination and reform. Idei's concern to prepare his followers to accept defeat graciously, with pride intact, is evident. Defeat is no more shameful than victory, but rather both must be handled in accordance with the "will of God." Appeal is made to a unique cultural identity, an identity expressed in concepts such as the "Land of the Gods" or Japanese spirit, but these are now used as indications of high moral achievement, a morality that must be cultivated. And it is this moral cultivation that will lead to the establishment of world peace.

With the end of the war, Idei began to call Shūyōdan Hōseikai's facilities "Homelands of Peace" and proclaimed that the purpose of the organization would be precisely the establishment of world peace. This

149

orientation towards world peace was reinforced with the introduction of a prayer for peace offered every day at noon at Hōseikai's Tokyo headquarters, a practice begun in 1952. From 1958 Hōseikai also began to erect Peace Stone Monuments in various locations at home and abroad.[40] Finally, since the mid-1970s an annual peace march can also be counted among this group's peace activities. All of these activities, however, are ordered to the attainment of peace through the moral cultivation of the individual members.

PEACE THROUGH MORAL CULTIVATION

Shūyōdan Hōseikai's teaching is summarized in the ten Essential Points reproduced in the members' handbook and read out at worship services.[41] Here the followers are called upon to realize that they are children of God and to strive to learn the law of nature that they may live correctly. They are told to be thankful in all things, and to remember the value of labor. The head of the house is to be respected, children are to be loved, and the harmony of the household should be maintained by striving for mutual understanding. They are to be aware of their words and actions and relate to others with a bright and warm heart. They are not to begrudge others their wealth nor to envy them their virtue. They should neither allow themselves to be discontent nor voice their displeasure, but instead humble themselves, avoid conflict with all, and cultivate a spirit that respects all people. They should take seriously their own responsibility, readily accept the instruction of their superiors, and follow their direction unwaveringly.

This is an example of the "ethic of daily life" common to many of the New Religions.[42] What is interesting here, however, is that Hōseikai explicitly makes this the foundation of their work to establish world peace. In the collections of short sayings of the founder that are given to the believers as the main points of Idei's thought, one often finds reference to "the foundation of peace" or "the establishment of peace."[43] What is offered here as the foundation or building block for peace is generally the injunction to give thanks, to use kind words, or to cultivate a spirit of service, as called for in the Essential Points. For example, a typical phrase would be, "Offering thanks to all of existence and aiming at friendly relations with people is the teaching of Shūyōdan Hōseikai, and this is the road to world peace."[44]

The apparent banality of this teaching is somewhat abated by Hōseikai's emphasis on *jikkō*, or practice. As a more general concept this indicates that the cultivation of thankfulness, friendliness, and other virtues is to take concrete expression. However, often the founder would prescribe a specific *jikkō* for the member, on the basis of the founder's intuition and reading of the member's character. In conversations I participated in as part of an earlier research project, members who had received such an instruction would often say how the *jikkō* had cut to the core of their own particular character weakness and had thus become a vehicle for comprehensive change, the concrete expression of individual moral cultivation that is to serve as a building block of peace.[45]

The advanced average age of the members of Hōseikai calls into question whether this teaching is being adequately passed on to a new generation in the absence of the founder. This is not only a matter of attracting new members; an interview with one young believer raises concern that even within the group those with little personal contact with Idei might have shallow or confused understandings of the practice of their faith.[46]

Andō Daisuke is a third-generation member of Shūyōdan Hōseikai in his late twenties and he tells us that the normal practice in the group is not to place much emphasis on "learning" while in the Youth Division, because youth is a time to play. Serious study of Hōseikai's teaching starts when the member graduates to the Men's Division, a transition that Andō was in the process of making, since he was married in the previous year. An additional motivation for increased seriousness in his faith is the fact that his wife is now pregnant, and, as young parents are wont to be, he is more and more concerned about what he should teach his own child.

When asked about the Hōseikai activities for peace outlined above, Andō replied that he really hadn't ever given them much thought. As a child he remembers participating in the Peace Walk that Hōseikai sponsors every year, but he doesn't recall being especially conscious of the fact that this activity was in some way contributing towards world peace.

Somebody would say, "Okay we're going to start now, so line up!" Although it was called a Peace March, we weren't really aware of any connection with peace.... I never really thought about why it was called a Peace March before.

Likewise, in regard to Hōseikai's Peace Stones, Andō says the question never really occurred to him before, but perhaps the founder erected these stones to give people an opportunity to be reminded about peace. Regarding the appellation "Homelands for Peace" applied to Hōseikai facilities, Andō gives an explanation more in line with the group's fundamental teaching on peace.

> The founder probably used that name to indicate that with this place as the starting point we should enlarge the circle of peace. Or maybe he wanted to remind the people who enter here about peace, and tell them, "Do your best to establish world peace!"

Andō's study of Hōseikai's teaching will no doubt give him the tools to better explain the meaning of these activities. His befuddlement at the time of our conversation, however, illustrates a problem with making work for peace perhaps too commonplace by associating it with all sorts of daily activities; there comes a point when such association no longer promotes awareness of peace but actually hinders it. This is especially so for someone who, like Andō, has been raised in an environment that too readily makes those associations.

Given the emphasis on individual moral cultivation it is not surprising that nearly two-thirds of the respondents to my survey indicated that cultivation of the mind and heart is the most important way to work for world peace. Indeed, the survey results indicate that the overall mean score for this response, including all seven groups that were the object of my research, approaches 60%. This testifies to the high level of importance placed on individual moral cultivation by the Japanese New Religions as a whole. However, it is also important to point out that nearly one-fourth of the Hōseikai respondents replied that international organizations such as the United Nations are *more* important for the establishment of world peace than individual moral cultivation. It would seem, therefore, that while the importance placed on individual moral cultivation as a means to world peace remains strong, it is clearly rejected as a sufficient means by a significant minority of the believers of this group.

This tendency is also illustrated by an interview I conducted with Fukuhara Reiko. Her opinion on the efficacy of individual moral cultivation as a sufficient means to world peace is all the more noteworthy for the fact that, at the time of our conversation, she was in her late seventies and had been recruited directly by the founder. As a matter of fact, she claims a special relationship with Idei, given that her father died shortly after the family entered Hōseikai in the immediate postwar period, and Idei himself subsequently "took responsibility" for the family. Fukuhara does profess belief in Hōseikai's teaching that personal moral cultivation leads to world peace, saying, "Individual peace is closely tied with world peace." For her, the cultivation of personal peace means specifically the abandonment of selfish desires. She says,

> When I visit a shrine or temple, I always think first of world peace. It's normal for someone, when they throw their money into the offering box, to pray for their family, or for the success of their business.... But when I go to worship the Kannon, or some other god, first I always pray, "May there be peace in the world." That's what I pray for first. And only after that I might pray, "Let everyone be healthy" or so on. [The founder] taught that personal desires are a kind of sin.

When asked what the meaning of "Homelands of Peace," the title given to Hōseikai's facilities, might be, Fukuhara responds that they are a place to reaffirm Hōseikai's selfless teaching, an oasis in the often inhumane urban environment. They are not an escape from the nitty-gritty of personal relationships and personal growth, however, for the core of the teaching presented there is an emphasis on personal responsibility. As Fukuhara explains,

> Hōseikai teaches that you should think of others before yourself. But with the world we live in now, if you think of others first you're likely to end up being left behind, too late to get a seat on the train, for example. Even if you are able to keep that kind of an attitude while you are here [at one of the Hōseikai facilities], as soon as you step out the door there is no telling what might happen.... But even though there is no guarantee that you'll be able to maintain the same feeling once you get home, at least while you are here it is a place where you can refresh your spirit.... Some people would be willing to give tens of thousands of dollars if you tell them that you'll pray for them and can guarantee them happiness. But here they teach that it is up to you to keep the teachings, that happiness

is something that you have to gain for yourself. Unless you have a great deal of patience and generosity you won't last long here.

However, steeped in Hōseikai's teachings on personal responsibility and personal cultivation as she is, and convinced that peace does start from inner transformation of each individual person, Fukuhara cannot avoid criticizing the quietism this idea can lead to, a tendency that she sees in her fellow believers.

> Although they say that peace starts from the heart of each individual, and then that affects other people and eventually becomes world peace,...they are not willing to take any initiative and say, "Let's do this" or "Let's take a stand on that." There is no action.... Unless you show it in action, even if you have peace in your heart people won't know it.

This tendency towards quietism can also be seen in further results from the questionnaire survey. On several of the questions dealing with pacifism, Hōseikai believers indicated a greater degree of isolationism than we see in the other groups included in this research. For example, when asked their views on the Persian Gulf War, 15% of the Hōseikai respondents offered the opinion that as long as Japan wasn't involved they really didn't care what happened there. This was the highest percentage of any of the seven groups covered here, and almost three times the overall average of 6%. Also regarding the passage of the Peacekeeping Operations Bill, allowing participation by Japanese Self-Defense Forces in United Nations operations, 30% attributed passage to outside pressure on Japan, once again the highest rate of any group covered and nearly ten points more than the overall average of 21%. To a higher degree than any of the other groups studied here, Shūyōdan Hōseikai respondents seem to be saying that they want to be left alone, to cultivate peace in their own hearts, or, at best, in their own country.

The advanced age of the membership and an apparent problem in passing down the teaching to younger generations call into question the future of Shūyōdan Hōseikai. More in line with our own concerns, the tendency to identify all activity with the establishment of world peace contributes to a banalization of the term and leads ultimately to quietism. This problem could be addressed from within Hōseikai's own doctrine and practice through the use of the concept of *jikkō*, but the accounts of the members and results of the questionnaire survey indicate that this is not being done sufficiently. There seems to be a significant minority among the membership, however, who are aware of the limits of moral cultivation as a means to world peace and are interested in exploring other channels. One wonders, however, whether this group will be able to find the energy and resources to answer this challenge. I conclude this chapter with some further thoughts on the limits of this part of the "civilizational" concept of peace.

THE LIMITS OF MORAL CULTIVATION

Moral cultivation is an important part of the concept of peace promoted by all of the groups included in this survey, although it takes a variety of expressions. In Byakkō Shinkōkai moral cultivation means the recitation of the Prayer for World Peace, for it is through such action that one is released from the lingering effects of karma and becomes a purer spiritual entity, and thus a vehicle of peace. Nipponzan Myōhōji, while it retains a belief in the spiritual power of, for example, the relics of the Buddha, emphasizes concretely the cultivation of the virtues of faith and trust. However, as an advocate of nonviolent action towards structural change in society, the emphasis placed on moral cultivation is somewhat tempered in this group. Sōka Gakkai, Risshō Kōseikai, and Shōroku Shintō Yamatoyama all emphasize the cultivation of interpersonal relations, the former two groups through a self-abnegating abandonment of negative emotions and desire, and Yamatoyama through physical self-sacrifice and solidarity in suffering. Shūyōdan Hōseikai offers a prototypical example of the worldview common to many of the Japanese New Religions: the concentric circles of action, starting with internal cultivation, and an emphasis on the common virtues of thanksgiving, selflessness, and thoughtfulness.

Concern with detail, and endless practice to ensure that every detail is just right, is one of the common characteristics of modern Japanese culture. Perhaps more than most people, the Japanese really do believe that "Practice makes perfect," an adage that can also be used to describe the emphasis placed on moral cultivation as a means to peace that we have been exploring in this chapter. One cannot disagree with the proposition that the cultivation of common virtues such as thanksgiving, sacrifice, trust, and thoughtfulness will make the world a better place, a more peaceful place for all of humankind. Nor is this truth recognized only in Japan; the emphasis on individual conversion can be found broadly in religious approaches to peace. Certainly, in the end, it is only such cultivation by every single human individual—the perfection of the human character—that will lead to a world that no longer needs armies or police, if, indeed, such a world can ever be realized. It can also be an empowering concept, as we saw in evaluating the peace activities of Sōka Gakkai, Risshō Kōseikai, and Shōroku Shintō Yamatoyama.

Acknowledging that there are some problems with the comparison, in evaluating moral cultivation as a means to peace I am reminded of a popular account of the Japanese approach to baseball. In his book contrasting baseball as played in Japan with that in the United States, Robert Whiting points to an almost fanatical belief in Japan that great players are made, not born.[47] It is believed that with endless repetitions—swinging a bat, pitching, going for grounders—not only will physical form improve but, perhaps more importantly, the proper winning spirit will be instilled. Players begin training for the season in January, and often special postseason training camps are held in November and December as well. During the season more hours seem to be spent in practice than in actually playing the game. It is a system that has produced some outstanding players, and the level of play in Japan overall has arguably improved over the years. But it has its problems, with pitchers, especially, worn out before their time, and a cautious type of play that makes one wonder sometimes if too much attention is being placed on details and not enough on the broader picture—the game itself.

Moral cultivation as a means to peace likewise has its successes. The emphasis placed on individual attitudes and behaviors certainly contributes to the safety and order of Japanese society, perhaps unparalleled in the world. In addition, it offers people the assurance that their efforts, no matter how insignificant they seem, make their own contribution towards the perfection of peace. But one must also fault it for its narrowness. Concentrating on the details of human perfection, it tends to lose sight of the fact that wars occur as a result of a political process that cannot always be reduced to individual, or collective, greed, envy, hate, or whatever. In other words, it often loses sight of—or perhaps deliberately closes its eyes to—the wider picture. While moral cultivation is certainly indispensable for peace, until the concentric waves of morality have perfected every human being, arguably more will be done to avoid war—if not to establish true and lasting peace—by seeking to influence political processes.

The emphasis on social and political processes is often interpreted as a product of Western culture, over against the Asian or oriental culture that we are dealing with here. It is to the question of a civilizational divide reflected in such arguments, and how this divide is expressed in the concept of peace offered by these groups, that we turn in the following chapter.

Six

The Mission to Spread Peace

Robert Sharf, Bernard Faure, and others have pointed to the presence of what is variously called occidentalism, secondary orientalism, or reverse orientalism in modern Japanese studies of Zen, as represented particularly in the work of Nishida Kitarō and D. T. Suzuki.[1] What they mean by these terms is that some of the leaders of the so-called New Buddhism movement in modern Japan stood the rhetoric of orientalism on its head in their attempt to preserve a place for their religious tradition in the increasingly hostile cultural and political environment of Meiji Japan. Orientalism was identified by Edward Said in his groundbreaking, and controversial, book of that title as a political, academic, and cultural discourse that established the "otherness" of the peoples from the Middle East to the Far East by portraying them as mysterious, sensual, irrational, inscrutable, fatalistic, and childlike, as opposed to the clear, chaste, rational, optimistic, mature peoples of the West. Such rhetoric is intimately connected with Western colonial activities, establishing the "truth" of Oriental inferiority and turning the Western enterprise into a noble mission to extend the benefits of civilization. Occidentalism and its cognates adopt many of the stereo-types of orientalist discourse, but in their turn claim superiority for the irrational, direct, spiritual East over the too-rational, dualistic, material-istic West, and, in the case of the modern Zen thinkers, place Japan at the center of a new mission to save the world from the dead end of Westernization.

Such rhetoric is not limited to Zen; it also plays a major part in the thought of Fujii Nichidatsu, the Nichiren monk and founder of Nipponzan Myōhōji highlighted in Chapter Two. In the following pages, as we explore the confrontational aspect of the civilizational concept of peace presented by the Japanese New Religions, we turn our attention first to the occidentalism of Fujii and Nipponzan Myōhōji, where the world is divided into a spiritual civilization and an opposing material civilization, and the former is identified as the only hope for establishing world peace. Similar terms are used in Byakkō Shinkōkai, but with its dualistic ontol-ogy they take on a sharply different meaning, a development that will be our second point of focus. From there, we will take a look at how the discourse of occidentalism is reflected in the mainstream groups included in this study, Sōka Gakkai and Risshō Kōseikai. Finally, concentrating on Shōroku Shintō Yamatoyama and Shūyōdan Hōseikai, we will turn to a consideration of discourse on Japan's mission in the postwar era. Paralleling the work done in the previous chapter on moral cultivation, we will be concerned here with showing both how the rhetoric of cul-tural superiority has a continuing influence on these groups, as well as how it has been transformed by them in the postwar period.

REVERSE ORIENTALISM IN NIPPONZAN MYŌHŌJI

Fujii's judgment on the Vietnam War presented in Chapter Two, that the North Vietnamese and Viet Cong forces obtained a great victory for nonviolent pacifism, is astounding for the lack of understanding that it betrays regarding even the most obvious meaning of the term. I believe that this contradiction in Fujii's teaching can be attributed to a more encompassing worldview, one that pits Oriental civilization against the West, especially as it is represented by the United States in the postwar period. Although worldviews are constructed out of numerous and varying experiences, in Fujii's writings one experience stands out as the linchpin in his thought and teaching—the United States' use of the atomic bomb on Japan.

As we saw in Chapter Two, Fujii is often identified with Mahatma Gandhi in relation to the nonviolent pacifism that he preached in the postwar period. This identification is in good part the result of Fujii's own activity: he emphasizes his interviews with Gandhi in his autobiography, the completion of Myōhōji's first Peace Pagoda at Kumamoto was celebrated by hosting a conference of pacifists associated with Gandhi's movement, and the first Peace Pagoda outside of Japan was inaugurated in India in 1969, to mark the one-hundredth anniversary of Gandhi's birth. Despite this identification with Gandhi and his work, however, in the following passage Fujii explicitly attributes his postwar position more to the atomic bombing of Hiroshima and Nagasaki than to his encounter with Gandhi.

> The reason I came to espouse nonviolent resistance and the antiwar, antiarms position was not because I met with Mr. Gandhi. Rather, it was because the atomic bomb was dropped on Hiroshima and Nagasaki, killing hundreds of thousands of innocent women and children, burning and poisoning [the population], a tragedy without precedent in human history, leading Japan to sue for unconditional surrender. In this we see the mad, stupid, barbaric nature of modern warfare.[2]

The horror of Hiroshima and Nagasaki is thus the primary motivation for Myōhōji's postwar activities: building Peace Pagodas, nonviolent protest against military bases, participation in disarmament and antiwar movements. Fujii believed, however, that it would not be sufficient to destroy only the weapons that humanity had accumulated. In addition, he advocated the more radical step of eradicating the culture that had developed these weapons in the first place, a culture that he called "scientific civilization."

> Since scientific civilization will cause the destruction of humanity, along with nuclear weapons scientific civilization itself must also be eliminated. In place of scientific civilization, the teaching of peace must rule the world. And the teaching of peace is found in religion more than any place else.[3]

Similar warnings concerning certain technological advances can no doubt be found broadly in the religious world. Fujii's condemnation of scientific civilization, however, is more encompassing, as we saw in the previous chapter. It is not merely a critique of technological excesses but targets scientific methodology itself, finding there the roots of contemporary distrust and suspicion. Furthermore, in Fujii's preaching scientific civilization becomes identified with the West and "religious civilization" with the Orient—a contemporary expression of occidentalism that looks to Eastern spirituality to save humanity from Western science. This connection is made explicit in a sermon entitled "Scientific Civilization and Religious Civilization."

> Scientific civilization continues its stampede, advancing rapidly in the countries of Europe since the sixteenth century. And with the development of each new machine, wars of aggression have increased. As a result, the countries of Asia, Africa, the Americas, and Australia all became colonies of Europe, and their peoples were either killed or enslaved as the new masters wanted. In the end, the development of scientific civilization is preparing for the destruction of the world and the extinction of the human race. And the first experiment in that destruction was the explosion of atomic bombs over Hiroshima and Nagasaki, by order of the President of the United States.... Asia is the place of birth of religious civilization. The Buddhism of Śākyamuni has been like a beacon [lighting the way] towards peace in the nations and among the peoples where it has spread. Therefore, the blot of wars of invasion and the subjugation or massacre of another people is extremely rare in the history of India or the other countries of Asia. These countries have been continually successful in creating peace.[4]

We have seen similar sentiments expressed in Japanese nativist thought since the seventeenth century, where a peaceful civilization was attributed to imperial and ethnic beliefs rather than to Buddhism. In his prewar letter to Gandhi on the occasion of their second interview, Fujii already makes the transformation from imperial to Buddhist beliefs, attributing Japan's pacifist nature to the spread of Buddhism to the country. His postwar sermon continues this transformation, now emphasizing the pan-Asian aspect of Buddhist belief. Thus, in Fujii's postwar thought the oppositional schema included in his concept of peace has been shifted from one anchored in specifically Japanese ethnocentrism to one that discriminates between science and religion, the West and the East, other religions and Buddhism. In this worldview, it is the spread of the culture of faith, specifically Buddhist faith, that is seen as the necessary condition for the establishment of peace in the world.

Fujii Nichidatsu and Nipponzan Myōhōji make use of the rhetoric of occidentalism to describe their mission of spreading peace: the spiritual East will save the scientific West from destruction. In Fujii's thought this is tied to a decidedly anti-American outlook that explains his comments regarding the Vietnam War above, where the United States is portrayed as the perpetrator of perhaps the worst crime in the history of warfare, the atomic bombing of Hiroshima and Nagasaki. In other remarks alluded to in Chapter Two, the United States is regarded as the new colonial power in Asia, with occupation forces stationed in Japan preparing for the invasion of the continent. In this way the United States has become the representative of scientific, Western civilization in the postwar period, continuing that civilization's policy of colonization and oppression. Indigenous peoples who stand up to this would-be colonizer, whether in Asia or in the Americas, are to be supported, even praised for their own restraint in the struggle against the oppressor. It is this line of thought, I believe, that leads Fujii to describe the North Vietnamese and Viet Cong as nonviolent pacifists.

In this attitude we see reflected the defiant spirit that the Myōhōji monk Katō Hiromichi described as characteristic of the group, much more than the tranquil and serene image that we might ordinarily have of pacifist Buddhist monks. Such defiance is perhaps necessary in order to maintain the antiestablishment posture that motivates Myōhōji's nonviolent activism. And the image of the tranquil and serene Buddhist monk is perhaps more an illusion, a product of a pervasive contemporary occidentalism, than a reflection of reality. In the end, however, Myōhōji emerges as the clearest example among the groups studied here of a lingering oppositional schema of civilization as part of the Japanese concept of peace. Here the terms are broadened from Japan to Asia, and Buddhism replaces imperial rule as the content of the civilization to be spread in order to establish peace, but the basic ideational framework remains intact.

The other groups in this study seem to have moved further away from the oppositional aspect of the civilizational concept of peace found in the prewar period, although the effects of occidentalist rhetoric can be found to some extent in some of the groups. We turn now to a consideration of the transformation of this concept in the other groups, beginning with the one that has made perhaps the most complete change, Byakkō Shinkōkai.

THE MATERIAL AND SPIRITUAL WORLDS IN BYAKKŌ SHINKŌKAI

Goi Masahisa, the founder of Byakkō Shinkōkai, uses terminology similar to Fujii Nichidatsu to indicate a very different reality. In his writings as well we can find an opposition between material culture and spiritual culture. However, rather than being identified with certain areas of the globe, Goi envisions universal growth from one to the other.

As in the case of Fujii and Nipponzan Myōhōji, the development and use of nuclear weapons is also of major concern here. We have seen how Goi was keen to develop a simple teaching that could move the masses. Part of his concern here was the empowerment of the masses: in the face of the nuclear standoff between the superpowers how could the common person feel that he or she was making some contribution to the peace and safety of the world? His answer was, of course, the Prayer for World Peace, working for the elimination of these weapons by attuning oneself to the harmonies of the divine world, and thus wiping away the shadows of the mistaken thoughts that have created the situation in which humanity now finds itself.

The development of nuclear weapons is also taken as an indication that material scientific culture has reached a dead end. This is not primarily because such weapons threaten the destruction of the material world, but rather it is one part of Goi's rather elaborate view of human evolution. Goi argues that it is in humanity's nature to evolve from material science through mental science to the goal of "spiritual science."

His terminology indicates a positive evaluation of science, in contrast to Fujii's rejection of science as part of the materialistic Western civilization. Like many of the latest wave of New Religions in Japan, as well as contemporary movements in other parts of the world, Byakkō Shinkōkai teaches that there is no fundamental opposition between science and religion. Instead, they believe that science can be used to prove the existence of a spiritual reality, that "true" science will lead humanity to spiritual truth.

In Goi's view, material science has, in general, served humanity well, leading to inventions and developments that have advanced the quality of life in the material world and promoted humanity's self-preservation. However, scientific development has been one-sided, in favor of the material world, and has tended to ignore humanity's spiritual development. The instinct for self-preservation, directed solely towards the material world, has led to a nuclear standoff between the superpowers, leaving no way out for humanity and signaling the end of material scientific development.

> Unless the instincts of self-preservation and self-defense are overcome, war will not be prevented by either a strategy of strength or one of compromise. In a strategy of strength neither side will be able to give, which will lead to tragedy. In a strategy of compromise, once one side yields the other will take advantage of the situation and invade.[5]

What is needed then is further evolution, beyond the limits of material science. Goi sees signs of such evolution already in the development of psychology and psychiatry, what he calls "the mental sciences." Through the discovery of the subconscious, humanity has already become aware that it possesses more than a material existence. Mental science has its own limits, however, because it does not recognize the presence and activity of God.

> Considering the amount of time this method [psychiatry] takes, its results are slim.... Since it doesn't recognize God, the Absolute, as the foundation of existence, it remains incomplete.[6]

The recognition of the limits of mental science leads to a discussion of the next stage of evolution, that of spiritual science, or spiritual culture. Spiritual science is to reveal the true nature of humanity as a spiritual existence. Such an awakening will transform the instincts of self-defense and self-preservation from their merely material pursuits to a fuller understanding of human evolution and human destiny.

> The human being does not live only in the physical body. The human being also exists in other worlds, such as the astral and spiritual world. In these worlds, the thoughts and actions of physical existence appear as one's destiny—for example, if you hate you will be hated; if you injure you will be injured. Once this is shown by scientific proof, thoughts of self-preservation and self-defense will be overturned at their foundation. They will be transformed into a kind of self-preservation and self-defense that takes account of both

the physical and spiritual worlds. Such concepts of self-preservation and self-defense in the higher worlds are vastly different from those in the physical world. They will not be based on the shallow desire of preserving one's own physical existence. In other words, they will be focused on making one's thought and action bright and pure, set free from spite, jealousy, and hate, manifesting peaceful love and truth.[7]

Finally, Goi maintains that this development is at hand, and, importantly, that it is something in which all of humanity will participate. Although Byakkō Shinkōkai has a central role to play in the dawning of spiritual science, through the popularization of the Prayer for World Peace, there is no indication of a unique role for Japanese, or even Asian, civilization. As part of the Prayer for World Peace, the believers pray that their "missions be accomplished," but this mission clearly is not limited to any ethnic group or civilization; in prayers at the group's headquarters the Prayer for World Peace is adapted to make mention of the mission of every nation. Byakkō Shinkōkai's ontological dualism has seemingly erased all trace of ethnocentric ideas of civilization and mission, replacing them with an opposition taken as universal for humankind, that between the material and the spiritual.

The belief in an imminent spiritual awakening, the dawning of a new age, is a common theme in contemporary religious movements throughout much of the industrial world. The adoption of this spiritist rhetoric seems to have enabled Byakkō Shinkōkai to completely overcome prewar ideas concerning the establishment of peace through the spread of Japanese civilization. We need to question once again, however, just how useful this path to the overcoming of ethnocentric ideas can be; Byakkō Shinkōkai itself would have to be called a fringe group in Japanese society. Despite Goi's dream of a religion that would "move the masses," it would seem that few people are yet prepared to opt for the spiritist worldview that Byakkō Shinkōkai offers.

Let us now consider how mainstream Japanese society has dealt with ideas of cultural superiority as part of the concept of peace in the postwar period. In order to do that we turn first to the two mainstream New Religions, Sōka Gakkai and Risshō Kōseikai, to see how their varying approaches to peace have influenced their view of Japan's role in the world today.

MULTINATIONALISM AND DIALOGUE

Despite its roots in Nichiren Buddhism, a religious tradition that was identified with nationalism in the prewar period, from its birth Sōka Gakkai has taken a stance against the Japanese establishment, and in the postwar period it has advocated multinationalism as the road to world peace. A closer look at some of the rhetoric employed by the group and its believers, however, reveals that it is not completely free of the idea of national mission, expressed in terms of Japan's unique position in the world. However, this is presented as part of an inclusivistic concept, a paradigm characteristic of Sōka Gakkai's doctrine, to which we now turn.

Sōka Gakkai's Life-Force theory was introduced in Chapter Three as the foundation of this group's concept of peace. All of existence is conceived as participating in one overarching Life-Force that permeates the universe and enlivens all beings. In the *Sōka Gakkai nyūmon*, which has been used as the doctrinal text for the group since the 1970s, this theory is explained in reference to other common theories of life in the following way.

First of all, theories regarding life are divided into materialistic and spiritual conceptions, with a further division in the materialistic category into mechanical and dialectical theories. In both the mechanical and dialectical approach, however, life is ultimately reduced to merely a material phenomenon. Opposed to this, spiritual theories of life look beyond the phenomena and posit a supernatural power as the source and ruler of life. The *Nyūmon* maintains that Sōka Gakkai's Life-Force theory fits into neither materialistic nor spiritual categories, but rather incorporates both of them.

> The Buddhist theory of life differs from both of these, or, rather, it completes and incorporates both of them. Life cannot be conceived as merely a material phenomenon, as it has been in the past. One has to think also of the fundamental principle lying behind phenomena that puts them in motion. However, that principle cannot be found outside of life itself; Buddhism looks for that principle within life. The author of life is not some outside force; life itself is the author, the director, the actor.[8]

Life-Force theory surpasses materialist theories by focussing on the animator of material substance, but it does not identify that force as something apart from material existence, as spiritual theories do. In this way, Sōka Gakkai claims, it transcends and incorporates both theories, offering a new, inclusive, choice.

In another example of this inclusivistic paradigm, Sōka Gakkai maintains, like Byakkō Shinkōkai, that there is no essential contradiction between science and religion. Once again, Life-Force theory is presented as a concept that illustrates the unity of science and religion by incorporating both.

> This profound Buddhist speculation is by no means inconsistent with science; rather it is one step ahead of science. In fact, current speculation that there are numerous planets in the universe like the earth that can sustain life supports the Buddhist teaching concerning innumerable Buddha-lands. Also, the fact that life has evolved out of the earth indicates that the earth itself, the universe itself, is life [as Buddhism teaches].[9]

In Sōka Gakkai's doctrine this inclusivistic paradigm is also used in speaking of a new world order, beyond the divisions of East and West, a fusion that is described as a "third civilization." In rhetoric reminiscent of Nipponzan Myōhōji's occidentalism, Sōka Gakkai argues that the tide of history has turned against Western materialism and towards Eastern, Buddhist spiritualism. However, this will not issue in the victory of one over the other, but rather in a fusion of the two—and historical circumstances have determined that Japan is to play the central role in that fusion.

> At the present time, when the tragic contradictions and distortions of the Western materialistic emphasis have begun to appear, the course of history has focused on the importance of Eastern Buddhism. The English historian Arnold Toynbee has gone so far as to say that the post-twentieth century will be a period when non-European civilization will make a counterattack on European civilization. At any rate, it is clear that the unstoppable tide of history calls for a civilization founded on humanity's awakening to a higher dimension, transcending Western, rationalistic culture.... Here, let me say a word or two about the fusion of Eastern and Western civilization and Japan's mission. Since the Meiji Period, Japan has chosen the path of Europeanization, and has taken on Western sensibilities. Oriental traditions have also come to rest in Japan, as if it were the final stop on a train line.... Japan is the only country that

has suffered an atomic bombing. In addition, geographically it is located as a bridge between East and West, a favorable place to contribute to world peace. If Japan were to take a position of leadership toward peace, on the basis of a sure philosophy, an unprecedented new world will be born. As the meeting point of Western and Eastern civilization, Japan possesses the call and responsibility to take the leadership in building a new civilization.[10]

Sōka Gakkai, therefore, explicitly sees itself as presenting a third way, encompassing the divisions in both philosophical thought and civilizations. It is this doctrine that motivates the multinationalism Sōka Gakkai proposes as the means to peace: overcoming the concept of the nation-state to build a new awareness of oneself as a citizen of the world. Politically, this awareness is to be expressed in new structures that embrace all of humanity, a truly international government. However, one can still finds traces of the rhetoric of ethnic mission, based on Japan's uniquely tragic experience of war, or on Japan as the meeting place of East and West. In the end we must question whether these sentiments constitute a major current in Sōka Gakkai's teaching, although the idea of a national mission does resonate with broader cultural trends that we will turn to in a moment.

A more important aspect of Sōka Gakkai's teaching, at least until recently, is that their inclusivism implies the ultimate victory of Buddhism, particularly Nichiren Buddhism as taught by this group. It will be interesting to see how this will ultimately be reconciled with their recent decision to engage in dialogue and cooperation with other religious groups. Risshō Kōseikai, in contrast, has been engaged in interreligious work for a number of years and actively promotes this work as the means to overcome cultural divisions and establish world peace. The group's founder, Niwano Nikkyō, has been central to Kōseikai's activities in this area, and his portrayal in the group's literature leaves one with the impression that his personality has played a key role in directing Kōseikai towards interreligious dialogue and cooperation.

In pointing out the influences on Niwano's religious outlook in Chapter Four, special mention was made of his family upbringing in the countryside of Niigata. Niwano himself claims that his childhood experiences had a definitive influence on his character, and, along with the Buddhist faith that he encountered as an adult, contributed greatly to his own personal concept of peace.

> I consider myself, humbly, as a man of peace. Let me describe some of the influences that have gone into my life to make me a "man of peace." First, I am blessed in having been able to grow up in a country village, surrounded by nature. Second, I was raised in a happy and warm family atmosphere. The third great influence on my life was my encounter with the Lotus Sutra.... As I see it, the first and second influences are the elements that have contributed to forming my peaceful nature. But the support and source of strength for that nature has come from my encounter with the Lotus Sutra.[11]

This natural disposition towards tolerance and harmony with others is provided as the motivation for his work in the area of interreligious cooperation. Indeed, they become the central virtues in the worldview presented by Niwano and are identified as Buddhist or Asian virtues in his own type of occidentalism.

Niwano's interreligious work began early in his career, with the founding of the New Japan Federation of Religious Organizations in 1951, a development that he was instrumental in bringing about. The New Japan Federation of Religious Organizations is an ecumenical group comprising more than forty new religious movements that, despite some divisions—mainly over their response to LDP efforts to make Yasukuni Shrine a national shrine for the war dead[12]—has become one of the longest-lasting and most effective examples of interreligious cooperation. In 1952, the New Japan Federation of Religious Organizations joined the Japan Religious League, an umbrella body that encompasses Buddhist, Shinto, and Christian groups. Niwano became the chairman of the board of directors of this latter group in 1969, and it was in that capacity that he became instrumental in the founding of the World Conference on Religion and Peace, mentioned in Chapter Four.

Previous to these developments, however, in 1963 Niwano participated in a delegation of eighteen religious leaders from Japan who traveled to countries in Europe and the United States to encourage nuclear disarmament. This was the beginning of Niwano's interreligious activities on the international stage, and the trip included meetings with the leaders of the Russian Orthodox Church and the Roman Catholic Church. Two years later he participated in a session of the Second Vatican Council of the Roman Catholic Church, at which time he was invited for an audience with the Pope. Niwano says that it was this encounter that encouraged him to devote his efforts to interreligious work, in the conviction that:

> As Shakyamuni insisted, the true teaching is only one. From the time of my visit to Rome, I began to see that the idea of one true teaching embracing all teachings might be the bridge that could connect Christianity and Buddhism and perhaps all religions.[13]

As the above quotation indicates, Niwano is convinced that all religions are essentially one, and that attachment to the particular expressions of one religion, that is the individual religious faiths, is a fundamental human error. As a result, intolerance is included among the most serious vices, arising as it does from human selfishness. Niwano says repeatedly that intolerance is clearly against the will of God or Buddha, which is expressed as love in Christianity and compassion in Buddhism.[14] Niwano's emphasis on tolerance is so great that he even interprets Nichiren's criticism of the other Buddhist sects of his day within this framework. That is, Niwano maintains that Nichiren's criticism was specifically against the mutual intolerance of these other sects. Niwano claims that in their emphasis on sectarian differences, on the basis of the teachings of their individual founders, these groups had introduced the scandal of intolerance into Japan, and that this was the focus of Nichiren's criticism. Finally, he explains that Nichiren's plan for correcting this situation, contained in the *Risshō ankokuron*, was to gather the leaders of the various sects together to discuss their faith, so that they might come to the conclusion that it is essentially one. Thus Nichiren is lauded as the first person in history to propose a religious meeting for the purpose of dialogue.[15]

Niwano's interpretation of Nichiren's motives is certainly at odds with the common perception of the twelfth-century Buddhist leader, and I mention it here as further indication of how thoroughgoing the emphasis on tolerance is in Risshō Kōseikai. Furthermore, intolerance is identified as a vice not only of the Buddhist sects of Nichiren's day, but of the Christian churches as well.

> The history of the Roman Catholic Church is a long one, filled with glory and with trouble. The Protestant sects that arose at the time of the Reformation and developed rapidly thereafter have been branded as godless heretics and demons by the Catholics. The disputes and strife between Rome and the Protestant Christian groups

led to warfare and great suffering. But how significant are the fundamental differences among these factions? The African native who has been exposed to the missionary activities of Catholics and Protestants probably thinks, "We have heard the teachings of all kinds of pastors and priests; but in the final analysis, they all seem the same to us." This simple attitude penetrates to the very heart of religion and sharply reveals the ugliness and foolishness of exclusivism.[16]

We see again here the idea that all religion is one, and that intolerance, or exclusivism, is the result of a selfish, sectarian outlook. Although, in principle, sectarianism can be seen in all religions, in other contexts we see hints that in Niwano's thought the vice of exclusivism is identified as characteristic of Christianity, in contrast to a fundamental tolerance characteristic of Buddhism.

Christianity, with its long history and tradition, has contributed greatly to the elevation of human culture, and continues to exert a great deal of influence. Although Christianity will undoubtedly play a significant role in humanity's future, I believe that the balance is now shifting towards Buddhism. Buddhism, with its rationality and tolerance, is what people are searching for, and thus Buddhism is the most important religion for humanity.[17]

Despite the evidence that intolerance crosses religious and cultural boundaries, evidence that Niwano himself alludes to in other contexts, in his remarks here he falls back on a common form of occidentalism that identifies the East, and especially Japan, with a history of religious tolerance, as opposed to the intolerant West. Once again, however, we must be careful not to read too much into these remarks. The final quote above, for example, is taken from a new year's address to Risshō Kōseikai believers, and is perhaps similar in character to homilies in Christian churches given on Christmas or Easter that emphasize Christianity's role in world salvation. The occidentalist attitudes expressed here, however, do indicate, on some level, the continuing influence of this particular discourse in Risshō Kōseikai, as well as mainstream Japanese society.

While we can thus see traces of notions of occidentalism or a unique mission for Japan as the bridge between East and West in Sōka Gakkai and Risshō Kōseikai, in the end I think we must conclude that these elements remain in the background, a subtheme to their interest in

171

promoting unity, either through multinationalism or dialogue, as the means to peace. In this way they have largely overcome prewar ethnocentrism. Indeed, the traces of that discourse found in these groups' doctrines would seem to point out more the pervasiveness of occidentalist, or more specifically *nihonjinron*,[18] thinking than any conscious adoption of such a framework by these groups.

The concept that peace is to be established through the spread of civilization is essentially a concept of mission. In the same way that the rhetoric of orientalism provided Western colonialism the ideology of a mission to spread civilization, prewar Japanese discourse provided a mission ideology for that nation's colonial exploits. This prewar discourse has been transformed into a type of occidentalism in the postwar period by some of the groups that we have been looking at here, identifying more broadly Asian, or specifically Buddhist, concepts as the content of their mission, in place of the ethnocentric concept of stability under Japanese imperial rule. But there is also a sense in which all of these groups, as well as Japanese society at large, participate in promoting the idea of a distinctively Japanese mission in the postwar world. It is to that idea of mission that we turn next.

JAPAN'S MISSION

A major concern of Shōroku Shintō Yamatoyama, as we have seen, has been to preserve Japanese identity in the face of the postwar changes in society. Under the influence of its postwar leader, Tazawa Yasusaburō, the members have cultivated an unabashed patriotism and reverent sentiments towards the person of the emperor. This has been achieved by reinterpreting prewar cultural items in line with postwar realities and understandings, and has been combined with an international awareness that is unusual for a small, fundamentally folk-religious group such as Yamatoyama.

An interview with Tazawa provided a telling example of this reinterpretation of Japanese cultural items, indicating how such an interpretation can be used to redirect discourse on Japan's mission in the postwar period. *Hakkō ichiu* was used as a popular political slogan during the war years to indicate Japan's mission to Asia and the world, namely, to unify the world under Japan's rule. We have seen in Chapter One how it became an important part of the nationalist rhetoric of Tanaka Chigaku's Nichirenism. Literally "eight cords, one roof," the phrase is adapted from a quotation attributed to the mythical founder of the Japanese imperial line, Jinmu, found in the third chapter of the *Nihon shoki*. The eight cords refer to the "eight directions" and are meant to refer to the whole world. According to the chronicle presented by the *Nihon shoki*, Jinmu is supposed to have united the tribes of the Japanese islands and was planning to build his capital. The relevant passage from the *Nihon shoki* is rendered in English as follows:

> ...[I]t will be well to open up and clear the mountains and forests, and to construct a palace. Then I may reverently assume the Precious Dignity, and so give peace to my good subjects. Above, I should then respond to the kindness of the Heavenly Powers in granting me the Kingdom, and below, I should extend the line of the Imperial descendants and foster rightmindedness. Thereafter the capital may be extended so as to embrace all the six cardinal points, and the eight cords may be covered so as to form a roof.[19]

Following its popularization by the Nichirenists as an expression of Japan's mission to bring peace to the world by spreading the benefits of Japanese civilization, dissolving national boundaries, and uniting the world under the rule of the emperor, the phrase was adopted as official national policy when a new cabinet was formed by Prime Minister Konoe Fumimaro on 1 August 1940. The Fundamental National Policy announced by the cabinet begins with the following declaration:

> The basic aim of Japan's national policy lies in the firm establishment of world peace in accordance with the lofty spirit of *hakkō ichiu* in which the country was founded, and in the construction, as the first step, of a new order in Greater East Asia.[20]

The quintessential expression of the aspect of the prewar civilizational concept of peace that we are exploring in this chapter—that is, the establishment of peace through the spread of the benefits of one's own civilization—*hakkō ichiu* is one more element of the Japanese cultural identity that Tazawa Yasusaburō attempts to retrieve in the postwar period, as we can see in the following quote from my interview with him.

> During the war the term was misunderstood, and the military at the time used *hakkō ichiu* to mean that Japan should rule the world. However, the original meaning is that everything under the heavens

comprises one house.... In other words, the whole universe is one house. Therefore, since it is one house, it should be completely in harmony. This harmony is the wish of the Japanese people for a world without conflict.

In Chapter Four we saw that Tazawa took as his own personal mission the preservation of a Japanese cultural identity in the postwar period, and to this end he reinterpreted various aspects of that culture to fit the postwar realities. His reinterpretation of *hakkō ichiu*, from an expression meaning military conquest and colonization to one indicating the spread of peace through the recognition of a fundamental human unity, retains the rhetoric of peace as the goal, but replaces the means used to achieve that goal. I believe this reflects the transformation in the understanding of national mission found more broadly in Japanese society, a point I will return to shortly.

The case of Shūyōdan Hōseikai also illustrates this new understanding of mission in postwar Japan. Shūyōdan Hōseikai and its founder, Idei Seitarō, share Yamatoyama's concern with preserving Japanese cultural identity. In the previous chapter we looked at Idei's address entitled "World Peace," delivered on 21 August 1945. In this address he introduces many of the themes of Hōseikai's postwar teaching: the recovery of cultural items previously associated with Japanese ethnocentrism, such as the concept of the Land of the Gods and the Japanese spirit or *yamato damashii*; the emphasis on personal moral cultivation and human relations as the road to peace; and the dedication of Hōseikai to the goal of establishing world peace. From the perspective of postwar Japanese social history we can say that Idei was prescient regarding the common themes of that society in the dedication of his religious group to the cause of peace.

The spread of peace as a unique mission of the Japanese people is a part of not only specifically religious but also secular social discourse in postwar Japan. This sense of cultural mission is illustrated by the meanings attached to two developments whose importance has emerged time and again throughout this study, namely, Japan's status as the only country to suffer from the use of atomic weapons and the adoption of the so-called Peace Constitution early in the postwar period.

From an early stage, rites commemorating the destruction of Hiroshima and Nagasaki moved beyond memorializing of the dead to a plea for peace. Details of the destruction caused by the atomic bombs on Hiroshima and Nagasaki, as well as commemorative rites, were suppressed during the Allied Occupation of Japan. James Foard reports that although some kind of memorial rite has been conducted at Hiroshima on the anniversary of the bombing every year since 1946, a "Peace Festival" planned in conjunction with these rites was banned by the Occupation authorities in 1950. It was only in 1952, after the restoration of Japanese autonomy earlier that year, that the annual Hiroshima rites took on the characteristic of both a memorial rite for the dead and a prayer for peace.[21]

Since that time the rites at Hiroshima and Nagasaki have been conducted as part of a civic religion, reaffirming the unique mission of postwar Japan to advocate the destruction of all atomic weapons and to pray for the establishment of peace. Leaders of government attend the official ceremonies, held at the times that the bombs exploded (6 August, 8:15 A.M. in Hiroshima; 9 August, 11:02 A.M. in Nagasaki), and the events are carried live on national television. The mayors of the cities deliver an annual appeal for peace, a number of names of victims are added to the list of the dead, and representatives of families of victims offer bouquets of flowers at the memorials near the epicenters of the explosions.

Outside of the contexts of these annual rites as well, the memorial parks that mark the bombings have become almost national, secular shrines.[22] For example, every year groups of school children from around the country visit the parks and the museums found there as part of their annual excursions. These school groups often hold private ceremonies to remember the dead and pray for peace. In Hiroshima these ceremonies frequently involve the laying of bouquets of origami cranes at the Memorial to the Atomic Bomb Children, recalling the story of Sasaki Sadako, a seventh-grade girl who died of leukemia in 1955 as a result of the bombing.[23]

These public celebrations and the other customs that have developed in connection with the Peace Parks in Hiroshima and Nagasaki have served to reinforce the idea of a unique national mission in the postwar era. A further enhancement of this sense of mission was the adoption of the postwar constitution in 1946, with its war-renouncing Article 9. Constitutional renunciation of war did not begin with Japan, nor has it been restricted to Japan in the post–World War II era. However, arguments are made that Article 9 of the Japanese constitution is unique in its thoroughgoing nature, as in the following quote from a Japanese constitutional scholar.

> Certainly Japan is not the first country to raise pacifism to a constitutional imperative. The French constitution of 1791 contained a war renunciation clause. In addition, the post-war constitutions of Italy, West Germany and Brazil, among others, contain war renunciation provisions. It is aggressive war, however, that is renounced by these foregoing constitutions. The Japanese constitution is distinct from these other constitutions in that it renounces all forms of war, including wars of self-defense. This is epochmaking pacifism that no other nation's constitution has established to date.[24]

In this way, these two developments have instilled in Japanese society the idea that Japan's postwar national mission is to be the world peacemaker. To a certain extent, the doctrine and practice of the groups we have been looking at in this study merely reflect this larger social concern; in one sense we can say that all of these groups have adopted this national mission as their own. Each group has been influenced, to varying extents, by prewar discourse that emphasized the spread of peace through the spread of Japanese civilization, and each group has made its own transformation in this discourse. For Nipponzan Myōhōji that has amounted to changing the terms of discourse while keeping its basic framework. Byakkō Shinkōkai universalized the terms of discourse through its ontological dualism. For Sōka Gakkai and Risshō Kōseikai the discourse remains more as an unconscious influence as they work for an all encompassing unity. Shōroku Shintō Yamatoyama and Shūyōdan Hōseikai actively try to reinterpret prewar cultural elements to fit the postwar reality of Japan as one nation among equals. But in a larger sense, all of these groups participate in the transformation of the prewar concept of peace seen more broadly in Japanese society. In this transformation, stability as the content and hallmark of civilization has been changed into the ideal of pacifism; the national mission is no longer the spread of unparalleled stability and order under imperial rule but rather the spread of pacifism.

The imperative of this new national mission is a major reason for the confusion regarding the implications of pacifism seen broadly in Japanese society and reflected in the groups that we have studied. Clearly Japan has opted to provide the means for its self-defense, by building one of the largest armed forces in the world and entering into security arrangements with the United States. The obvious conclusion to be drawn from these choices is that force will be used if the need ever arises, but any attempt to seriously consider that eventuality is shunned, since it is contrary to postwar Japanese identity. By hiding the reality of the choices made, the emphasis on the pacifist ideal thus masks fundamental problems inherent in that postwar identity. We will consider those problems, and the role that religion could play in highlighting and resolving them, in our conclusion.

Conclusion

M ore than fifty years on, the legacy of World War II is still a matter of considerable controversy in Japan. In his comparison of reactions to the war in Germany and Japan, Ian Buruma offers several reasons for Japan's apparent inability to come to terms with the war: the atomic bombings have made the Japanese victims and relativized their responsibility as aggressors in the war; judgments in the Tokyo war crimes trial are seen as arbitrary, little less than victors' justice; although the Japanese army may have engaged in atrocities, there is nothing to rival the horror of the Holocaust; Japanese political development has been stunted by the postwar constitution, which prevented any serious discussion of matters of war and peace.

A book recently published in Japan highlights many of the same points that Buruma has made, to a very different end. Kobayashi Yoshinori is a popular contemporary *manga* (comic) writer. The genre of *manga* is by now well known in the West as an important element of Japanese popular culture. Kobayashi is the author of the *Gōmanizumu sengen* [Declaration of pride] series, a biting critique of contemporary society.

A recent volume, offered as a *Gōmanizumu sengen* special, is entitled *Sensōron* [Theory of war]. There Kobayashi criticizes the postwar intellectual elite for instilling in the Japanese a sense of self-hate and a facile pacifism. He claims that the Japanese as a nation have been brainwashed into believing that what their fathers and grandfathers did in the war was inherently dishonorable, or that as a nation they are guilty of hideous crimes against humanity. He argues that this brainwashing was begun by the War Guilt Information Project, established by the Allied Occupation officers, in order to deflect attention from their own crimes—primarily the use of atomic weapons—and to make the populace docile and easy to control. He contends that this brainwashing has been so effective that there is almost a knee-jerk reaction among contemporary Japanese that all war is bad, that there can be nothing worth fighting for.

While I disagree with, even find distasteful, much of Kobayashi's analysis, his argument brings into relief many of the same problems that my own research has indicated: an uncertain cultural identity, the inability to deal in any realistic way with their own actions in the war, and an unreflective pacifism. And I believe the key to all of these is the problem of pacifism, or more properly, the view of Japan's postwar mission as a pacifist nation.

As narrative theorists point out, we all seek to impose some order on our experiences and to discover an underlying meaning to our lives—that is, to establish our identity—through the use of stories. These narratives are woven both personally and culturally. In the absence of such a story, individual life as well as cultural life will disintegrate into a series of discrete experiences, without meaning or direction, offering no guidelines for future directions.

Of all the narratives that could have been adopted in postwar Japan to give meaning to the experience of destruction and defeat, and define the nation's role in terms of the new international realities, it would appear to be most difficult to find fault with one focusing on the spread of peace as the national mission. However, the analysis of the concept of peace presented by the groups under study here indicates several problems with this narrative, specifically connected with its culturalism and romantic notion of the pacifist option.

In constructing our narratives, either individual or cultural, we look for threads of continuity, reading back into our history the foundations of current choices. We have seen examples of this in the biographies of some of the founders examined here, for example Fujii Nichidatsu's attempts to establish a prewar pacifism. On a national level this phenomenon is expressed in understandings that credit Japan's postwar mission of spreading peace not so much to the result of its recent wartime experiences but rather to the enduring character of Japanese culture; Japanese are portrayed as, by nature, empathetic, group-oriented, and eager to preserve harmonious relationships, in contrast to the logical, individualistic, and aggressive Westerner.[1] Instances of intolerance or violence are ignored, or blamed on the Westernization of society.[2] The indications of occidentalist rhetoric that we looked at in the previous chapter offer several examples of how the concept of a national mission takes on these culturalist overtones.

The idea of Japan as a pacifist nation is also inherently a romantic concept. Clinging to the pacifist ideal has made it impossible to deal realistically with issues of security. Although most people would agree that some kind of armed force is necessary to preserve order and provide for self-defense, questions about situations when force might be necessary are avoided, for to provide answers would violate the ideal image of the pacifist nation. Ironically, of the groups we looked at in this survey it is only Nipponzan Myōhōji, the pacifist monastic group, that offers any criteria for the use of force, e.g., in wars of liberation against an oppressor.

This romanticism has also made it impossible to deal forthrightly with the questions of responsibility for World War II. Partly this is due to the selective nature of narratives; we tend to downplay or ignore those parts of our history that do not fit with the identity we have chosen for ourselves, and war guilt becomes problematic for a pacifist people. I believe, however, that there is also a more subtle reason for this avoidance.

In the end, I think, most people would agree that the causes of war are rarely one-sided. There is evidence that from early in the postwar period perhaps a majority of Japanese have had ambivalent feelings concerning their country's actions in war. While they might deplore some of the excesses, they would not see the basic policies that led to war as singularly unjust or wrong. An early evaluation of the Occupation, published by an independent foreign relations institute, indicates the presence of these attitudes in assessing the results of the Tokyo war crimes trial.

> Although a genuine feeling of national shame swept the country
> with the revelation of the atrocities committed by their fellow coun-

trymen, shame or guilt over the initiation of the war itself, although not entirely lacking, was not widespread and it did not appear to be materially increased by the trial. To the extent that guilt was admitted on this score it was believed by the people to rest with their leaders.... Disgust and disillusionment with the former leadership increased as the trial progressed, due not to what the defendants had done, however, but to their efforts each to shift the blame to the other. By refusing to adopt this course and by assuming full responsibility for the war, absolving the Emperor of any direct responsibility therefor, Tojo, on the other hand, in large measure reestablished his reputation among the people as a man of loyalty and courage. The responsive chord struck by his deposition, copies of which had a wide popular sale, in which he maintained that Japan had no choice but to embark on the war despite all odds in order to insure its continued existence, indicated that this view continued to be widely held.[3]

Any realistic accounting of Japan's war responsibility would need to acknowledge these sentiments. However, postwar pacifist rhetoric, with its facile dismissal of all reasons for war, has made any rational explanation for Japan's actions untenable. To the pacifist there can be no extenuating circumstances; all war is bad. It is small wonder then that Kobayashi and others end up defending the opposite extreme, arguing that the war was completely righteous and that talk of atrocities are lies fabricated in accordance with Occupation policy.

Narratives are constantly revised in line with new experiences and understandings, offering more nuanced—or, occasionally, more self-serving—identities and purposes. Often we choose to focus on and embellish one part of the story in order to face a new reality, or when a reassessment of some part of our heritage is called for. The United States' Congressional apology for the incarceration of Japanese-Americans during World War II is one example of a revised narrative along the lines of a newly emphasized multiculturalism in the United States. The uproar over the proposed reexamination of the atomic bombing by the Smithsonian Museum in 1995, on the other hand, is an example of a failed revision in the national narrative. The Japanese post-war narrative, emphasizing peace as the national mission, can likewise be refined to more accurately reflect cultural and historical realities, as well as the fundamental universality of the mission proposed. It would need to deal forthrightly with the radical implications of pacifism, recognizing it as an ideal and thus opening up the possibility of a realistic appraisal of security needs and Japan's role in international arrangements to fulfill those needs. It would also need to provide a healthy way of dealing with questions of cultural identity and the meaning of Japan's modern history.

The groups that we have looked at here do provide some positive directions for the needed revision of the postwar Japanese story. The pacifist witness of Nipponzan Myōhōji and Byakkō Shinkōkai can be an important contribution to social discourse in Japan on issues of war and peace. Absolute pacifism is a powerful witness in any age. The images of Civil Rights demonstrators under assault from a hostile police force in Selma, Alabama, or a lone man in Peking facing down a line of tanks, are moving not primarily because of the sympathy or concern that they elicit, but rather because of the witness to overriding values that they make. It is important in any age that society have such witness, to remind us that there are values worth the ultimate sacrifice, and that there are human beings willing to make that sacrifice. The presence of those who have taken the pacifist position is also important to act as a brake on the tendency to resort to the use of force too easily. Pacifist witness, therefore, is important precisely because it is an extreme, even fringe, position, and in order to preserve its witness value it must be clearly seen as such.

Efforts to preserve cultural identity and cultural pride, as seen in the doctrine and practice of Shōroku Shintō Yamatoyama and Shūyōdan Hōseikai can also be positively evaluated. Particularly in Yamatoyama, we see evidence that such efforts have had a salutary effect in allowing the members to deal more realistically with some of the issues involved in this survey, and that they do not hinder an international outlook. While we may question whether prewar cultural items can be retrieved and reinterpreted as easily as these groups seem to assume, clearly there is a need for some continuity in the narrative if the nation's history is to be realistically assessed.

The mainstream groups of Sōka Gakkai and Rissho Kōseikai have also pioneered international efforts to deal with the question of world peace, through political and interreligious means respectively. In this they have, for the most part, overcome the bounds of culturalism and provided a model of activity that breaks through the borders of the nation-state or religious group. Recent movements towards the strengthening of regional alliances in the political realm, as well as attempts such as that to describe a common global ethic in the religious sphere, serve to indicate the increasing importance given to the path taken by these groups.

Clearly more needs to be done, however. Perhaps most fundamentally, the quest for peace must be redeemed from banality in popular discourse. Regretfully, influenced by the idea of a postwar national mission, "world peace" has become a catchphrase among some Japanese religionists. As in the case of Shūyōdan Hōseikai, the purpose of establishing world peace is attached to all sorts of disparate activities. For example, I recently viewed a videotape of a television program covering a fertility festival at a Shinto shrine in the suburbs of Nagoya. The festival is among the better known of its genre in Japan, and every year busloads of tourists come from as far as Tokyo to view the festival, where phalluses are prominently displayed and "sex goods" are on sale. In an interview, the head priest of the shrine explained the meaning and significance of the festival by saying that the people were praying for a good harvest, prosperity, and world peace.[4] While, on reflection, the connection between prosperity and peace is one of the traditional understandings of the concept of peace, the ease with which such attributions are offered by seemingly any religious group in postwar Japan can only contribute to the banality of the term, as well as the dismissal of religion in contemporary society, an issue that I will return to in a moment.

Although Shūyōdan Hōseikai, and perhaps Byakkō Shinkōkai, exhibit some tendencies towards this banality, the activity of the other groups in this survey attests to the seriousness with which the quest for world peace is taken. There is still need, however, to overcome the romanticism with which many of these groups approach the issue of peace, and deal seriously with the question of the use of force. Many of these groups allow that force is sometimes necessary in a world not yet made perfect. The question of what circumstances might make the use of force necessary, at least in terms of broad categories or principles, is a moral question that is quite proper for religion to address. Indeed it is a question that no religious group that is not strictly pacifist should avoid.

Additionally, some of these groups have made positive contributions towards an honest evaluation of Japan's action in World War II. We have seen how Shōroku Shintō Yamatoyama has financed the construction of welfare facilities in China and Korea as a sign of reparation, and how

Risshō Kōseikai has organized trips to countries in Asia and Southeast Asia for its youth group, to raise their consciousness regarding the war. All of the groups in general also exhibited a relatively high awareness of the issues of war guilt contained in the questionnaire survey. While commendable, these attitudes and activities do not appear to have had much of an effect yet on overall social discourse in Japan, where the issues are left to fester. This is yet another area where these religious groups could take a role of moral leadership in public debate.

The issue of religion in public debate in Japan is a difficult one. Religion, as an institution, is not regarded highly in Japanese society. In a recent survey conducted by the Nanzan Institute for Religion and Culture, people were queried on the level of trust placed in seventeen national or international institutions, such as the Parliament, the police, the press, and the United Nations.[5] Religion was ranked as least trustworthy of all the social institutions, with 45% of the respondents saying they had little trust in religion, and an additional 40% saying they had no trust at all.

The release of poison gas by a religious group on the Tokyo subways in 1995 obviously has contributed greatly to this mistrust. The problem in the perception of religion in Japan, however, is not recent, but rather has its roots in the historical position of religion in Japanese society beginning at least in the Tokugawa period. At that time the Buddhist establishment was pressed into service to enforce the ban on Christianity, and as a result it became little more than the purveyor of funeral rites, a position it still maintains in Japanese society. Religious policy in the Meiji period abandoned the Buddhists in favor of the creation of State Shinto. The modern creation of a national religious ideology as a vehicle to promote cultural identity could only be maintained by the use of increasingly oppressive force, and ultimately failed when that force could not be sustained following the defeat of the nation in 1945. Some of the New Religions (such as Tenrikyō and Konkōkyō) that emerged at the same time that State Shinto was being created were arguably more effective at preserving cultural identity in the face of the massive importation of foreign cultural items in the modern period. However, these movements were subject to a highly critical press and varying levels of oppression from the authorities. They ultimately sought recognition from the government as sects of Shinto, willingly purveying the nationalistic creed right up through to the end of the war.

The press also played a major role in how new religious movements were perceived in the postwar period. Religious freedoms guaranteed by Occupation policy and the new constitution contributed to a proliferation of new movements, often dismissed by intellectuals and the press as preying on the superstitions and alienation of the lower classes, little more than a cynical attempt to amass fortunes by bilking their believers and avoiding tax laws.[6] This situation changed somewhat in the 1970s and 1980s when, riding a wave of popular interest in the occult, print and televised media began to play up the mysterious and "odd" nature of religious groups. Occasionally the media and some religious groups would feed off each other to boost their ratings or membership. Such coverage came to a crashing end with the Aum Shinrikyō case, however, with the media now focusing on the scandal-ridden and dangerous nature of these "cults," a term popularized in the post-Aum era.[7]

Surveys indicate both a widespread antipathy towards religion in contemporary Japan and that this antipathy is based primarily on the popular images of religion outlined above. For example, in a nationwide survey of university students conducted annually since 1995, consistently almost 60% of the respondents say that they have little or no interest in religion. Significantly, only 3% of the students attribute this negative attitude to a direct experience with a religious group, with the rest presumably drawing on the media for their image of religion.[8] Results from a survey conducted by the *Yomiuri Shinbun* in 1995 also attest to the influence of the above negative popular images. Given the opportunity for multiple responses to a question on their image of religion, 40% answered that religious groups were only out to make money and 37% expressed the opinion that religions prey on people's unease in order to increase their membership. Only 6% expressed the opinion that religious groups were making a positive contribution to society.[9]

Religion in contemporary Japan plays a subservient role in society. In such a hostile environment it is perhaps understandable that religious groups would conclude that they have no voice in society. Their reluctance to speak out, however, could itself contribute to the poor image of religion. For example, in the Nanzan Institute survey mentioned earlier, when asked if religions were providing an adequate response to social problems, only 9% of the respondents answered positively, indicating that there is some expectation that religious groups should do more to provide answers to those problems.

There is also positive evidence that people will respond to social initiatives on the part of religious groups, as occurred in the lead-up to the Persian Gulf War. At that time, in opposition to the proposal by the Japanese government to send Self-Defense Force planes to the Gulf to help in the evacuation of civilians—which would have amounted to another ad hoc extension of the use of the Self-Defense Forces—religious leaders called for contributions from the public in order to charter civilian planes to carry out the mission. The move was so popular that the government was forced to withdraw its proposal.

Helping to shape public debate on moral issues is clearly a legitimate role for religion in contemporary society. However, I would make a distinction between this role and direct participation in political activities. I would agree with Stephen Carter that such political activity actually endangers religion's role as moral teacher or guide.[10] When engaged in direct political activities religions are seen as just one more power bloc, promoting their own agenda for their own ends. Debate on the value of that agenda often becomes secondary to the more immediate need to engage in political power struggles, either for or against the religious group. And if a religion should emerge as winning and become part of the ruling establishment, it then has a stake in preserving the status quo and thus loses its critical role in society.

The case of Sōka Gakkai is a clear example of what happens when religion engages in direct political activity, rather than limiting itself to the promotion of a moral point of view. In its support of the Kōmeitō not only has it compromised the pacifist principles that it would like to uphold, it is perceived by many as a group more interested in political power than religious activities. In general, people reject such a directly political role for religion,[11] and it is for that reason that Sōka Gakkai and the Kōmeitō have occasionally become an albatross around the neck of their coalition partners in the Japanese political realignment of recent years.[12]

Sōka Gakkai argues that political involvement is the only way to prevent further exploitation of religion by the state, and that it offers a platform to those who were left out in the postwar Japanese political structure.[13] I personally believe that a different forum needs to be found for religious groups to participate in public debate in a way that is seen to be clearly not self-serving, and morally uncompromised. It is only in this way that religion will find its voice in social debate and be able

186

to make its contribution towards the revision of the postwar Japanese narrative.

The need for involvement in this debate can be expressed in terms of the cultural emphasis given moral cultivation. In our treatment of this aspect of the concept of peace offered by these groups we have seen that the choice is often presented as one of individual moral cultivation or direct political action. What is overlooked is that religion can play a role in the moral cultivation of society, not only by preaching a personal ethic of honesty, tolerance, and cheerfulness, but also by participating in public debate, helping to clarify the moral issues involved in the questions facing society. In terms of the concept of peace presented by this research, religion can contribute specifically towards the overcoming of culturalism and a facile pacifism.

In their identification of harmony, tolerance, and a peace-loving nature as national characteristics, many of the religious groups looked at in this study seem to adopt the clichés of Japanese culturalism too easily. Within the dynamics of the discourse that we have looked at here, that is, preaching addressed to the members of these groups, such emphases are, to a certain extent, understandable, for the items of popular discourse are the building blocks of good preaching. As religious leaders, however, the preachers need to be more critical and discriminating in their use of that discourse. In this way they might contribute towards the development of the Japanese cultural narrative in positive directions, towards a balanced acceptance of responsibility for past actions and a more realistic idea of national mission. Such developments will depend on an integral sense of self, a construct that religion, at its best, has traditionally provided within cultures.

Finally, although society needs the witness of absolute pacifism as provided by groups such as Nipponzan Myōhōji, honestly grappling with moral ambiguity and the dilemmas arising from the need to preserve the conflicting values of an integral view of life—encompassing the broad spectrum of human rights—is an equally necessary witness. With the limits of traditional just war theory now apparent, there is a need for new approaches to these moral questions. A too-easy pacifism both cheapens the witness of its authentic expression and amounts to an abdication of moral responsibility on the part of these religious groups.

The mission of establishing world peace should issue in unique initiatives as Japan considers its role in the world today. It is only a realistic assessment of the world situation, beyond the blinders of culturalism and a too-easy pacifism, that will lead to the development of these new initiatives. The title of this study, *Prophets of Peace*, draws inspiration from a passage in the Jewish and Christian scriptures (Jer. 28: 8–9), where it is used as a criticism of those who would find peace too easily.[14] Perhaps it can serve as a challenge not only for these groups but for all in Japanese society and elsewhere to deal with situations of conflict more realistically, and thus provide new intiatives towards the establishment of a true and lasting peace.

Questionnaire Survey on Peace Attitudes

Aquestionnaire survey of seven new religious groups was carried out between December 1992 and March 1993, in most cases with the cooperation of the groups chosen as research subjects. In all cases a stamped self-addressed return envelope was included with the questionnaire, to ensure the anonymity of the respondents.

Two priests from Nipponzan Myōhōji assisted in distributing 120 copies of the survey instrument to other priests, nuns, and believers who visited their temples. Of these, 31 questionnaires were returned, giving us a response rate of 26%. Five hundred questionnaires were distributed through Sōka Gakkai's Cultural Affairs Division, one hundred each to the Young Women's Group, Young Men's Group, Student Group, Women's Group, and Men's Group. 339 of these were returned, for a response rate of 66%. 510 questionnaires were distributed at a service held at Risshō Kōseikai headquarters in December 1992, ten each to members of fifty-one churches represented there. 365 responses were obtained, for a return rate of 70%. Four hundred questionnaires were distributed at a meeting of believers at the Shōryoku Shintō Yamatoyama

189

headquarters early in 1993, with 173 returns, for a response rate of 44%. In the case of Shūyōdan Hōseikai, one hundred questionnaires were distributed through the Niigata branch church, one hundred-fifty at a ceremony held at the Tokyo headquarters in January 1993, and an additional one hundred-fifty at a meeting of older believers, the most active group in the church. Two hundred-ten responses were obtained, giving us a return rate of 52%. My request for cooperation was turned down by the central administration of Byakkō Shinkōkai. One believer who cooperated greatly in my research helped me to distribute 210 questionnaires to people returning from services held at the group's headquarters, and of these 57 were returned, for a response rate of 26%. In addition, four hundred questionnaires were distributed at a ceremony held at the headquarters of Shinnyoen, a new religious group not directly involved in peace work. 286 responses were obtained, for a return rate of 71%. These were meant to serve as a control group, and, indeed, their responses consistently followed the mean of all the groups included in the survey.

None of the groups involved sought to exercise control over the contents of the survey. The survey questions were made in consultation with Professor Shimazono Susumu of the Department of Religious Studies at Tokyo University and several of my fellow graduate students at that same university. In devising the questions I sought, where appropriate, to offer three possible choices, covering what could be identified as the two extremes on the issue as well as a middle position. Many of the questions were based on topics of current interest at that time, and the terms of rhetoric employed in the media or more broadly in common discourse in Japan were used in forming the possible answers. For that reason, some of the choices given may seem odd to those unfamiliar with that discourse. Despite the idiosyncrasies of this approach, the generally high response rate could be taken to indicate that it succeeded in making the survey instrument readily comprehensible to the targeted audience.

Given my limited resources, in almost all cases I had to rely on the various groups to distribute the questionnaire to a sample of their members. Clearly, more active members were generally targeted to respond to the survey, and the results must be read with this fact in mind. Furthermore, the fact that a random sampling was not used limits the conclusions that can be drawn from the results. At best what we can hope for from these results is indications of trends leading to the formation of theories or hypotheses in need of further testing. Previous research on Japanese New Religions has followed similar procedures.[1]

A translation of the questionnaire and a summary of results are included below. Percentages have been rounded off.

SURVEY ON ATTITUDES REGARDING PEACE ISSUES

1. How old are you?

0) No answer	5) 50–59
1) Nineteen or younger	6) 60–69
2) 20–29	7) 70–79
3) 30–39	8) 80–89
4) 40–49	9) Ninety or older

	NA	10s	20s	30s	40s	50s	60s	70s	80s	90s
Byakko Shinkōkai	1 2%		6 10%	4 7%	14 25%	10 17%	17 30%	5 9%		
Sōka Gakkai		6 2%	135 40%	91 27%	61 18%	34 10%	12 3%			
Shūyōdan Hōseikai	3 1%	2 1%	8 4%	6 3%	30 14%	35 17%	61 29%	50 24%	15 7%	
Risshō Koseikai	2 1%		8 2%	23 6%	118 33%	115 32%	66 18%	24 7%		
Nipponzan Myōhōji	1 3%	2 6%	5 16%	4 13%	13 42%	3 10%	2 6%	1 3%		
Shinnyoen			48 17%	75 26%	100 35%	50 17%	13 4%			
Yamato-yama		3 2%	39 22%	78 45%	45 26%	2 1%	7 4%	1 0%		
Totals	7 0%	13 1%	249 17%	281 19%	381 26%	249 17%	178 12%	81 6%	15 1%	

2. Are you male or female?

    0) No answer

    1) Female

    2) Male

	NA	Female	Male
Byakko Shinkōkai		42 74%	15 26%
Sōka Gakkai	1 0%	144 42%	194 57%
Shūyōdan Hōseikai	9 4%	155 74%	46 22%
Risshō Koseikai	4 1%	310 87%	42 12%
Nipponzan Myōhōji		12 39%	19 61%
Shinnyoen	1 0%	166 58%	119 42%
Yamato-yama		53 30%	122 70%
Totals	15 1%	882 61%	557 38%

3. What is your occupation?

0) No answer
1) Agriculture/forestry/fishing
2) Owner of your own business
3) Full-time employee
4) Part-time employee

5) Employed in a family business
6) Self-employed
7) Housewife
8) Student
9) Unemployed/retired

3-1. For those who answered "housewife" to number 3: What is your husband's occupation?

The following is an aggregate table, including the husband's occupation for those who answered "housewife" to question 3 and responded to question 3-1 with the appropriate information. Only those who answered "housewife" to question 3 and did not respond to question 3-1 are included in "housewife" below.

	NA	1	2	3	4	5	6	7	8	9
Byakko Shinkōkai			2 3%	25 44%	6 10%		6 10%	8 14%		10 17%
Sōka Gakkai			25 7%	178 52%	15 4%	3 1%	13 4%	17 5%	85 25%	3 1%
Shūyōdan Hōseikai	1 0%	1 0%	23 11%	54 26%	14 7%	13 6%	18 9%	13 6%	5 2%	68 33%
Risshō Koseikai	2 1%	18 5%	31 9%	121 34%	32 9%	11 3%	29 8%	62 17%	1 0%	49 14%
Nipponzan Myōhōji	2 6%		3 10%	5 17%	4 14%		8 28%		2 7%	7 24%
Shinnyoen	1 0%	3 1%	48 17%	144 50%	35 12%	8 3%	21 7%	15 5%	6 2%	5 2%
Yamato-yama	2 1%	20 12%	21 12%	94 54%	11 6%	3 2%	8 5%		9 5%	7 4%
Totals	8 1%	42 3%	153 11%	621 43%	117 8%	38 3%	103 7%	115 8%	108 7%	149 10%

193

4. What is the highest level of education that you have achieved?
 0) No answer
 1) Prewar lower primary school
 2) Prewar higher primary school
 3) Prewar junior high/vocational/normal school
 4) Prewar senior high/higher vocational/higher normal school
 5) Prewar university (including graduate school)
 6) Postwar junior high
 7) Postwar senior high
 8) Postwar junior college/vocational
 9) Postwar university (including graduate school)

	NA	1	2	3	4	5	6	7	8	9
Byakko Shinkōkai	1 2%		2 3%	5 9%	9 16%	2 3%	2 3%	14 25%	9 16%	13 23%
Sōka Gakkai	4 1%		1 0%	6 2%	6 2%		6 2%	97 29%	39 11%	180 53%
Shūyōdan Hōseikai	1 0%	7 3%	16 8%	57 27%	38 18%	2 1%	2 1%	38 18%	20 9%	29 14%
Risshō Koseikai	1 0%	18 5%	45 13%	24 7%	14 4%	1 0%	67 19%	153 43%	22 6%	11 3%
Nipponzan Myōhōji	3 10%	1 3%	2 6%	1 3%			1 3%	13 42%	2 6%	8 26%
Shinnyoen			2 1%	6 2%	5 2%	1 0%	18 6%	110 38%	62 22%	82 29%
Yamato-yama	2 1%	3 2%	2 1%	5 3%	5 3%		14 8%	91 52%	25 14%	28 16%
Totals	12 1%	29 2%	70 5%	104 7%	77 5%	6 0%	110 8%	516 35%	179 12%	351 24%

194

5. How long has it been since you entered this religious group?
   0) No answer
   1) Five years or less
   2) Six–ten years
   3) Eleven years or more

	NA	~5	6~10	11~
Byakko Shinkōkai	3 5%	5 9%	11 19%	38 67%
Sōka Gakkai	1 0%	7 2%	12 3%	319 94%
Shūyōdan Hōseikai	3 1%	8 4%	8 4%	191 91%
Risshō Koseikai	4 1%	19 5%	36 10%	297 83%
Nipponzan Myōhōji		5 16%	2 6%	24 77%
Shinnyoen	1 0%	31 11%	177 62%	77 27%
Yamato-yama	1 1%	8 5%	29 17%	137 78%
Totals	13 1%	83 6%	275 19%	1083 74%

6. Do you hold a position within this religious group?

   0) No answer
   1) Yes
   2) No

	NA	Yes	No
Byakko Shinkōkai	4 7%	7 12%	46 81%
Sōka Gakkai	3 1%	318 94%	18 5%
Shūyōdan Hōseikai	5 2%	67 32%	138 66%
Risshō Koseikai	14 4%	287 81%	55 15%
Nipponzan Myōhōji	1 3%		30 97%
Shinnyoen	3 1%	25 9%	258 90%
Yamato-yama	5 3%	72 41%	97 56%
Totals	35 2%	776 53%	642 44%

7. What is your opinion regarding the Japanese Constitution?
   0) No answer
   1) The present constitution should not be revised.
   2) The present constitution should be revised.

	NA	Retain	Revise
Byakko Shinkōkai	5 9%	33 58%	19 33%
Sōka Gakkai	6 2%	215 63%	118 35%
Shūyōdan Hōseikai	23 11%	112 53%	75 36%
Risshō Koseikai	40 11%	225 63%	91 26%
Nipponzan Myōhōji	1 3%	21 68%	9 29%
Shinnyoen	14 5%	138 48%	134 47%
Yamato-yama	9 5%	74 42%	92 53%
Totals	98 7%	818 56%	538 37%

7-1. For those favoring revision of the constitution: Please choose one of the following.

   0) No answer

   1) The emperor should be made the sovereign of the nation.

   2) The emperor should remain the symbol of the unity of the nation, and sovereignty should remain with the people.

   3) The emperor system should be abolished and the sovereignty of the people made more explicit.

	NA	Sovereign	Symbol	Abolish
Byakko Shinkōkai	6 27%	1 4%	15 68%	
Sōka Gakkai	11 8%	1 1%	77 60%	40 31%
Shūyōdan Hōseikai	10 8%	18 15%	92 75%	2 2%
Risshō Koseikai	22 14%	29 18%	98 62%	9 6%
Nipponzan Myōhōji	1 7%		5 36%	8 57%
Shinnyoen	17 11%	9 6%	115 78%	7 5%
Yamato-yama	5 5%	17 16%	82 77%	3 3%
Totals	72 10%	75 11%	484 69%	69 10%

7-2. For those favoring revision of the constitution: Please choose one of the following.

   0) No answer

   1) Article 9 of the constitution renouncing war as a sovereign right of the nation is unrealistic and should be abolished.

   2) Article 9 of the constitution renouncing war as a sovereign right of the nation should not be revised, and the posture of a "peace nation" should be maintained.

   3) The pacifism of Article 9 should be further strengthened.

	NA	Abolish	Retain	Strenghten
Byakko Shinkōkai	1 4%	2 8%	9 37%	12 50%
Sōka Gakkai	4 3%	4 3%	53 41%	67 52%
Shūyōdan Hōseikai	10 9%	7 6%	55 51%	36 33%
Risshō Koseikai	10 6%	1 1%	66 41%	82 52%
Nipponzan Myōhōji			1 7%	13 93%
Shinnyoen	8 5%	8 5%	70 47%	62 42%
Yamato-yama	2 2%	12 11%	54 52%	36 35%
Totals	35 5%	34 5%	308 45%	308 45%

8. Which of the following is closest to your opinion regarding the war with China following the Manchurian Incident?

    0) No answer

    1) It was wrong for the Japanese army to invade the territory of another country.

    2) Although in some ways the advance into the continent could not be avoided, there should not have been a war with China.

    3) The war was necessary to protect China from the Western Powers.

	NA	Invasion	Inevitable	Protect
Byakko Shinkōkai	9 16%	33 58%	13 23%	2 3%
Sōka Gakkai	7 2%	310 91%	18 5%	4 1%
Shūyōdan Hōseikai	16 8%	121 58%	68 32%	5 2%
Risshō Koseikai	41 11%	203 57%	93 26%	19 5%
Nipponzan Myōhōji	3 10%	27 87%		1 3%
Shinnyoen	17 6%	193 67%	67 23%	9 3%
Yamato-yama	14 8%	92 53%	61 35%	8 5%
Totals	107 7%	979 67%	320 22%	48 3%

9. Which of the following is closest to your opinion regarding the Second World War?

    0) No answer

    1) We Japanese were the aggressors.

    2) We Japanese were the victims.

    3) We Japanese were both aggressors and victims.

	NA	Aggressors	Victims	Both
Byakko Shinkōkai	2 3%	3 5%		52 91%
Sōka Gakkai		43 13%	7 2%	289 85%
Shūyōdan Hōseikai	2 1%	29 14%	8 4%	171 81%
Risshō Koseikai	12 3%	31 9%	9 2%	304 85%
Nipponzan Myōhōji		6 19%		25 81%
Shinnyoen	6 2%	41 14%	5 2%	234 82%
Yamato-yama	7 4%	7 4%	6 3%	155 89%
Totals	29 2%	160 11%	35 2%	1230 85%

10. Which of the following is closest to your opinion regarding the issue of the comfort women?

    0) No answer

    1) The facts of the issue have been established, and the Japanese government should apologize and compensate the victims.

    2) Although the facts of the issue have been established, sufficient apologies and compensation have already been made for the war.

    3) Since the facts of the issue have not been established, there is no need for apology or compensation.

	NA	Apologize	Finished	No need
Byakko Shinkōkai	8 14%	24 42%	24 42%	1 2%
Sōka Gakkai	7 2%	304 90%	24 7%	4 1%
Shūyōdan Hōseikai	20 9%	100 48%	77 37%	13 6%
Risshō Koseikai	39 11%	221 62%	81 23%	15 4%
Nipponzan Myōhōji	4 13%	26 84%	1 3%	
Shinnyoen	26 9%	205 72%	49 17%	6 2%
Yamato- yama	11 6%	106 61%	53 30%	5 3%
Totals	115 8%	986 68%	309 21%	44 3%

11. Which of the following is closest to your opinion regarding the 1991 Persian Gulf War?

    0) No answer

    1) Since invasion of another country cannot be allowed under any circumstances, the war was necessary to maintain world peace.

    2) Since the use of force against another country cannot be allowed under any circumstances, the situation should have been resolved by nonviolent means.

    3) We can't do anything about other countries going to war, but at least Japan should not get involved.

	NA	Necessary	Nonviolent	Not Japan
Byakko Shinkōkai	3 5%	6 10%	44 77%	4 7%
Sōka Gakkai	4 1%	79 23%	255 75%	1 0%
Shūyōdan Hōseikai	12 6%	62 29%	105 50%	31 15%
Risshō Koseikai	23 6%	65 18%	231 65%	37 10%
Nipponzan Myōhōji	1 3%	1 3%	29 93%	
Shinnyoen	10 3%	72 25%	195 68%	9 3%
Yamato-yama	7 4%	76 43%	83 47%	9 5%
Totals	60 4%	361 25%	942 65%	91 6%

12. Do you believe that Japan has the right to defend itself against invasion from another country?
    0) No answer
    1) Yes
    2) No

	NA	Yes	No
Byakko Shinkōkai	6 10%	45 79%	6 10%
Sōka Gakkai	6 2%	300 88%	33 10%
Shūyōdan Hōseikai	9 4%	178 85%	23 11%
Risshō Koseikai	29 8%	280 79%	47 13%
Nipponzan Myōhōji	3 10%	25 81%	3 10%
Shinnyoen	12 4%	240 84%	34 12%
Yamato-yama	4 2%	149 85%	22 13%
Totals	69 5%	1217 84%	168 12%

12-1. For those who responded "yes" to the previous question: In that case, do you believe that an armed defense is necessary?

    0) No answer

    1) Yes, it is necessary.

    2) No, it is not necessary.

	NA	Yes	No
Byakko Shinkōkai	2 4%	17 38%	26 58%
Sōka Gakkai	8 3%	157 52%	135 45%
Shūyōdan Hōseikai	11 6%	126 69%	46 25%
Risshō Koseikai	14 5%	132 46%	141 49%
Nipponzan Myōhōji	1 4%	1 4%	24 92%
Shinnyoen	12 5%	136 56%	94 39%
Yamato-yama	4 3%	121 80%	26 17%
Totals	52 4%	690 56%	492 40%

13. Which of the following is closest to your opinion regarding the Self-Defense Forces?

    0) No answer

    1) The existence of the Self-Defense Forces is itself unconstitutional and they should be disbanded immediately.

    2) The existence of the Self-Defense Forces is not unconstitutional and they have my full support.

    3) In the present situation some kind of means of defense such as the Self-Defense Forces is necessary, but it should be limited in size and activity.

	NA	Disband	Support	Limited
Byakko Shinkōkai	4 7%	2 3%		51 89%
Sōka Gakkai	3 1%	27 8%	5 1%	304 90%
Shūyōdan Hōseikai	9 4%	6 3%	16 8%	179 85%
Risshō Kōseikai	13 4%	8 2%	26 7%	309 87%
Nipponzan Myōhōji	1 3%	27 87%		3 10%
Shinnyoen	13 4%	10 3%	10 3%	253 88%
Yamato-yama	5 3%		26 15%	144 82%
Totals	48 3%	80 5%	83 6%	1243 85%

14. Which of the following is closest to your opinion regarding the Peacekeeping Operations Law?

    0) No answer

    1) Deployment of Self-Defense Forces outside Japan is unconstitutional, and the law should be revoked.

    2) Participation in Peacekeeping Operations is an important contribution to world peace and it has my full support.

    3) Because of pressure from outside the country, the enactment of the Peacekeeping Operations Law couldn't be stopped.

	NA	Revoke	Support	Pressure
Byakko Shinkōkai	11 19%	7 12%	30 53%	9 16%
Sōka Gakkai	3 1%	10 3%	312 92%	14 4%
Shūyōdan Hōseikai	18 9%	35 17%	93 44%	64 30%
Risshō Koseikai	33 9%	55 15%	170 48%	98 27%
Nipponzan Myōhōji		30 97%		1 3%
Shinnyoen	19 7%	52 18%	131 46%	84 29%
Yamato-yama	8 5%	20 11%	112 64%	35 20%
Totals	92 6%	209 14%	848 58%	305 21%

15. In the event that Japan ever becomes involved in another war, what would be your reaction? Please choose one of the following responses.

0) No answer
1) If it is necessary for Japan's defense, I would willingly participate in the war.
2) I would avoid cooperating in the war as much as possible, and quietly pray for peace.
3) I would express my opposition to the war and participate in antiwar activities.

	NA	Participate	Pray	Oppose
Byakko Shinkōkai	4 7%	1 2%	39 68%	13 23%
Sōka Gakkai	6 2%	14 4%	12 3%	307 91%
Shūyōdan Hōseikai	20 9%	24 11%	87 41%	79 38%
Risshō Koseikai	19 5%	18 5%	112 31%	207 58%
Nipponzan Myōhōji	3 10%		2 6%	26 84%
Shinnyoen	7 2%	18 6%	129 45%	132 46%
Yamato-yama	8 5%	45 26%	75 43%	47 27%
Totals	67 5%	120 8%	456 31%	811 56%

16. What is most important for the establishment of peace?
    0) No answer
    1) That each individual pray for peace in his or her heart.
    2) Building a peaceful society through participation in civic movements.
    3) Discussions between nations through organs such as the United Nations.

	NA	Heart	Civic	UN
Byakko Shinkōkai	2 3%	50 88%	2 3%	3 5%
Sōka Gakkai	36 11%	147 43%	47 14%	109 32%
Shūyōdan Hōseikai	19 9%	135 64%	7 3%	49 23%
Risshō Koseikai	29 8%	206 58%	22 6%	99 28%
Nipponzan Myōhōji	5 16%	19 61%	5 16%	2 6%
Shinnyoen	15 5%	180 63%	12 4%	79 28%
Yamato-yama	8 5%	143 82%	5 3%	19 11%
Totals	114 8%	880 60%	100 7%	360 25%

17. Have you participated in any of the following peace activities? Please answer yes for each activity that you have ever participated in.

   1) Peace prayers or peace ceremonies sponsored by your religious group
   2) Individual prayer for peace on a daily basis
   3) The Atomic Bomb/Peace Ceremonies in Hiroshima or Nagasaki
   4) Signing petitions to ban nuclear weapons
   5) Peace marches
   6) Fasting for a period of several days
   7) The One-Meal Campaign
   8) Antiwar demonstrations
   9) Demonstrations opposing military bases
  10) Charity bazaars
  11) Distribution of Peace Stickers
  12) Erection of Peace Poles

	1	2	3	4	5	6	7	8	9	10	11	12
Byakko Shinkōkai	49	53	3	4	39	29	8	1		13	39	37
	86%	93%	5%	7%	68%	51	14%	2%		23%	68%	65%
Sōka Gakkai	220	321	30	152	17	1	2	11		127	10	2
	65%	95%	9%	45%	5%	0%	1%	3%		37%	3%	1%
Shūyōdan Hōseikai	173	131	15	68	58	1	3	2	1	43	2	
	82%	62%	7%	32%	28%	0%	1%	1%	0%	20%	1%	
Risshō Koseikai	315	181	38	159	121	12	332	5	2	234	21	5
	88%	51%	11%	45%	34%	3%	93%	1%	1%	66%	6%	1%
Nipponzan Myōhōji	29	22	26	28	29	22	2	22	25	4	3	2
	93%	71%	84%	90%	93%	71%	6%	71%	81%	13%	10%	6%
Shinnyoen	102	145	11	61	8	2	2	7	3	72	3	
	36%	51%	4%	21%	3%	1%	1%	2%	1%	25%	1%	
Yamato-yama	144	101	2	15	8	3	159	1	1	153	1	
	82%	58%	1%	9%	5%	2%	91%	1%	1%	87%	1%	
Totals	1032	954	125	487	280	70	508	49	32	646	79	46
	71%	66%	9%	33%	19%	5%	35%	3%	2%	44%	5%	3%

Notes

[1] Despite some reservations, I use this term to refer to the war in deference to its familiarity in the West. The more common term in Japan would be the Pacific War, or Asian-Pacific War, because it more accurately reflects the fact that, for Japan and its neighbors, the war began already in 1931 with Japan's invasion of China. See the Preface in Ienaga 1979 for arguments regarding this usage.

[2] Casualty figures are taken from Harries and Harries 1991, p. 443.

[3] Figures regarding religious affiliation in Japan are notoriously unreliable. Almost every Japanese is nominally a member of one of the major Buddhist sects, a holdover from a seventeenth-century government policy that resulted in the monopolization of funeral rites by the local Buddhist temples. Additionally, the entire population is automatically counted as parishioners of the local Shinto Shrine, issuing in a total religious membership of well over two hundred million, nearly double the total population of the country (Ministry of Education 1996). Membership figures for new religious groups are likewise based on the self-reporting of the groups, and wildly varying criteria for membership often leads to clearly inflated results. On the other hand, there is little dispute that several groups counted among the New Religions can rightly claim a membership in the millions, so a total figure of fifteen percent would not be unreasonable. Total religious membership has been measured at regular intervals throughout the postwar period by several independent social surveys, such as the *Nihonjin no kokuminsei chōsa* (Tōkei Sūri Kenkyūjo 1991) and the *Nihonjin no shūkyō ishiki chōsa* (NHK Yoron Chōsabu 1984). Ishii Kenji (1997) provides a useful summary of postwar survey results.

[4] See, for example, Robert Sharf's argument regarding the classification of Sanbōkyōdan as a New Religion in "Sanbōkyōdan: Zen and the Way of the New Religions" (1995a).

[5] Because I have chosen to highlight the religious traditions predominantly represented by the New Religions that emerged in the different periods of modern Japanese history, my classification here differs from the three waves that Hardacre

identifies (1986, p. 4) or the four waves proposed by Nishiyama (1988, p. 177) and Shimazono (1992b, p. 9).

6 A short report on my research into the social ethic of the Japanese New Religions can be found in Kisala 1994b. A more complete account has been published in Japanese (Kisala 1992).

7 *Shinshūkyō jiten*, Inoue et al., eds., 1990.

8 Pye 1994.

9 Details on the questionnaire survey can be found in the appendix to this volume. For the structured interviews I had planned on a sample of five from each group, for a total of thirty. However, only four interviews could be arranged with Nipponzan Myōhōji and Shūyōdan Hōseikai members in the time I set aside for my research. An attempt was made to find believers who were either themselves active in their group's peace activities or who could otherwise articulate the group's teaching on peace. Except for Sōka Gakkai and Shūyōdan Hōseikai, who arranged interviews for me, the interviews were set up through my own personal contacts in the various groups.

Because of the small size of the sample, and the fact that some of the interviews were arranged by the groups themselves, I cannot claim that the interviews presented here are necessarily representative of the views of the believers of these groups. They do, however, illustrate aspects of the doctrine or practice of these groups and personalize what could be a very abstract discussion, and it is for that reason that they have been included.

10 Richard Miller (1991) makes this argument.

11 Martin 1965 and Marty 1996.

12 Martin argues that this position should properly be called "pacificism," rather than "pacifism" (1965, p. 73).

13 Tsuneoka 1993, p. 140.

14 Martin 1965, p. 201.

15 Bainton 1960, pp. 152–72.

16 President George Bush and other political leaders made use of just war rhetoric in arguing for the necessity of facing down Saddam Hussein and the Iraqi army with force, and consequently popular news magazines picked up on the theme and ran feature reports on the ethical arguments involved. Furthermore, while the war was being conducted early in 1991, the American military made repeated reference in their briefings to the purported accuracy of their bombs and consequent low levels of civilian casualties, a prime condition set on the conduct of war by the just war theory.

17 Bainton 1960, pp. 17–20.

18 Ishida 1983, pp. 117–36.

CHAPTER 1: ELEMENTS OF A JAPANESE CULTURAL CONCEPT OF PEACE

[1] The most comprehensive postwar peace study is the twenty-volume *Nihon hei-waron taikei* [Outline of Japanese peace theory], published under the direction of Ienaga Saburō (1993–1994). Bamba and Howes (1978) provide a useful summary in English of the thought of some of the major figures from this period in *Pacifism in Japan: The Christian and Socialist Tradition*. The one pre-Meiji figure normally identified as part of this pacifist tradition is Andō Shōeki (1703?–1762), an egalitarian who wrote antimilitary tracts and was the focus of an early postwar study by E. H. Norman (1949).

[2] William Farris, for example, argues against facile comparisons with the emergence of feudalism in Europe, what he calls the Western-analogue theory, precisely because "warriors acted more like mercenaries than vassals, repeatedly betraying their lords and switching their loyalties to the winning side" (Farris 1992, p. 312).

[3] Ooms 1985, p. 66.

[4] Ibid., p. 68.

[5] Ibid., p. 69. Ooms points out that discourse on *jihi* helped to mask the controlling character of the Tokugawa administration, based as it was on military might.

[6] This translation is provided in Maruyama 1974, p. 82.

[7] Translation provided as above.

[8] Yasumaru 1974. A concise English summary of Yasumaru's argument can be found in Shimazono 1981.

[9] In her study of *shingaku* Janine Anderson Sawada points out that Buddhist, Shinto, and Taoist elements were also incorporated in its teaching, and that by the end of the eighteenth century it was already making significant inroads in the countryside (Sawada 1993, pp. 4, 9).

[10] Motoori 1969, p. 281.

[11] Ibid., p. 283.

[12] Ibid., pp. 285, 288.

[13] Ibid., p. 291.

[14] Ibid., pp. 304–5.

[15] *Kokutai* normally refers specifically to beliefs in the unbroken imperial reign and analogies of the state as a family, with the emperor in the position of father, as the unique characteristics of the Japanese polity. Satomi Kishio was the son of Tanaka Chigaku, a famous Nichiren nationalist whose ideas on national mission are taken up later in this chapter. The material on *shinkoku* summarized here can be found in two sections of his study (Satomi 1992, pp. 217–19 and 282–91).

16 These two frameworks are offered in Wakabayashi 1986, p. 18. Much of the following discussion regarding the development of the concept of *jōi* in Tokugawa Japan is also dependent on Wakabayshi's reading of the subject.

17 The translation is taken from Wakabayashi 1986, p. 149.

18 Ibid., p. 150.

19 Ibid., p. 200.

20 Ibid., p. 201.

21 Ibid., p. 258.

22 See Hardacre 1989 for a description of developments in the Meiji government's religious policy.

23 The official translation, as found in Gluck 1985, p. 121.

24 Gluck 1985, pp. 120–21.

25 Lee 1975, p. 26.

26 Ibid., p. 30.

27 Ibid., p. 33.

28 In addition to Lee, see Tanabe 1989 and Stone 1994 for discussions of Tanaka's Nichiren nationalism.

29 Once again, this is not the first time that these ideas are expressed in Japanese intellectual history. An earlier specific expression of these ideas, connected with the concept of *shinkoku* and used to justify military invasion, can be found in documents relating to the invasion of the Korean peninsula at the end of the sixteenth century. In April 1592, after conquering the remaining opposition warlords in Japan, Toyotomi Hideyoshi launched an assault on Korea. In a letter written to the Portuguese ambassador in India the year previous, Hideyoshi explained that he has already succeeded in uniting Japan under the rule of the emperor, ending long years of strife, and now he meant to extend that stability and order to the countries of Asia, including, eventually, India. The reason given for this determination is that "Our Court is the Land of the Gods." See Nakura 1976, p. 30, for the pertinent portions of Hideyoshi's letter.

30 Nitobe 1969, p. xii.

31 Ibid., p. 25.

32 Ibid., p. 26.

33 Ibid., p. 27.

34 Ibid., p. 29.

35 Ibid., pp. 31–32.

36 Ibid., p. 41.

[37] Ibid., p. 9.

[38] Ibid., p. 136.

[39] Ibid., p. 128.

[40] See Mullins 1998 for an examination of the influence that Uchimura and Mukyōkai had on the development of several indigenous Christian movements in Japan.

[41] *Uchimura Kanzō zenshū* [The collected works of Uchimura Kanzō], vol. 3, p. 39. This collection will be abbreviated as CWUK in subsequent entries. Emphasis in original.

[42] Ibid., pp. 42–43. Emphasis in original.

[43] Ibid., pp. 45–46.

[44] CWUK, vol. 36, p. 414. Emphasis in original.

[45] CWUK, vol. 5, p. 3. Uchimura goes on to give then-current examples of the tendency to compromise in Japanese society. Much the same argument was made in a short English essay published earlier in the year entitled "Peace, Peace!" (CWUK, vol. 4, pp. 64–65).

[46] CWUK, vol. 11, p. 296.

[47] "Thoughts on the War" (CWUK, vol. 12, pp. 37–40).

[48] CWUK, vol. 12, p. 425.

[49] CWUK, vol. 12, p. 447.

[50] This scandal plays a central role in the development of the thought and social awareness of Idei Seitarō, the founder of Shūyōdan Hōseikai, as we will see in Chapter Five.

[51] Kinoshita 1973, pp. 419–20.

CHAPTER 2: THE PACIFIST OPTION

[1] For a consideration of pacifism in the Catholic Church see Musto 1986. Bainton 1960 presents the case of the historic peace churches in Chapter 10.

[2] Martin 1965, p. 201.

[3] Article 9 of the Japanese constitution reads as follows:

Aspiring sincerely to an international peace based on justice and order, the Japanese people forever renounce war as a sovereign right of the nation and the threat or use of force as means of settling international disputes.
In order to accomplish the aim of the preceding paragraph, land, sea, and air forces, as well as other war potential, will never be maintained. The right of belligerency of the state will not be recognized.

4 *Waga hibōryoku*, 1992b (originally published in 1972). A shortened version of his autobiography is available in English under the title *My Non Violence: An Autobiography of a Japanese Buddhist* (1975). In the following examination of Fujii's beliefs and activities I quote where possible from the English translation of his autobiography, although, from time to time, it is necessary to supplement this with material found only in the Japanese edition.

5 The chanting of the *daimoku*, that is, the phrase *namu myōhō rengekyō* in praise of the *Lotus Sutra*, is a religious practice popularized by Nichiren.

6 *Gyakku shōdai* is a characteristic practice of Nipponzan Myōhōji. In Fujii's autobiography it is connected with a vision he had after completing a week of fasting and cold water austerities at Mt. Kasuga in Nara in November 1916. In the vision he saw a pilgrim carrying on his back an infant, identified as Śākyamuni, while beating a drum (Fujii 1975, pp. 29–36).

7 Fujii 1992b, p. 103.

8 Fujii 1975, pp. 15–16.

9 Interviews with Myōhōji monks, nuns, and believers were arranged through visits to several Myōhōji temples in Japan and abroad. To ensure privacy, the names of the people interviewed have been changed, both here and in subsequent chapters. However, each name used does refer to a specific person.

10 Fujii's letter, written in Japanese, was translated into English before being delivered to Gandhi by one of Fujii's disciples. However, I have only been able to find a copy of the Japanese original, reproduced in *Byakuju*, a collection of Fujii's sermons published in 1983 (pp. 74–83).

11 Tokoro 1976, p. 582.

12 Fujii 1992b, pp. 163–64.

13 Fujii 1975, p. 86.

14 Fujii 1992b, pp. 171–72.

15 Fujii 1975, p. 91. The translation is as found in the English edition of the autobiography.

16 Ibid., p. 118.

17 Fujii 1985, p. 15. The translation is as found in the pamphlet prepared by Myōhōji's foundation in the United States.

18 Ibid., pp. 20–21.

19 Only 31 of 120 questionnaires distributed to Myōhōji followers were returned, yielding a response rate of 26%, the lowest of the groups included in the survey. The monks' loose organization and generally itinerant lifestyle made it difficult to obtain greater cooperation with the survey, and thus the results obtained can only be considered suggestive of the opinions of Myōhōji followers.

Owing to the methodology employed in conducting the survey, as explained in the Appendix, the survey results as a whole do not lend themselves to solid conclusions as much as they can be used to indicate possible hypotheses and trends in need of further testing. Therefore, the material based on the survey in this and the following chapters will be presented primarily in the form of comparisons with the results of other groups or with the survey sample overall, in order to point out these possible trends. Tables displaying the results of the survey can also be found in the Appendix.

[20] In addition to the six groups treated in this book, a seventh group not directly involved in peace work, Shinnyoen, was included in the questionnaire survey for comparative reasons. Combining the five questions in this way, requiring a pacifist response across the board, is perhaps not the most elegant way to handle the results statistically. It does offer a stark comparison, however, for the next highest response on this scale is merely 1.4%, shared by Shūyōdan Hōseikai and Shinnyoen. That the other group identified as pacifist in this chapter, Byakkō Shinkōkai, does not appear on the scale raises an important question, and an attempt at an answer will be made when we treat their survey results later in the chapter.

[21] Fujii 1992a, pp. 49–50.

[22] I am indebted to Tsushiro Hirofumi, a colleague in the Graduate School of Arts and Letters at Tokyo University, for helping to arrange interviews with Byakkō Shinkōkai members. The interviews were conducted on several occasions following services at the Byakkō Shinkōkai headquarters.

[23] Saionji Masami is the adopted daughter of the founder of Byakkō Shinkōkai, Goi Masahisa, and the present leader of the religion.

[24] The complete English text of the prayer is as follows:

May peace prevail on earth.
May peace be in our homes and countries.
May our missions be accomplished.
We thank thee, Guardian Deities and Guardian Spirits.

[25] Autobiographical information on Goi Masahisa is taken from *Ten to chi o tsunagu mono* (Goi 1955).

[26] Goi 1955, p. 27.

[27] Jōrei is a development of the practice of *chinkon*, a spiritualistic healing ritual of Ōmotokyō. On the development of *chinkon* see Tsushiro 1990. In Western literature this term is often transliterated as "johrei," as in the name of the Johrei Fellowship, a group active in the United States and elsewhere.

[28] Goi 1955, p. 54.

[29] Ibid., pp. 60-61.

[30] Ibid., pp. 90–91.

[31] Goi 1985, p. 23.

[32] Goi 1974, p. 13. An English translation of this work is available under the title *The Future of Mankind* (1985), but because of the uneven quality of that translation I have chosen to present my own based on the original.

[33] Ibid., p. 60.

CHAPTER 3: COMPROMISED PACIFISM

[1] See Astley 1992, Métraux 1992, and Van Bragt 1993 concerning the split with Nichiren Shōshū. Stone 1994 suggests that at least part of the reason for the split might have been the adoption of an attitude more tolerant of other religions by Sōka Gakkai.

[2] Sōka Gakkai's official account can be found in the fortieth-anniversary history of the group (Sōka Gakkai Yonjūnenshi Hensan Iinkai 1970). For outside sources on Makiguchi see Bethel 1973 and Shimazono 1992a.

[3] Reflecting the pragmatic emphasis of Sōka Kyōiku Gakkai, these meetings were call *taizen seikatsu jikken shōmei zadankai*, or "forums on practical experimentation for abundant life."

[4] This figure is taken from Bethel 1973, p. 99, as representative of Toda's worth at prewar exchange rates.

[5] For an explanation of this development see Shimazono 1999.

[6] The vitalistic conception of the salvation is an optimistic view of the universe as giving abundant life, manifested in immediate benefits, to anyone who seeks to maintain their natural connection with this source of life. See Tsushima et al. 1979 for a more complete description of this concept.

[7] See Stone 1994 for a discussion of the use of *shakubuku* throughout the history of the Nichiren sects.

[8] Murata 1969, p. 99.

[9] Quote taken from Murata 1969, p. 100.

[10] Stone 1994. The policy of religious tolerance was made explicit in the Charter adopted at the Twentieth General Assembly of Soka Gakkai International in October 1995. That charter states that

SGI shall, based on the Buddhist spirit of tolerance, respect other religions, engage in dialogue and work together with them toward the resolution of fundamental issues concerning humanity.

[11] This particular interpretation of *ōbutsumyōgo* and the establishment of the *Kokuritsu kaidan* led to a split in Nichiren Shōshū, as Métraux points out (1980, pp. 59–60). As a matter of interest I might mention that, as one result of the split with

Sōka Gakkai the worship hall at Taisekiji is being torn down, apparently because the maintenance costs have become prohibitive now that the numbers of worshippers at the temple have fallen dramatically. Billed as the largest religious structure built in the twentieth century, construction of the worship hall cost almost one hundred million dollars, and its demolition is estimated at over forty million dollars.

[12] See my article on the 1995 revision of the Religious Corporations Law (Kisala 1997) for a discussion of some of these political developments.

[13] Métraux 1996, p. 388.

[14] The crew of a Japanese tuna boat, the *Dai go fukuryū maru* or Lucky Dragon No. 5, was exposed to radiation from the test of a hydrogen bomb on Bikini Atoll conducted on 1 March 1954, resulting in the death of one of the crew members.

On the occasion of the Sōka Gakkai rally held in 1957, Toda in effect joined his voice to a popular antinuclear campaign that had begun rather spontaneously in the wake of the accident three years earlier. While advocating disarmament, however, his remarks reflect more the militant posture of Toda and the group he led, rather than a nonviolent, pacifist approach, as the following quote illustrates.

Although the movement to ban the testing of atomic and nuclear weapons has taken off throughout the world, I want to deal with an issue that remains hidden in the background of that movement. The issue I refer to is the fact that no matter what country they might be from, whether they be the victors or the vanquished in war, if anyone has used a nuclear weapon, they should be subject to the death penalty. Why? Because we citizens of the world enjoy the right to life. Any person who threatens that right is the devil, a Satan, a monster. Therefore, anyone who has used these weapons against human society, regardless of country, regardless of the reason for that use, should be condemned to die (Sōka Gakkai Yonjūnenshi Hensan Iinkai 1970, p. 219).

[15] Ikeda 1991, p. 66.

[16] Ibid., p. 66.

[17] Ibid., p. 132.

[18] Ibid., p. 9.

[19] Ibid., p. 132.

[20] Ibid., p. 129.

[21] Sōka Gakkai Kyōgakubu 1977, p. 44.

[22] Ibid., pp. 61, 79.

[23] Ibid., pp. 111–12.

[24] Interviews with Sōka Gakkai members were arranged by the Sōka Gakkai Public Relations Office. In response to my request, people from a variety of backgrounds reflecting various approaches to peace were chosen for the interviews. A member of the Public Relations Office sat in on some of the early interviews, ostensibly

to observe what kinds of questions I intended to ask. I observed little change in the demeanor of the interviewees regardless of whether an official representative of the group was present or not.

25 "They have healed the wounds of my people lightly, saying, 'Peace, peace,' when there is no peace" (Jer 6:14, Revised Standard Version).

26 The survey was conducted with the cooperation of Sōka Gakkai's Public Relations Office. The Appendix offers an account of how the questionnaires were distributed. Because of the method of distribution, youth were perhaps overrepresented in the Sōka Gakkai sample; the percentage of respondents in their twenties (40%) and thirties (27%) was considerably higher than the overall averages (17% and 19%, respectively).

27 This interpretation can be found, for example, in Sōka Gakkai Yonjūnenshi Hensan Iinkai 1970, pp. 71, 74.

28 This private fund is itself a source of controversy, with many of the women forced into sexual slavery refusing to receive compensation from the fund, since it is an obvious ploy on the part of the Japanese government to avoid direct acknowledgment of responsibility for the sufferings of these women.

29 Martin 1965, p. 77.

30 Pauling and Ikeda 1990, p. 226.

CHAPTER 4: THE JUST WAR AND ITS DISCONTENTS

1 There was some speculation in the wake of the Persian Gulf War that the Catholic Church might abandon the just war theory, on the basis of an editorial published in the semiofficial Church organ *La Civiltà*. The editorial questioned whether it was possible to speak of a just war anymore, because of modern historical developments culminating in the practical recognition of the right of the nation-state to wage war. An analysis of the argument in the editorial can be found in Shannon 1993. The *Catechism of the Catholic Church*, published in 1994, however, acknowledges the right, and duty, of national self-defense, making reference to the just war doctrine (par. 2308–10).

2 I use this word deliberately, despite its irony, for clearly such a promise was the basis for the deterrent strategy of Mutual Assured Destruction promoted for much of this period.

3 The principle of proportionality holds that the prospective suffering and costs to be incurred by war must be commensurate with the values to be defended. Discrimination holds that only combatants can be targeted in war.

4 See, for example, paragraphs 127–28 of *Pacem in terris*, issued by John XXIII in 1963, or paragraphs 79–82 of the *Pastoral Constitution on the Church in the Modern World*, adopted by the Second Vatican Council in 1965.

[5] United States Catholic Conference 1983, par. 143.

[6] Ibid., par. 174–75.

[7] See Miller 1991, pp. 13–15, for his list of *ad bellum* and *in bello* criteria.

[8] Bainton presents this as one element of the nuanced Quaker allegiance to the pacifist position (1960, pp. 160–61).

[9] Yoder 1996, pp. 50–51.

[10] Information on Niwano Nikkyō is taken largely from his autobiographies, *Lifetime Beginner* (1978), and *Mugen e no tabi* (1963), as well as the account found in the history of Risshō Kōseikai published by the group (Risshō Kōseikai 1983).

[11] The Naval Armament Limitation Treaty, signed by the United States, Britain, Japan, France, and Italy on 6 February 1922, restricted the number and tonnage of naval vessels.

[12] Risshō Kōseikai 1983, p. 48.

[13] Niwano 1978, p. 58.

[14] Ibid., p. 63.

[15] Tengu Fudō is one example of the syncretistic nature of much of Japanese folk belief. It is an amalgamation of beliefs in a mountain spirit (Tengu) with extraordinary powers that has a human form, with a red face, long nose, and wings, and a form of popular Buddhism that calls on the protection of a fierce-looking Buddhist guardian spirit (Fudō) who carries a sword and was originally associated with the Hindu god Shiva. Belief in the Buddhist guardian spirit Fudō was also instrumental in the religious experiences of Tazawa Seishirō, the founder of Shōroku Shintō Yamatoyama, dealt with later in this chapter.

[16] Niwano 1978, p. 74.

[17] It is common practice in Japan that the deceased be given a new name in death, and parallels can be drawn here with the taking on of a religious name during initiation or ordination rituals in other religions. Different statuses are often assigned to *kaimyō*, depending on the choice and number of characters used to write the name, and prices are charged accordingly. The practice is often criticized for its blatant financial connections, and because it can be a means of carrying on discriminatory practices even after death. See, for example, William Bodiford's research on such practices in the Sōtō Zen sect (1996).

[18] Kubo and Reiyūkai also introduced the innovation of reverencing the ancestors of both the husband and wife in the increasingly more common urban nuclear family, a break with the traditional practice of exclusively patrilineal veneration.

[19] See Hardacre 1984, chapter one, for an account of the early history of Reiyūkai.

[20] The *hōza*, as a neighborhood association of believers, remains important in Risshō Kōseikai. In its emphasis on the sharing of religious experience it corresponds to

the *zadankai* in Sōka Gakkai and other new religions. In addition to their religious function, these groups also serve the social function of offering a solidarity group to people who have left the closer social bonds of the town or village for the anonymity of the city. The *hōza* as practiced in Risshō Kōseikai also serves as a popular form of counseling, as Kenneth Dale's study indicates (1975).

21 Risshō Kōseikai was the fifth of these splinter groups since Reiyūkai's founding just thirteen years earlier. As Hardacre points out, Reiyūkai's organizational structure, which emphasized the personal relationship with one's own recruiter and local branch head over the group's central authority, contributed to this schismatic tendency (Hardacre 1984, p. 45).

22 Niwano 1963, pp. 146–47.

23 Tokoro 1970, p. 94.

24 Niwano 1963, pp. 150–51.

25 Niwano 1978, p. 121.

26 After conducting their own investigation, Risshō Kōseikai and The New Japan Federation of Religious Organizations denied that Kōseikai was responsible for the suicides, citing four contributing factors to a nervous breakdown on the part of the woman, none of which were traceable to her membership in the group. See Morioka 1994 for a detailed analysis of the controversies surrounding Risshō Kōseikai in the mid-1950s.

27 Niwano 1977, pp. 36–37.

28 Ibid., pp. 17, 31.

29 Niwano 1972, pp. 76–77.

30 Niwano 1978–1981, vol. 6, pp. 275–76.

31 Interviews with Risshō Kōseikai members were arranged through contacts that I had developed within the group over the course of several years of research on Kōseikai's social welfare activities.

32 Shōroku Shintō Yamatoyama traces its founding to a revelation experienced by Seishirō in 1919, but it was not until 1930 that a group of followers was organized, and 1940 when the group was officially registered as a religion.

33 Inari is yet another popular folk belief in Japan. Originally the god of grains, Inari is usually associated with foxes. On Inari see Smyers 1999.

34 Yamato 1991, p. 54.

35 Ibid., p. 55.

36 The only biography available is published by Yamatoyama (Yamato 1991).

37 Yamato 1991, p. 267.

38 Ibid., p. 97.

[39] Ibid., pp. 136–37.

[40] Ibid., p. 93.

[41] Tazawa 1991, p. 265.

[42] Yamato 1991, p. 272.

[43] Interviews with Yamatoyama believers were arranged through contacts I had developed by attending interreligious conferences and in the course of previous research on New Religions in Japan.

[44] Tazawa 1991, pp. 266–67.

[45] Ibid., p. 314.

[46] Article 1 of the postwar constitution describes the emperor's role as follows.

The emperor shall be the symbol of the State and of the unity of the people, deriving his position from the will of the people with whom resides sovereign power.

[47] This activity belies the fact that in the questionnaire survey Yamatoyama members exhibited relatively little interest in the acknowledgment of war guilt. On the issue of the war in China, Yamatoyama believers were least likely to call Japan's military activity an invasion (53%). Thirty percent of Yamatoyama believers also expressed the opinion that any necessary apology or reparation for the so-called Comfort Women had already been taken care of, compared to a 21% overall average.

CHAPTER 5: PEACE THROUGH MORAL CULTIVATION

[1] Hardacre 1986, p. 23.

[2] See, for example, my article on reinterpretations of karmic beliefs in Tenrikyō and Risshō Kōseikai (Kisala 1994a).

[3] Goi 1974, pp. 13–14.

[4] Ibid., p. 96.

[5] Ibid., pp. 59–61.

[6] Fujii 1980a, pp. 176–77. I have amended the translation here on the basis of the original in Fujii 1980b, pp. 173–74.

[7] Fujii 1992a, p. 164.

[8] Sōka Gakkai Kyōgakubu 1977, pp. 14–15.

[9] Niwano 1978–1981, vol. 6, p. 107.

[10] Ibid., p. 151.

[11] Ibid., p. 138.

[12] Hardacre 1986, pp. 22–23.

13 This optimistic view of human nature is one aspect of the vitalistic worldview common to many of the Japanese new religious movements, as argued in Tsushima et al. 1979, previously cited in Chapter Three.

14 The expression of this emphasis can at times, however, be comical, if not disturbingly smug. Headlines in the *Seikyō Shinbun*, Sōka Gakkai's daily newspaper, refer almost daily to the international contacts of the group, and especially its leader, Ikeda Daisaku. On 11 November 1997, the newspaper carried a picture on its front page of Ikeda meeting with two academics. In the subheadlines accompanying the story, the academics were identified as from England and China, in contrast to the identification of Ikeda as of "the world."

15 I thank Ian Reader for pointing out the possibility of deleterious consequences resulting from cross-cultural contacts.

16 These results might have been skewed somewhat by the method used to distribute the survey. Out of four hundred questionnaires distributed to members of the group, one hundred fifty were distributed at a meeting of elder members, a decision taken because this particular group is one of the most active in Hōseikai. A survey conducted by Shimazono et al. several years prior to the current research, however, produced similar results, so we can be fairly confident that the age of the overall membership is accurately reflected here (Shimazono 1992c).

17 Information regarding Idei Seitarō is largely based on that provided in Shimazono 1992c. Hōseikai has also published a semiautobiographical work under Idei's name (Idei 1965), but Kaminogō reports that this account was greatly embellished by Idei's ghostwriter (1987, p. 179).

18 Kōbō Daishi, or Kūkai, was the founder of the Shingon sect of Buddhism in Japan. He is widely associated with miracle stories, and has become the object of much popular belief.

19 Idei 1965, pp. 48–50.

20 Ibid., p. 48.

21 Ibid., p. 50.

22 Shimazono 1992c, pp. 10–11.

23 Idei 1965, p. 73.

24 Ibid., pp. 75–85.

25 Later called Tenri Honmichi, and finally Honmichi.

26 The *kanrodai* is a pillar erected at the center of the Tenrikyō main temple, thought to be the place of origin for humankind. It is believed that when humanity has been perfected, sweet nectar, or *kanro*, will pour from heaven and fill the top, bowl-shaped, part of the *kanrodai*, ushering in a golden age when all people will live in happiness until the age of one hundred fifteen.

27 Idei 1965, pp. 166–68.

28 A collection of his wartime teachings was published by Shūyōdan Hōseikai in three volumes as *Idei Seitarō kunwashū* [*The collected moral lectures of Idei Seitarō*], 1980–1982.

29 Idei 1980–1982, vol. 1, p. 52.

30 Ibid., vol. 1, p. 181; vol. 3, p. 57.

31 In Hōseikai, this use of puns (in Japanese called *goroawase*, or, more pejoratively, *dajare*) bears some connection with *kotodama*, the belief in the power of sounds or words. Idei often employed it in his teaching, as in the case cited here, for rhetorical effect—with a great deal of success, judging from the stories that believers still recall and recount. Beliefs more directly connected with *kotodama* can also be found in this group. For example, the believers avoid the use of the sound *ga*, meaning the ego or self and associated with selfish desires, using "*otanomishimasu*" in requests rather than the more common "*onegaishimasu*."

32 Idei 1980–1982, vol. 1, p. 181.

33 Ibid., vol. 1, p. 204.

34 Shimazono further recounts that Idei would tell his followers to bow to the incoming American bombers and say, "*Gokurōsama*," a polite expression used to thank someone for their service. By greeting them in this way, recognizing that they are only doing their job, rather than harboring enmity towards them, Idei said that they would be protected from the destruction of the bombing (Shimazono 1992c, p. 15). Even in the face of the destruction of Japanese cities as a result of the bombing, the emphasis is placed on individual motives and responsibility in order to promote understanding and acceptance of the other.

35 Shimazono calls it a "bold move [while] under the control of GHQ" (Shimazono 1992c, p. 15). Controversy over the use of the national flag and national anthem continues until the present day in Japan because of their identification with Japanese militarism and colonialism. In the late 1980s, for example, the Education Ministry caused an outcry when it decreed that the flag and anthem be used at all school entrance and graduation ceremonies. Norma Field also recounts at length the story of the struggle of one native of Okinawa against the Japanese national flag (1993).

36 Idei 1980–1982, vol. 3, p. 71.

37 Ibid., p. 73.

38 *Yamato damashii* is a phrase that took on definite ethnocentric and militaristic connotations in the immediate prewar period, when it was used to describe spiritual qualities that were supposedly unique to the Japanese people. The phrase was used in mediaeval Japanese literature, from around the eleventh to the fourteenth centuries, usually to distinguish native ideas and patterns of behavior from those of China. It was revived by National Learning scholars in the latter half of the Tokugawa period as part of their reaction against Chinese influences. By late Tokugawa it had become associated with nationalistic beliefs centered on the role of

the emperor, and it was in this context that it became a rallying call for the nationalists and militarists in the modern period. See the entry in the *Kodansha Encyclopedia of Japan* (Reischauer 1983), vol. 8, p. 309.

[39] Idei 1980–1982, vol. 3, p. 74.

[40] As of 1992 a total of twenty Peace Stones had been erected in Japan and four overseas. Overseas the Peace Stones are located in San Francisco, Achibaya (Brazil), Berlin, and Sydney.

[41] *Shūyōdan Hōseikai kōryō* [The essential points of Shūyōdan Hōseikai's teaching].

[42] The term "ethic of daily life" is used by Fujii Takeshi to describe the ethic commonly taught by the Japanese New Religions (1990). The ethic of daily life can be seen as an extension of the worldview of these groups that emphasizes internal moral cultivation in order to achieve a transformation of the external environment. In this ethic the believer is encouraged to reflect on his or her daily life and relationships within the family, with neighbors and coworkers, and to repent of any selfishness that has led to disharmony. It is often thought that by such a change of heart illness can be cured, wounded relationships healed, and prosperity attained.

[43] The collections of these sayings in my possession are Idei 1964, Idei 1973, and Shūyōdan Hōseikai Tōkyō Misesu no Tsudoi 1980.

[44] Shūyōdan Hōseikai Tōkyō Misesu no Tsudoi 1980, p. 306.

[45] See, for example, the interview with Matsumoto Seiji presented on pp. 102–3 of Shimazono 1992c. Matsumoto says that he was instructed to polish his older brother's shoes as his *jikkō*, a practice that he eventually came to interpret more broadly as helping others to "look good," instilling within him an understanding for others' weakness and a resulting compassion that he now judges had been deficient in his character development.

[46] Interviews with Hōseikai members were arranged by the assistant director of the group, Idei Shigeru, the adopted son of the founder. I had made Idei's acquaintance in the course of the earlier research project directed by Shimazono, and am confident that he attempted to meet my criteria in suggesting members as my informants.

[47] Whiting 1989.

CHAPTER 6: THE MISSION TO SPREAD PEACE

[1] See Sharf 1995b and Faure 1993, 1995.

[2] Cited in Tokoro 1976, p. 594. Tokoro makes the argument here that Japan's defeat in the war was indeed a turning point in Fujii's thought and activities, and later claims by Fujii to a prewar pacifism should be dismissed.

[3] Fujii 1992a, p. 92.

[4] Ibid., pp. 22–25.

[5] Goi 1974, p. 48.

[6] Ibid., p. 51.

[7] Ibid., p. 49.

[8] Sōka Gakkai Kyōgakubu 1977, p. 44.

[9] Ibid., p. 61.

[10] Harashima 1969, pp. 88–89. Harashima Takashi was the head of the doctrinal department of Sōka Gakkai and held several other administrative positions within the group when this book was published. He later left the group, but it would be safe to assume that his words, while not official Sōka Gakkai doctrine, can be taken to reflect at least one influential strand of thought in Sōka Gakkai.

[11] Niwano 1977, p. 13.

[12] Yasukuni Shrine was established in Tokyo early in the Meiji period, with the purpose of venerating the spirits of those who had given their lives for the imperial cause. Although the shrine was disestablished by decree of the Occupation forces in the immediate postwar period, legislation to nationalize the shrine as a veterans' war memorial has been introduced in parliament by members of the Liberal Democratic Party a number of times since 1969.

[13] Niwano 1978, p. 225.

[14] See, for example, Niwano, 1978–1981, vol. 6, pp. 294–95; and Niwano 1978, pp. 220, 225.

[15] Niwano 1978–1981, vol. 3, pp. 472–80.

[16] Niwano 1978, p. 219.

[17] Niwano 1978–1981, vol. 6, p. 305.

[18] *Nihonjinron* refers to discourse on the uniqueness of Japanese culture that emerged in the 1970s. For a dispassionate and thoughtful analysis of *nihonjinron* and its significance in contemporary Japanese culture see Yoshino 1992.

[19] The translation is taken from Aston 1997, p. 131. The *Nihon shoki* is also known as the *Nihongi*, the word used in the title of Aston's translation.

[20] Found in the entry on *hakkō ichiu* by Robert Spaulding in the *Kodansha Encyclopedia of Japan* (Reischauer 1983), vol. 3, p. 85.

[21] Foard 1994, p. 26.

[22] The treatment afforded non-Japanese victims of the atomic bombings in these memorials indicates how these tragedies have been associated with notions of a unique victimization and consequent national dedication to ban these weapons and establish peace. Until recently, for example, a memorial to victims of Korean descent

was not allowed within the confines of the park in Hiroshima. Information on this incident can be found in Foard 1994, p. 40, n. 5.

23 The story of Sadako and how she believed she might recover by folding one thousand paper cranes—a symbol of longevity and good fortune—has since found its way into school textbooks around the world, becoming itself a symbol of Japan's mission to establish world peace.

24 Tsuneoka 1993, p. 138.

CONCLUSION

1 See, for example, the brief review of some *nihonjinron* literature on this subject in Yoshino 1992, pp. 17–22.

2 For example, the *Yomiuri Daily News* carried this quote from the father of a murder victim, reacting to the decision against imposing the death sentence on one of the defendants in the Aum Shinrikyō case: "I find it hard to understand why there are fewer death sentences and lighter penalties despite the rise in the number of Western-style violent criminal offenses" (27 May 1998).

3 Fearey 1950, pp. 19–20. Fearey's report was published under the auspices of the International Secretariat, Institute of Pacific Relations.

4 The program, "Tagata Jinja Hōnensai," was broadcast on PerfecTV on 16 March 1997. I am grateful to Karen Smyers for making the videotape of this program available to me.

5 The survey was conducted by the Nanzan Institute for Religion and Culture, in collaboration with other sociological and religious researchers. A random sample of three hundred adults from the Tokyo and Osaka areas responded to the survey. Results of the survey are available from the author.

6 The presentation in van Wolferen (1989, pp. 361–63) is a good example of the enduring quality of this view.

7 See Watanabe 1997 for an analysis of how the Aum Affair contributed to the popularization of an anticult movement in Japan.

8 The survey is conducted by The Japanese Association for the Study of Religion and Society's Religious Awareness Project. The annual reports on the results of the survey are available from the author.

9 These results are taken from Ishii 1997, pp. 179–81.

10 Carter argues that, "If the religiously devout come to treat their faith communities as simple interest groups, involved in a general competition for secular power, it should come as no surprise if everybody else looks at them the same way" (1993, p. 68). Furthermore, the danger is not only one of public perception of religion; it goes to the core of its role in society: "The closer the religions move to the center of

secular power (as against influence), the less likely they are to discover meanings that are in competition with those imposed by the state. The simple reason for this is that if the religions are able to impose their own meanings, there is no longer any distinction, and, thus, no longer important work for the triumphant religions as autonomous agencies to do" (p. 273).

[11] In the recent survey conducted by the Nanzan Institute for Religion and Culture mentioned above, 77% of the respondents agreed with the statement that "religious leaders should not attempt to influence politics."

[12] I have argued this point in Kisala 1998. The new political party founded by many of the anti-LDP coalition partners in 1995 was dissolved two years later, with many of the former Kōmeitō members eventually forming a new party of their own, the New Kōmeitō.

[13] In a policy memorandum titled "Soka Gakkai's Political Stance in Japan," dated 29 July 1998.

[14] "The prophets who preceded you and me from ancient times prophesied war, famine, and pestilence against many countries and great kingdoms. As for the prophet who prophesies peace, when the word of that prophet comes to pass, then it will be known that the Lord has truly sent the prophet" (Jer 28:8–9, Revised Standard Version).

APPENDIX: QUESTIONNAIRE SURVEY ON PEACE ATTITUDES

[1] See, for example, Hardacre 1984 and Davis 1980.

Bibliography

Astley, Trevor. 1992. A Matter of Principles: A Note on the Recent Conflict between Nichiren Shōshū and Sōka Gakkai. *Japanese Religions* 17: 167–75.

Aston, W.G., trans. 1997. *Nihongi: Chronicles of Japan from the Earliest Times to A. D. 697.* Complete Works of W. G. Aston, Vol. 3. Bristol: Ganesha Publishing Ltd. (originally published in 1896).

Bainton, Roland H. 1960. *Christian Attitudes Toward War and Peace: A Historical Survey and Critical Re-evaluation.* Nashville: Abingdon Press.

Bamba, Nobuya, and John F. Howes, eds. 1978. *Pacifism in Japan: The Christian and Socialist Tradition.* Kyoto: Minerva Press.

Bethel, Dayle M. 1973. *Makiguchi the Value Creator: Revolutionary Japanese Educator and Founder of Soka Gakkai.* New York: Weatherhill.

Bodiford, William. 1996. Zen and the Art of Religious Prejudice: Efforts to Reform a Tradition of Social Discrimination. *Japanese Journal of Religious Studies* 23: 1–27.

Buruma, Ian. 1995. *The Wages of Guilt: Memories of War in Germany and Japan.* New York: Meridian.

Carter, Stephen L. 1993. *The Culture of Disbelief.* New York: Basic Books.

Chūō Gakujutsu Kenkyūjo, ed. 1992. *Heiwa no kadai to shūkyō.* Tokyo: Kōsei Shuppansha.

Dale, Kenneth J. 1975. *Circle of Harmony: A Case Study in Popular Japanese Buddhism with Implications for Christian Mission.* Tokyo: Seibunsha.

Davis, Winston. 1980. *Dojo: Magic and Exorcism in Modern Japan.* Stanford: Standord University Press.

Farris, William Wayne. 1992. *Heavenly Warriors: The Evolution of Japan's Military, 500–1300.* Cambridge: Harvard University Press.

Faure, Bernard. 1993. *Chan Insights and Oversights: An Epistemological Critique of the Chan Tradition.* Princeton: Princeton University Press.

———. 1995. The Kyoto School and Reverse Orientalism. In *Japan in Traditional and Postmodern Perspectives,* ed. Charles Wei-Hsun and Steven Heine. Albany: State University of New York Press.

Fearey, Robert A. 1950. *The Occupation of Japan: Second Phase, 1948–50.* Westport, Connecticut: Greenwood Press.

Field, Norma. 1993. *In the Realm of a Dying Emperor: Japan at Century's End.* New York: Random House (originally published in 1991).

Foard, James. 1994. The Universal and the Particular in the Rites of Hiroshima. In *Asian Visions of Authority: Religion and the Modern States of East and Southeast Asia*, ed. Charles F. Keyes, Laurel Kendall, and Helen Hardacre. Honolulu: University of Hawai'i Press.

Fujii Nichidatsu. 1975. *My Non Violence: An Autobiography of a Japanese Buddhist.* Yamaori Tetsuo, trans. Tokyo: Japan Buddha Sangha Press.

———. 1980a. *Buddhism for World Peace: Words of Nichidatsu Fujii.* Miyasuku Yumiko, trans. Tokyo: Japan-Bharat Sarvodaya Mitrata Sangha.

———. 1980b. *Bukkyō to sekai heiwa.* Tokyo: Nichi-In Sarubodaya Kōyūkai.

———. 1983. *Byakuju.* Tokyo: Nipponzan Myōhōji.

———. 1984. *Itten Shikai Kaiki Myoho.* Tokyo: Japan-Bharat Sarvodaya Mitrata Sangha.

———. 1985. *Kill Not Life: Fusessho.* Miyazaki, Yumiko, trans. Everett, Mass.: Nipponzan Myohoji New England Sangha.

———. 1992a. *Tenku.* Tokyo: Nipponzan Myōhōji.

———. 1992b. *Waga hibōryoku.* Yamaori Tetsuo, trans. Tokyo: Shunjūsha.

Fujii Takeshi. 1990. Seikatsu kiritsu to rinrikan. In *Shinshūkyō jiten*, ed. Inoue Nobutaka et al. Tokyo: Kōbundō.

Gluck, Carol. 1985. *Japan's Modern Myths: Ideology in the Late Meiji Period.* Princeton: Princeton University Press.

Goi Masahisa. 1955. *Ten to chi o tsunagu mono.* Ichikawa: Byakkō Shinkōkai Shuppankyoku.

———. 1974. *Jinrui no mirai.* Ichikawa: Byakkō Shinkōkai Shuppankyoku.

———. 1985. *The Future of Mankind.* Ichikawa: Byakkō Shuppan.

Groner, Paul. 1989. The *Lotus Sutra* and Saichō's Interpretation of the Realization of Buddhahood with This Very Body. In *The Lotus Sutra in Japanese Culture*, ed. George J. Tanabe, Jr. and Willa Jane Tanabe. Honolulu: University of Hawai'i Press.

Harashima Takashi. 1969. *Sōka Gakkai.* Tokyo: Seiki Shoten.

Hardacre, Helen. 1984. *Lay Buddhism in Contemporary Japan: Reiyūkai Kyōdan.* Princeton: Princeton University Press.

———. 1986. *Kurozumikyō and the New Religions of Japan.* Princeton: Princeton University Press.

———. 1989. *Shintō and the State, 1868–1988.* Princeton: Princeton University Press.

Harries, Meirion, and Susie Harries. 1991. *Soldiers of the Sun: The Rise and Fall of the Imperial Japanese Army.* New York: Random House.

Hubbard, Jamie. 1995. Buddhist-Buddhist Dialogue?: The *Lotus Sutra* and the Problem of Accommodation. *Buddhist-Christian Studies* 15: 119–36.

Idei Seitarō. 1964. *Hōsei tokuhon.* Tokyo: Shūyōdan Hōseikai Kyōgakuin.

———. 1965. *Keireiki.* Tokyo: Heiwakyō Henshubu.

———. 1973. *Inochi no kate.* Tokyo: Shūyōdan Hōseikai Kyōgakuin.

———. 1980–1982. *Idei Seitarō kunwashū.* Tokyo: Shūkyō Hōjin Shūyōdan Hōseikai.

Ienaga, Saburō. 1979. *Japan's Last War: World War II and the Japanese, 1931–1945.* Oxford: Basil Blackwell.

Ienaga Saburō, managing ed. 1993–1994. *Nihon heiwaron taikei.* 20 volumes. Tokyo: Nihon Tosho Sentā.

Ikeda Daisaku. 1991. *Proposals on Peace and Disarmament: Towards the 21ˢᵗ Century.* Tokyo: Soka Gakkai International.

Inoue Nobutaka et al., eds. 1990. *Shinshūkyō jiten.* Tokyo: Kōbundō.

Ishida, Takeshi. 1983. *Japanese Political Culture: Change and Continuity.* New Brunswick, NJ: Transaction Books.

Ishii Kenji. 1997. *Gendai Nihonjin no shūkyō ishiki.* Tokyo: Shin'yōsha.

Kaminogō Toshiaki. 1987. *Kyōso tanjō.* Tokyo: Shinshiosha.

Kinoshita Naoe. 1973. *Kinoshita Naoe shū. Nihon kindai bunka taikei.* Tokyo: Kadokawa Shoten.

Kisala, Robert. 1992. *Gendai shūkyō to shakai rinri.* Tokyo: Seikyūsha.

———. 1994a. Contemporary Karma: Interpretations of Karma in Tenrikyō and Risshō Kōseikai. *Japanese Journal of Religious Studies* 21:73–91.

———. 1994b. Social Ethics and the Japanese New Religions: The Social Welfare Activities of Tenrikyo and Rissho Koseikai. In *New Religious Movements in Asia & the Pacific Islands: Implications for Church & Society,* ed. Robert C. Salazar. Manila: De La Salle University.

———. 1997. Reactions to Aum: The Revision of the Religious Corporations Law. *Japanese Religions* 22: 60–74.

———. 1998. The Fallout of Aum: New Religious Movements and Japanese Society in the Aftermath of the "Aum Affair." In *Croyances et sociétés,* ed. Bertrand Oullet and Richard Bergeron. Montreal: Fides.

Kitagawa, Joseph M. 1966. *Religion in Japanese History.* New York: Columbia University Press.

Kraft, Kenneth, ed. 1992. *Inner Peace, World Peace: Essays on Buddhism and Nonviolence.* Albany: State University of New York Press.

Lee, Edwin B. 1975. Nichiren and Nationalism: The Religious Patriotism of Tanaka Chigaku. *Monumenta Nipponica* 30: 19–35.

Martin, David A. 1965. *Pacifism: An Historical and Sociological Study.* London: Routledge and Kegan Paul Ltd.

Marty, Martin. 1996. *Modern American Religion.* Vol. 3. Chicago: University of Chicago Press.

Maruyama, Masao. 1974. *Studies in the Intellectual History of Tokugawa Japan.* Mikiso Hane, trans. Tokyo: University of Tokyo Press.

Métraux, Daniel. 1980. Why did Ikeda Quit? *Japanese Journal of Religious Studies* 7: 55–61.

———. 1992. The Dispute between the Sōka Gakkai and the Nichiren Shōshū Priesthood: A Lay Revolution against a Conservative Clergy. *Japanese Journal of Religious Studies* 19: 325–36.

———. 1996. The Soka Gakkai: Buddhism and the Creating of a Harmonious and Peaceful Society. In *Engaged Buddhism: Buddhist Liberation Movements in Asia,* ed. Christopher S. Queen and Sallie B. King. Albany: State University of New York Press.

Miller, Richard B. 1991. *Interpretations of Conflict: Ethics, Pacifism, and the Just War Tradition.* Chicago: University of Chicago Press.

Ministry of Education. 1996. *Shūkyō Nenkan.* Tokyo: Ministry of Education.

Morioka Kiyomi. 1994. Attacks on the New Religions: Risshō Kōseikai and the "Yomiuri Affair." *Japanese Journal of Religious Studies* 21: 281–310.

Motoori Norinaga. 1969. *Motoori Norinaga shū. Nihon no shisō,* vol. 15. Tokyo: Chikuma Shobō.

Mullins, Mark. 1998. *Christianity Made in Japan: A Study of Indigenous Movements.* Honolulu: University of Hawai'i Press.

Murata, Kiyoaki. 1969. *Japan's New Buddhism: An Objective Account of Soka Gakkai.* New York: Weatherhill.

Musto, Ronald G. 1986. *The Catholic Peace Tradition.* Maryknoll, NY: Orbis Books.

Nakamura Hajime. 1959. *Shūkyō to shakai rinri.* Tokyo: Iwanami Shoten.

Nakura Tetsuzō. 1976. Hideyoshi no Chōsen shinryaku to "shinkoku." *Rekishi hyōron* 314: 29–35.

Narayan, Sachindra, ed. 1990. *Buddhism and World Peace.* New Delhi: Inter-India Publications.

NHK Yoron Chōsabu, ed. 1984. *Nihonjin no shūkyō ishiki.* Tokyo: Nippon Hōsō Shuppan Kyōkai.

Nishiyama Shigeru. 1988. Gendai no shūkyō undō: Rei-jutsu kei shinshūkyō no ryūkō to "futatsu no kindaika." In *Gendaijin no shūkyō,* ed. Ōmura Eishō and Nishiyama Shigeru. Tokyo: Yuhikaku.

Nitobe, Inazo. 1969. *Bushido: The Soul of Japan.* Tokyo: Charles E. Tuttle Company.

Niwano Nikkyō. 1963. *Mugen e no tabi.* Tokyo: Tokisha.

———. 1972. *Heiwa e no michi.* Tokyo: Kōsei Shuppansha.

———. 1976. *Buddhism for Today: A Modern Interpretation of the Threefold Lotus Sutra.* Tokyo: Kosei Publishing Co.

———. 1977. *A Buddhist Approach to Peace.* Tokyo: Kosei Publishing Co.

———. 1978. *Lifetime Beginner: An Autobiography.* Tokyo: Kosei Publishing Co.

———. 1978–1981. *Niwano Nikkyō hōwa senshū*, 6 volumes. Tokyo: Kōsei Shuppansha.

Norman, Edgerton H. 1949. Ando Shoeki and the anatomy of Japanese feudalism. *Transactions of the Asiatic Society of Japan*, third series, 2.

Ooms, Herman. 1985. *Tokugawa Ideology: Early Constructs, 1570–1680*. Princeton: Princeton University Press.

Pauling, Linus, and Ikeda Daisaku. 1990. *Seimei no seiki e no tankyū*. Tokyo: Yomiuri Shinbunsha.

Pye, Michael. 1994. National and International Identity in a Japanese New Religion. In *Japanese New Religions in the West*, ed. Peter B. Clarke and Jeffrey Somers. Kent: Japan Library (Curzon Press).

Reischauer, Edwin, ed. 1983. *Kodansha Encyclopedia of Japan*. Tokyo: Kodansha.

Risshō Kōseikai. 1983. *Rissho Kōseikai shi*, vol. 1. Tokyo: Kōsei Shuppansha.

Said, Edward. 1978. *Orientalism*. New York: Random House.

Satomi Kishio. 1992. *Kokutai shisōshi*. Tokyo: Hentensha.

Sawada, Janine Anderson. 1993. *Confucian Values and Popular Zen: Sekimon Shingaku in Eighteenth-Century Japan*. Honolulu: University of Hawai'i Press.

Shannon, William H. 1993. Christian Conscience and Modern Warfare. In *Studying War—No More? From Just War to Just Peace*, ed. Brian Wicker. Grand Rapids, MI: William B. Eerdmans Publishing Company.

Sharf, Robert. 1995a. Sanbōkyōdan: Zen and the Way of the New Religions. *Japanese Journal of Religious Studies* 22: 417–58.

———. 1995b. The Zen of Japanese Nationalism. In *Curators of the Buddha: The Study of Buddhism under Colonialism*, ed. Donald S. Lopez, Jr. Chicago: The University of Chicago Press.

Shimazono Susumu. 1981. Religious Influences on Japan's Modernization. *Japanese Journal of Religious Studies* 8: 207–23.

———. 1992a. *Seikatsuchi to kindai shūkyō undō: Makiguchi Tsunesaburō no kyōiku shisō to shinkō*. In *Shūkyō to shakai kagaku*, ed. Kawai Hayao et al. Tokyo: Iwanami Shoten.

———. 1992b. *Shin-shinshūkyō to shūkyō būmu*. Tokyo: Iwanami Shoten.

———, ed. 1992c. *Sukui to toku*. Tokyo: Kobundo.

———. 1999. Sōka Gakkai and the Modern Reformation of Buddhism. In *Buddhist Spirituality: Later China, Korea, Japan and the Modern World*, vol. 9 of *World Spirituality: An Encyclopedic History of the Religious Quest*. New York: The Crossroad Publishing Co.

Shioiri Ryōdō. 1989. The Meaning of the Formation and Structure of the *Lotus Sutra*. In *The Lotus Sutra in Japanese Culture*, ed. George J. Tanabe, Jr. and Willa Jane Tanabe. Honolulu: University of Hawai'i Press.

Shūyōdan Hōseikai Tōkyō Misesu no Tsudoi. 1980. *Mujōken jikkō*. Tokyo: Shūyōdan Hōseikai Tōkyō Misesu no Tsudoi.

Smyers, Karen. 1999. *The Fox and the Jewel: Symbolizing Shared and Private Meanings in Japanese Inari Worship.* Honolulu: University of Hawai'i Press.

Sōka Gakkai Kyōgakubu, ed. 1977. *Sōka Gakkai nyūmon.* Tokyo: Daisan Bunmeisha.

Sōka Gakkai Yonjūnenshi Hensan Iinkai, ed. 1970. *Sōka Gakkai Yonjūnenshi.* Tokyo: Sōka Gakkai.

Stone, Jacqueline. 1994. Rebuking the Enemies of the *Lotus*: Nichirenist Exclusivism in Historical Perspective. *Japanese Journal of Religious Studies* 21: 231–59.

Tanabe, George J. 1989. Tanaka Chigaku: The *Lotus Sutra* and the Body Politic. In *The Lotus Sutra in Japanese Culture*, ed. George J. Tanabe, Jr. and Willa Jane Tanabe. Honolulu: University of Hawai'i Press.

Tazawa Yasusaburō. 1991. *Seiki no chōkoku: Tomoni ikiru sekai o mezashite.* Aomori: Yamatoyama Shuppan.

Tōkei Sūri Kenkyūjo Kokuminsei Chōsa Iinkai, ed. 1991. *Nihonjin no kokuminsei.* Tokyo: Idemitsu Shoten.

Tokoro Shigemoto. 1970. *Niwano Nikkyō ron.* Tokyo: Tokisha.

———. 1976. *Nichiren kyōgaku no shisōshiteki kenkyū.* Tokyo: Tomiyamabo.

Tsuneoka, Setsuko Norimoto. 1993. Pacifism and Some Misconceptions about the Japanese Constitution. In *The Constitution of Japan*, ed. Tsuneoka et al. Tokyo: Kashiwashobō Publishing Co.

Tsushima Michihito et al. 1979. The Vitalistic Conception of Salvation in Japanese New Religions. *Japanese Journal of Religious Studies* 6: 139–61.

Tsushiro Hirofumi. 1990. *Chinko gyohōron.* Tokyo: Shunjusha.

Uchimura Kanzō. 1981. *Uchimura Kanzō zenshū.* 40 volumes. Tokyo: Iwanami Shoten.

United States Catholic Conference. 1983. *The Challenge of Peace: God's Promise and Our Response.* Washington: United States Catholic Conference.

Van Bragt, Jan. 1993. An Uneven Battle: Sōka Gakkai vs. Nichiren Shōshū. *Bulletin of the Nanzan Institute for Religion & Culture* 17: 15–31.

van Wolferen, Karel. 1989. *The Enigma of Japanese Power: People and Politics in a Stateless Nation.* London: Papermac (Macmillan Publishers Ltd.).

Wakabayashi, Bob Tadashi. 1986. *Anti-Foreignism and Western Learning in Early-Modern Japan: The New Theses of 1825.* Cambridge: Harvard University Press.

Watanabe Manabu. 1997. Reaction to the Aum Affair: The Rise of the 'Anti-Cult' Movement in Japan. *Bulletin of the Nanzan Institute for Religion & Culture* 21: 32–48.

Whiting, Robert. 1989. *You Gotta Have Wa.* New York: Macmillan Publishing Company.

Yamamoto Tsunetomo. 1980. *The Hagakure: A Code of the Way of the Samurai.* Takao Mukoh, trans. Tokyo: The Hokuseido Press.

Yamato Komatsukaze. 1991. *Yamatoyama: Oitachi to oshie.* Morioka: Yamatoyama Shuppansha.

Yasumaru Yoshio. 1974. *Nihon no kindaika to minshū shisō.* Tokyo: Aoki Shoten.

Yoder, John Howard. 1996. *When War is Just: Being Honest in Just-War Thinking.* (Revised edition). Maryknoll, NY: Orbis Books.

Yoshino, Kosaku. 1992. *Cultural Nationalism in Contemporary Japan: A Sociological Enquiry.* London: Routledge.

Index

About the Author

Robert Kisala is a fellow at the Nanzan Institute for Religion and Culture and associate professor at Nanzan University in Japan. After receiving a Master of Arts degree in theology from Catholic Theological Union in Chicago, he did graduate work in religious studies at Tokyo University, where he received his Ph. D. in 1994. His publications include works in Japanese and English on the social ethic of the Japanese New Religions, religion and state in contemporary Japan, the Aum Shinrikyō incident, and Japanese apocalypticism.